Creativity, Religion and Youth Cultures

This book explores the rich intersection between faith, religion, and performing arts in culture-based youth groups. The co-constitutive identity-building work of music, performance, and drama for Samoan and Sudanese youth in church contexts has given rise to new considerations of diversity, cultural identity, and the religious practices and rituals that inform them. For these young people, their culture-specific churches provide a safe if "imagined community" (Anderson 2006) in which they can express these emerging identities, which move beyond simple framings like "multicultural" to explicitly include faith practices. These identities emerge in combination with popular cultural art forms like hip hop, R&B, and gospel music traditions, as well as performance influences drawn from American, British, and European popular cultural forms (including fashion, reality television, social media, gaming, and online video-sharing). This book also examines the ways in which diasporic experiences are reshaping these cultural and gendered identities and locations.

Anne M. Harris is Senior Lecturer at Monash University, and researches in the areas of creativity, performance, and diversity.

Routledge Advances in Critical Diversities
Series Editors: Yvette Taylor and Sally Hines

1 **Sexuality, Citizenship and Belonging**
Trans-National and Intersectional Perspectives
Edited by Francesca Stella, Yvette Taylor, Tracey Reynolds and Antoine Rogers

2 **Creativity, Religion and Youth Cultures**
Anne M. Harris

Creativity, Religion and Youth Cultures

Anne M. Harris

NEW YORK AND LONDON

First published 2017
by Routledge
711 Third Avenue, New York, NY 10017

and by Routledge
2 Park Square, Milton Park, Abingdon, Oxon OX14 4RN

Routledge is an imprint of the Taylor & Francis Group, an informa business

© 2017 Taylor & Francis

The right of Anne M. Harris to be identified as author of this work has been asserted in accordance with sections 77 and 78 of the Copyright, Designs and Patents Act 1988.

All rights reserved. No part of this book may be reprinted or reproduced or utilised in any form or by any electronic, mechanical, or other means, now known or hereafter invented, including photocopying and recording, or in any information storage or retrieval system, without permission in writing from the publishers.

Trademark notice: Product or corporate names may be trademarks or registered trademarks, and are used only for identification and explanation without intent to infringe.

Library of Congress Cataloging-in-Publication Data
Names: Harris, Anne M., author.
Title: Creativity, religion and youth cultures / by Anne M. Harris.
Description: 1st Edition. | New York : Routledge, 2017. | Series:
    Routledge advances in critical diversities ; 2 | Includes bibliographical
    references and index.
Identifiers: LCCN 2016030699 (print) | LCCN 2016033690
    (ebook) | ISBN 9781138923812 (hardcover : alk. paper) |
    ISBN 9781315684789
Subjects: LCSH: Religion and culture—Case studies. | Performing arts—
    Case studies. | Group identity—Case studies. | Youth—Case studies. |
    Creative ability—Case studies.
Classification: LCC BL65.C8 H385 2017 (print) | LCC BL65.C8
    (ebook) | DDC 201/.6791—dc23
LC record available at https://lccn.loc.gov/2016030699

ISBN: 978-1-138-92381-2 (hbk)
ISBN: 978-1-315-68478-9 (ebk)

Typeset in Sabon
by Apex CoVantage, LLC

This book is dedicated to my loving father Edward C. Harris (September 29, 1922–February 5, 2001), on whose birthday I finished this manuscript, and who taught me about faith, love, loyalty, and celebrating difference;

and to Greg Dimitriadis (August 27, 1969–December 29, 2014), whose creative and heartful scholarship has influenced me and so many others, and who has left us far too soon.

Contents

List of Figures		ix
Preface to Creativity, Religion, and Youth Cultures		xi
ANITA HARRIS		
Acknowledgments		xv
Introduction: About This Book		1

SECTION 1
Samoan Mediascapes and Faith-as-Performance **15**

Section 1 Overview		17
1	Education and the Creative Imaginary	33
2	God Culture and the Capacity to In/Aspire	62
3	Semblance and Praisesong	81

SECTION 2
Religion, Art, and a South Sudanese Post-National Imaginary **117**

Section 2 Overview		119
4	Imagining New Individualities/New Collectivities	135
5	The Art of Gender in South Sudanese Mediated Diasporas	160
6	Meaning and "Madolescence"	184
Conclusion		203
References		217
Index		233

Figures

I.1	Samoan fun at *Culture Shack* program	1
S1.1	Ana showing some digital love	17
S1.2	Rosada, double-selfie	26
1.1	Still image from *Samoan Youth Creativity and Religion*, 2016, Alta Truden/Anne Harris	37
1.2	Vineta and Ana, Samoan style, October 2014	43
1.3	Vineta's first *Culture Shack* poster, theatrical wizard	54
1.4	White Sunday goofing, 2015	56
2.1	Getting real with the spirit, at White Sunday, 2014	62
2.2	Spoofing Samoans	77
3.1	White Sunday, 2014	81
S2.1	Rap crew, *Culture Shack*	119
4.1	Hip-hopsters Dona and Rania	138
4.2	Lyrics review	143
4.3	Samoan and Sudanese collaborators and friends—Vineta, Achai, Rosada	147
4.4	In the studio—Andria, Abul, Aluel	156
5.1	Writing and recording original raps—Winnie and Dona	161
5.2	Loosening up and learning how to freestyle from Nantali	164
5.3	Afreem and Andria watching their hip hop video clips	171
6.1	Joyceline and Andria finish recording	192
6.2	Long days at the studio	201

Preface to *Creativity, Religion, and Youth Cultures*

Anne Harris's *Creativity, Religion, and Youth Cultures* is a much-needed intervention into debates about the identity practices and creative activities of diasporic youth. Her book offers deep insights into the creative community-building undertaken by young people who are too often cast as problem subjects, and too often apprehended via dated ideas about migrant integration and youth transition. There is no doubt that we urgently require more agile theorisation of youth identities, cultures, and communities in conditions of globalisation, mobility, super-diversity, and new life patterns. Young people's contemporary efforts for self-expression, community, and identity now extend us well beyond conventional frames in youth/migration studies, such as the outdated problematic of how young people overcome what is seen as their ethnically-induced deficit, as well as the rigidity of dichotomising home/host and 'torn between two cultures' paradigms of belonging. Young people are forging new, globalised, and/or transnational communicative practices, communities, and identities in the context of ever-diversifying patterns of diversity, the collapse of traditional pathways to and possibilities for conventional citizenship, and the advantages and demands of mobility and connectivity. In doing so, they draw on local and global networks and fields of power that privilege the currency of creativity.

How specific groups of young people are doing this work of creative practice, how faith and culture converge in the process, and what this means for theorising youth identity, citizenship, and cultures in new times, is the subject of this engaging, brilliant book. Through an extraordinary ten-year plus (auto)ethnographic project with South Sudanese and Samoan background Christian youth in Melbourne, Australia (a place simultaneously of the global North and South), Anne Harris brings us directly into youth faith-shaped creative practices, interweaving the scholarly work of the book with excerpts from their lyrics and poetry, photographic images, and links to their audio and visual performances, representations, and commentary. She demonstrates how they generate creative capital from a position of local embeddedness in a Southern, subaltern, disaporic context that nonetheless always intersects with global, mobile, and virtual networks.

xii *Preface to* Creativity, Religion, and Youth Cultures

Intersectionality drives Harris's approach in every respect, but especially noteworthy is that she never retreats from working at the juncture of faith, youth, and arts. Youth studies has had surprisingly little to say about faith, religion, and spirituality beyond documentation of generational shifts in membership of organised religions or research into youth and religious prejudice, predominantly investigations of young people's experiences of Islamophobia. Religion is often imagined as a pre-determined sociological category that functions as a layer or variable in youth identity, rather than a dynamic, processual experience. Harris instead opens a window onto the everydayness of the intertwining of faith and creativity in the lives of young people and a sophisticated understanding of the processual nature of the identities and practices that they produce.

The book puts substance and criticality into what are often abstract claims that diasporic youth cultures enable processes of creative hybridisation and animate the local-global nexus. It shows exactly how these processes unfold and are managed in the everyday lives of young people, and the implications this has for understanding youth aspirations, belonging, and identity in new times. We are invited to consider these young people's experience as 'madolescence': a glorious term coined by Harris to get at the condition of dissonance between creative forces and communities and the racist, adultist, bordered society (as well as the well-worn theoretical paradigms) through which youth are regulated. She draws on Hickey-Moody's notion of 'little publics' to understand how young people are building community outside, and at times in defiance of, highly managed institutional contexts and regimes of integration and transition. The concept of madolescence takes us straight to the heart of the wild intensity, excess, and untamed possibilities of youth creativity in the making of community and connection. But Harris is not excessively celebrationary or reductionist about young people's creative counterpublics as 'transformative'. Rather, she pushes us to think beyond the usual frameworks about how, with what resources, and against what barriers, youth construct connection, community, belonging, and identity projects in contexts that are simultaneously post-national, transcultural, locally embedded, and multiply networked.

Here we see how creative practices allow youth to simultaneously inscribe local maintenance of culture and religion, network globally, market themselves in transnational creative and cultural industries, and generate processes for individual and collective reflexivity about identity and community. And importantly, the book also explores the complexity faced by young people who seek to express agency, politics, connection, and creativity locally and at the same time pursue global visibility and cachet through the commodification and commercial applications of their image and output. As Harris so deftly demonstrates, these are not so much contradictory impulses as a reflection of the multiple meanings and uses of creative identities for young people in times that reward creative entrepreneurialism, aspiration, and display as signs of good youth citizenship and also offer unprecedented possibilities for empowering experiences of expression and connectivity.

Preface to Creativity, Religion, and Youth Cultures   xiii

Fundamentally, Anne Harris gives us vital new ways of understanding how diasporic youth act and are produced as creative subjects within and beyond old borders of identity, community, and belonging. I have long admired her work (and have been flattered to be mistaken for her on occasion owing to the double quirk of the similarity of our names [no relation] and the fields we work in), and would venture that *Creativity, Religion, and Youth Cultures* is her best yet. This theoretically sophisticated, intersectional analysis of youth creativity is an absolute game-changer: it takes youth studies just where it needs to go.

Anita Harris

Acknowledgments

First and foremost, I would like to acknowledge my creative collaborators in this work: Vineta, Ana, Newjoy, Rosa, Eseta, and all at the Wesleyan Methodist Samoan church in the western suburbs of Melbourne, Australia; and to Khamisa, Lina, Dona, Achai, Rania, Jaklin, Afreem, Winnie, Sunday, Jaclin, Achol, Aluel, Abul, Viviana, Joyceline, and Ashay. Also many thanks to Alta Truden, who continues to be a gifted and generous filmmaking collaborator, always ready to grab her camera and run—a great collaborator and ever-enthusiastic visual storyteller and ethnographer. Thanks to all the artists and scholars associated with this current collaboration and previous ones, including *Culture Shack*, *SAILing into University*, and *Teaching Diversities*. Thanks to Sheri M. Goldhirsch who, like Greg Dimitriadis, was a humble and passionate advocate of young people and their creativity, who took the work and lives of young adults seriously and not as a prelude to something more to come. Sheri, like Greg, was taken from us too soon and is deeply missed by many. Thanks to Footscray Community Arts Centre, a gloriously diverse and creative stalwart in a rapidly gentrifying region of Melbourne Australia, where many of these conversations, projects, and relationships were born and nurtured over many years. Thanks also to Mari Eleanor—consummate musician, teacher, friend, with whom I have co-taught, collaborated, and strived to better understand and make valuable arts experiences for many of the young people in these two communities.

I would like to acknowledge those who have influenced my thinking in this work: Enza Gandolfo, Ben O'Mara, Clare Hall, Scott Bulfin, Helen Forbes-Mewett; Lew Zipin, with whom I brainstormed some of the ideas about aspiration and minoritarian youth communities, particularly culturally diverse ones; Kathleen Gallagher, Megan Boler, Julia Gray, Noah Kenneally, Joe Norris, and other valued colleagues and collaborators in the rich Canadian research and creative community to whom I am indebted both intellectually and for their companionship as friends, makers, and scholars. My gratitude to Lisa Gordon, my sister-by-choice, whose love, laughter, and upstate New York home has provided a sanctuary for me since I moved

xvi   *Acknowledgments*

away from our shared hometown more than thirty years ago now, and where I wrote the important parts of this book. To Luna, my beloved and ever-present cocker spaniel companion of fifteen years, who is still teaching me about loyalty, creativity, and affect in these, her final months as she battles through stage four cancer. And to Stacy, Haddie, Murphy, and Tasha, for bringing all my chaotic and untamed creative dreams to life.

Introduction
About This Book

Figure I.1 Samoan fun at *Culture Shack* program. Photo and copyright, Anne Harris.

Critical Creative Cultures

This book takes a critical approach to the intersectional study of creativity, religion, and cultural practices, based in the rich youth cultures of Samoan and South Sudanese Australians. In it I also recognise the historicity of such enquiries, buried as they are in changing notions of culture, gender, spirituality, and especially these days, creativity. I draw heavily on Appadurai's scapes, his *capacity to aspire* and attention to global flows, and his *social imaginary*, an extension of Anderson's *imagined communities*—all of which I thread through my notion of *creative imaginaries*.

I also propose a notion of 'creative capital' that extends Bourdieu. I use the youth cultures scholarship of Dimitriadis (who himself used Appadurai) and Anita Harris for thinking about multicultural youth and urban youth.

2   Introduction

Less centrally, I draw on the religious/cultural scholarship of Yip, and the creative industries scholarship of O'Connor. I use these interwoven theoretical approaches in order to address the intersectionality of the multiple topics of culture, race, gender, digital cultures, and youth, which I introduce as a contextual landscape against which these youth rise up.

According to foundational creativity researcher E. Paul Torrance, at least from the time of Aristotle, it has been acknowledged that creative achievement is influenced by culture (1997). The ways in which creativity is distinct from artmaking, religion is distinct from faith, and culture is distinct from both ethnic and national subject positions inform the central questions of this text. Drawing on two groups of culturally, religiously, and creatively diverse youth in Melbourne, Australia (who know each other, and whose creative and religious pursuits bring them into contact), this book celebrates the complex intersectionality that characterises the lives of some migrant youth today. Here, South Sudanese and Samoan Christian youth discuss their faith-informed creative practices from a global south, Asia-Pacific perspective. By looking at the intersectionality of race, youth, culture, and music/performance-making as a nexus of social and cultural capital for youth cultures in the Asia Pacific, this book shows readers the increasingly digitally inflected, increasingly globally focused lives of even those who are mostly framed as 'local' in the discourses of global mobilities.

The threads that tie a gossameric link between creativity and spirituality are long and deep, and the things that make creativity both difficult to define and worth pursuing are some of the same characteristics of faith and spirituality. But here the intersection focuses on the ways in which contemporary young people from these two distinct diasporic communities pursue the meaning of Christian faith in their lives, in ways that might be considered both secular and religious. As Yip and Page remind us, the concepts of 'lived religion' (McGuire 2003) and 'everyday religion' (Ammerman 2007)

> capture the ways in which individuals interweave their religious faith with their everyday life, engaging with enabling and constraining potentials in explicitly religious spaces as well as secular spaces. This offers the possibilities of encountering religion in unexpected places, and opens the researchers' minds to the ways in which religion might not be bound up in institutions and/or sacred texts. Lived and everyday religion instead puts the focus on the ingenious ways individuals craft their faith in a complex world.
>
> (2013, 4)

These young people perform and also narrate their Christian faith in just that way. The intersectional approach used in this book is informed by several discourses, including post-structuralist, youth studies, creativity studies, and critical education. The use of multiple frameworks acknowledges the

Introduction 3

inextricability of these influences on the ways South Sudanese and Samoan youth in the global south understand community, cultural maintenance, creativity, and contemporary youth practices, which for them are embedded in their Christian values, and collective/individual creative and family-based rituals. Together, these sites of ritual form fields and habitus, co-constructing and enacting different forms of capital. These young people's ability to reflect upon and creatively reframe their experiences demonstrate a kind of emerging creative capital that can be understood as relational, agentic, and public. I argue that this emerging creative capital is a gateway to what Appadurai (1996) calls a new imaginary, constructed and maintained by these diasporic youth through an extension of his social mediascapes and Manning's (2009) 'relationscapes'.

The book is comprised of the written text and its digital assets, which were created by myself (and Alta Truden) and the young people you will meet here, with whom I have been working over the past ten years. The digital assets (video, sound, and still image files) are mostly self-generated graphic digital artefacts from these South Sudanese and Samoan Australian youth communities in order to foreground their particular kinds of critical approaches to their lived experiences, and which co-construct meaning alongside the more 'scholarly' arguments I advance in the text. These written and digital artefacts should be experienced together (as they were created), in order to fully enter into the multiple (though co-mingled) worlds which this book explores.

I have divided the book into two sections relating to community-building and creative becoming. These section introductions and headings provide, I hope, a fairly straightforward structure for working through this critical creative material without re-essentialising these disparate communities or practices, or suggesting they can be considered here individually and not in relation to one another. The book is divided by cultural group, not because of any culturally or ethnically essentialising goal or oversight, but rather because their primary communities of creative practice centre on these subjectivities. These two diverse youth communities are combined together in one work, as I outline in the introduction chapter, because they have known each other, performed together, and in some cases have been classmates for many years, and as such their stories (and mine) are intertwined. Their creative and religious identifications also provide a salient point of comparison and contrast due to them both being Christian, despite my original intention to include religiously diverse groups also. In the end, in conversation we came to decide that it was a good idea to include both Christian groups to see how they imagined and expressed their faiths differently, despite both being Christian.

It is my intention that these young people's voices lead us into a complex interrogation of the very rich ways in which they live the intersections between capitalism, faith-based practices, and creativity in their own lives—lives that are racially and culturally integrated but also productively segregated at times. It is written with a variety of audiences in mind, including the young people

4 *Introduction*

and their own peers, families, and other youth around the globe. But in it we also attempt to speak to practitioners, service-providers, and researchers in the fields of social work, gender, community arts, cultural and creativity studies, communications, arts and philosophy, sociology, health, and education. I have written it too with the intention of being relevant to policy-makers and practitioners within the voluntary and public sector working on gender, community development, religious studies, and cultural diversity in the fields of international relations, education, and youth work.

I hope this text fills a gap at the intersection between some important recent books on post-secularity (Lassander 2012), youth cultures (White and Wyn 2013), and cultural diversity, globalisation, and religion (Maira and Soep 2005; Rudowicz 2003) on the one hand, and creativity as it intersects with education, culture, and global creative industries on the other (Flew 2013; Araya and Peters 2010; Lubart and Sternberg 1998). Importantly, this book focuses on southern hemisphere and South Pacific perspectives and practices as a site of emergent creative practice, and represents an area of long-standing interest but a dearth of critical texts (Giuffre 2009), especially not self-generated. While not concerned primarily with digital culture beyond its role in the community-making labour of the young people featured here, the book acknowledges the links between DIY maker cultures, participatory and prosumer cultures, and creative communities (for the non-'creative class').

Overall, this text emerges from a rise in interest in recent years about racial, religious, and cultural diversity in youth cultures. It unpacks the social and cultural implications of such diversities, through the lens of creativity. The text's unique focus is on the ways that performance, creativity, and the arts both construct and simultaneously undermine those intersecting identities. It foregrounds Pacific and southern states geo-political subjectivities that remain under-represented in popular and scholarly discourses, and their influence on the cultural role of creativity globally.

Creativity studies researchers, social scientists, arts practitioners, and activists working intersectionally in intercultural contexts may also find some value between these covers, and it is my express wish that the observations and arguments advanced here will contribute to the very dynamic contemporary conversation about culture and creativity, and that readers will find something to 'speak back' to, with which to engage, and from which to launch their own interventions into understanding contemporary creativity that offer a more holistic and more sustainable way forward than we are seeing at the current time.

Defining Youth

This book spends intentional time defining the notion of 'youth', which in the case of migrant and refugee young people is often misunderstood and inconsistently named (not unlike creativity itself), a fact that too-often goes

Introduction 5

unremarked in mainstream western and academic literatures. It is also a category with permeable boundaries depending on cultural contexts, historical contexts, age, and genders. The United Nations delineates youth as those between fifteen and twenty-four years old (see www.un.org), but in the two predominant longitudinal projects featured in this book, the youth have ranged between thirteen and thirty years old. Of course, 'youth' as a category and as a discursive exercise is always culturally situated, and often constructed very differently in western culture than in non-western cultures. So for example the ways in which the category of youth is defined by the Samoan young people in this book is very different from the ways in which youth are defined in South Sudanese culture (both in western resettlement contexts and in Africa, as detailed extensively in my text on ethnocinema and South Sudanese girls, in Harris 2013a). In this book I once again draw on the cultural anthropology of Arjun Appadurai (2013, 2006, 2004,1999, 1996), on the new materialist work of Erin Manning (2014, 2013, 2009, 2007, 2003) and Brian Massumi (2013, 2011, 2002), on youth and girlhood studies literature especially from Amy Dobson (2015) and Anita Harris (2013, 2008, 2004), and most importantly I draw on the reflections and creative performances of my youth collaborators.

In defining youth though, I also want to make a clear distinction between the youth in this book who have emerged from diverse refugee and migrant experiences, and those who have not. Migrants too often get lumped together, as do people of colour, youth in general, and ethnic-based groupings like 'Africans' and 'Asians'. The South Sudanese and Samoan youth whose voices are featured here, like most of us, go to great pains to distinguish themselves from the others with whom they are overgeneralised and genericised in groupings, and so out of respect for them and for the requirements of vigourous scholarship, so too must we and I strive to do so in this book. The purpose of combining them in a book on religion, culture, and creativity is in order to show two distinct and dynamic groups of non-white western youth who are active in community in cosmopolitan Melbourne, but their pairing is not arbitrary: as mentioned, many of these young people are friends, former classmates, and are fellow Christians. For these and other reasons, there are overlaps and yet distinctions, and both offer rich axes for comparison and contrast.

The many differences between refugee-background and non-refugee-background migration are equally significant: the South Sudanese youth here (or for some who were very small upon arrival or born in Australia, their parents and/or siblings) have suffered unimaginable layers of trauma associated with their refugee experiences. Sometimes these layers are visible in their creative works, and sometimes they are not. The often-violent contexts from which they have emerged are substantively distinct from the migration experiences of the Samoan youth who have not emerged from war contexts. Yet some aspects of their experiences bear similarities too: in living as part of a global diaspora, the fractured and uprooted scattering of families, the racism and othering of brown people in a majority-white country of resettlement, the

6 Introduction

remoteness of geographic home, the cultural and familial experience of being born outside of one's family's country of origin.[1] The Samoan youth narrate the ways in which just moving from New Zealand to Australia (a small move compared to the initial migration from Samoa to 'the west') has further eroded their cultural and religious knowledges and community cohesion. For the South Sudanese, there are ways in which the migration out of South Sudan has increased the interconnectedness and commitment of their religious and cultural subjectivities, as well as scattered them.

Kathleen Gallagher's (2014) five-year multi-sited ethnography *Why Theatre Matters* similarly tackles some of these issues concerning young people who are most regarded as 'disadvantaged' and 'marginal' by calling her work a 'pedagogy of the real'. I too would consider what these Samoan and South Sudanese youth are doing here as a pedagogy of the real, albeit too often outside of schools. Gallagher takes a 'multi-dimensional' approach to student engagement, one which underscores social context and interpersonal relations, and one of her major contributions to the field is expanding what scholars and practitioners consider to be sites and practices of 'drama education'; similarly, this text asks readers to reconsider what sites and practices of culture might look like in a new global creativity.

What does it mean to 'globalise' the research imagination, as Appadurai and then Dimitriadis have asked us to do? For Gallagher, it is in both the construction of the knowledge created, as well as its circulation. Gallagher's 'data', like the data here, were relational, performative, and embedded in social relations. They included in-class work, live performances, digital performances, focus groups, interviews, and surveys. She deployed mixed methods with the explicit purpose of 'quantitatively exploring' what the richer data seemed to show, as I have done in my current four-nation creativity-in-schools research study (Harris 2015a). Yet what might be the value of global data sets if researchers seek to globalise our imaginations as well as our practices, rather than reduce such diversities into 'emergent themes' and foreclose the rich differences to which they bear witness?

For Gallagher, such a long-term, multi-sited mixed methods ethnographic study, from such vastly different contexts and processes and spaces, revealed the specificities of local practices, as the ongoing creative work of the Samoan and South Sudanese young people in this book does. She has also long drawn attention to what she calls the 'gendered material struggle' of urban youth in precarious employment, juggling various lives, and then having to endure stigmatizing representations of their lives in the popular media. Like the Samoan and South Sudanese youth here, Gallagher's co-participants have resorted to making their own self-representations because they see so few authentic reflections around them. And for every creative victory, these youth carry the weight of feeling responsible for what befalls them, being neoliberally programmed to believe that the global south matters less, is less interesting, less modern, networked, and less relevant to not only creative industries but creative and economic futures. And yet, the young people in this book respond, here we are. They see themselves as part of a global community, even if so many in that global community don't yet see them. They enact that global citizenship every day through social media and other online networks. Their resilience is interwoven into their expressions of culture, religion, and creativity, and the strength of this fabric protects them from the vicissitudes of racist, classist, and euro-centric society, and sustains them when these forces threaten to swamp their subcultural nests. They manage, somehow, to remain firmly rooted in local communities while reaching creative tentacles out into the global mediascape.

Lastly, while both groups of young people here experience racism, the South Sudanese report much more frequent and more aggressive forms of racism, and more directly tied to their skin colour, than the Samoan youth. As my earlier work has noted in detail (Harris 2014, 2013), in Australia the arrival of significant numbers of South Sudanese only dates back to about 2004, and the relatively sudden influx triggered ongoing and often ugly backlash from some sectors of the majoritarian white Australian community and media. In all of these ways, the youth featured in this book represent perhaps a different perspective on 21st-century youth cultures, both as migrant youth who use creativity to celebrate their particular hybrid brand of culture and religion and to speak back to everyday racism, and who connect with the global north for creative and cultural inspiration. These youth, while in some ways very different from their white peers in the global north (and the global south), are in many other ways exactly the same as they navigate adolescence, family, and the future, and I hope to highlight both these differences as well as the universalities of their experiences in these pages.

Defining Religion

At a time of so-called secularisation of the western world, set in a reassuringly neat binary opposite to the so-called fundamentalist rise of the non-western world, these youth groups show a more complex and more integrated picture, in which these supposed polarities meet and mingle in productive overlapping creative lived experience. As recent events in Russia have shown regarding the complexities of sexual/religious intersections, it is more important than ever to separate simplistic re-essentialising discourses of dogmatic religion from evolving global subjectivities and political agendas. The empirical data drawn on in this text, combined with the broad survey of the growing body of critical literature on secularism, religion, gender, and culture, enable this book to comment from both macro- and micro-perspectives on the ways in which these youth activities are powerfully shaping the political and cultural landscape of tomorrow, but also the ways in which simply secular/religious definitions may be missing the potency of faith orientations completely.

In approaching this book and the making of work for that purpose, I did consider and discuss with my youth collaborators whether it would be preferable to include diverse religious orientations as well as cultural ones.

8 *Introduction*

We agreed that while such an approach would have particular strengths, it also might lend itself to stereotyping about 'Christian' versus 'Muslim' or other youth practices, and we felt that offering two youth perspectives that were both Christian might bring other similarities and differences into sight. Working across well-established relationships on a topic of Christian faith expressions through creativity seemed simple and clear, for a topic that is messy and overlapping. Similarly, discourses themselves can be messy where youth, religion, and creativity are concerned. For example, current tensions between cultural industries and creative industries discourses show the ways that aspirational projects which seek to push forward into more intersectional approaches can become 'muddied' and lose momentum. Similarly, a book of this nature that criss-crosses so many complex realms of experience in the lives of young people points to the need for a more dynamic conversation about the differences between religion, faith, and spirituality—a conversation that (like creativity) often gets collapsed down into secular versus religious.

The role of religion and faith practices is also inextricably linked to aspiration and the ever-narrowing available paths to 'something better' (be that religious or material) for these minoritarian youth. While they sometimes speak explicitly about their Christian practices and beliefs as 'religion', they often consider it a more private 'faith' experience, or the less structured 'spirituality' they value. These nuances are important, and space limitations do not always allow me to explore them fully, but where possible they are noted and at least indicated as areas for further exploration. But I will also problematise the intersection between religious and youth cultures, especially within the Australian context, where greater criticality is indeed called for and can be heard in the voices of the youth themselves.

In another recent study of mine with culturally and linguistically diverse lesbian, gay, bisexual, transgender, and queer (LGBTQ) young people, the distinctions between religion and traditional culture were made by those youth who felt the brunt of homophobia was coming primarily from religious imperatives rather than cultural ones (Harris 2013d, 2011b). And in other work with some of the same youth collaborators featured here, I drew on Halberstam in order to problematise 'success' through her lens of the 'queer art of failure', "a resistance to the ubiquitous neoliberal notion that success and happiness are inexorably tied to individual liberty, achievement, resilience and ability, and that they are part of a liberating agenda in democratic society" (Harris 2013c, 123). By challenging the material success imperatives inherent in our American and Australian contexts, these young women from Samoan and South Sudanese backgrounds offer other kinds of success narratives than the singular one available in capitalist neoliberal discourses.

Some of the discussion here draws on *Culture Shack*, a previous collaborative creative project involving some of both these Samoan and also South Sudanese youth, in which "performers who ended up in the music video chose to sing in multiple languages, primarily English and Arabic. A majority of the lyrics included Christian faith-based content, which was surprising for the coordinators (some of whom knew the participants well) and for Nantali [the hip hop stream facilitator], who has run so many similar workshops in Montreal for the past several years" (Harris 2013c, 129). Such longitudinal involvement through artmaking allows the evolving notion of the intersectionality of the religious, cultural, and creative processes and perspectives of these youth to become clear to readers and sometimes to themselves.

Like Gallagher's multi-sited ethnographic co-participants, these youth speak confidently from 'insider' perspectives, in this case richly demonstrating the ways in which religion is not the constraining dogmatic institutional presence it may have been to their parents but rather the site of their hybrid emerging identities. Their creative activities represent a kind of post-political and post-proselytising engagement in which aspiration can be both grounded in lived experiences and communities (including families, church groups, cultural groups, and global youth movements), while at the same time representative of a 'capacity to aspire' (Appadurai) that offers them possibilities beyond their current circumstances. Faith-sharing and the arts offer them these possibilities in ways that more direct political and social activism do not.

It has been argued that a meta-narrative of secularity and extremism of this age masks a range of diverse experiences and relationships with the mundane, the divine, ecological and cultural formations, and social practices of praise (Taylor 2007) across the globe. Dimitriadis and Weis have written extensively about the "contested terrain of education, urban youth and globalization" (2008, 81), which includes popular culture, public pedagogies, and creative expressions of cultural and racial subjectivities. Building upon the southern postcolonial and critical gender scholarship of Connell (2007), Smith (2006), and others, this book highlights perspectives and practices specific to the Asia Pacific and Australia, as culturally, creatively, and spiritually diverse sites of modernity, and extends this scholarship to a critical consideration of the ways in which these social practices and diversities continue to evolve in emerging global digital cultures where young people perform and encounter creative role models, multiple forms of community-building, and material progress (Pollock 2005; Mitias 1985).

Defining Creativity

Since as far back as Stein (1953), scholars have tried to define and measure creativity and its relationship to culture (Niu and Sternberg 2001). Others more recently have highlighted new forms of creative enquiry in research contexts, especially new and emerging social science methods and methodologies (Spencer 2011; Mason and Dale 2010; Banks 2005; Giri 2004; Banks 2001/2005), including performative and digital ones. The power of

10 Introduction

visual and other evolving creative methods is increasingly well-documented (Harris 2015c; Spencer 2011), yet its impact on critical research and more broadly its implications for a paradigm shift regarding doing and disseminating research is yet to be deeply understood. This text goes some way toward advancing that agenda.

In defining how I'm grappling with the slippery notion of creativity for the purposes of this book, my in-depth discussion in Chapter One contextualises my use of it as a culturally constituted (or hijacked) neoliberal concept but also highlights the ways in which a kind of DIY ethic informs another kind of resilient cultural role of creativity—the 'maker' and practice-led approach to digital and other creativity that I have written about elsewhere as a resistant part of or opposition to commodified creativity (Harris 2014). Creativity as an industry has not replaced 'old school creativity' at all, but it is impacting on perceptions, definitions, and social functions of it, including these youths'. Mostly this contextual work is done in Chapter One, but before we get to it I must make explicit at the outset that while this book (in order to make those connections and distinctions) draws briefly on social media theory (connectivity, networked cultures, etc.), and also on creative and cultural industries discourses, it is primarily about youth cultures and how they interact with and use these two 'ecosystems' (O'Connor 2013) for their own ends, creating new 'imaginaries' as they do so, not for an examination of digital youth cultures per se. It is an exploration of how culture, creativity, faith, and gender diversities intersect in the online/offline worlds of these young people, and how their performance of creativity serves these ends. For that reason, the focus is squarely on the ways they express their creativity, and how that creativity is representative of their faith/religion and cultural values and perspectives.

These young people (many of whom I have been collaborating with since 2005) recognise the intersectionality between their arts, religious, and cultural practices. The co-constitutive identity-building work of music, performance, and drama for Samoan and Sudanese youth in church and outside-of-church (including online) contexts has given rise to new considerations of diversity, (multi/trans/inter)cultural identity, and the religious practices and rituals that inform them. These young people and their culture-specific churches provide a safe if 'imagined community' (Anderson 2006) in which they can express these emerging subjectivities, which move beyond simple framings like 'multicultural' to explicitly include faith practices. These identities emerge in combination with popular cultural art forms like hip hop, R&B, and gospel music traditions, and performance influences drawn from not only their specific cultural backgrounds but also American, British, and European popular cultural forms (including fashion, reality television, social media, gaming, and online video-sharing). In addition, there remains relatively little scholarship on the Pacific Islander and African youth experience (Chi and Robinson 2012) overall, particularly outside of the United States, the UK, and Europe, and the ways in which diasporic experiences are reshaping these cultural and gendered communities and geo-political localities.

Structure of the Book

This book takes a critical diversities approach to the study of creativity, religion, and cultural capital among today's youth. Section 1 draws on a Samoan Christian youth group and their award-winning musical performances across the Asia Pacific Christian community, highlighting the intersectionality of race, youth, culture, and music as a nexus of meaning-making and cultural capital, drawing on a Bourdieuian frame to look at the ways Samoan youth in Australia and New Zealand understand success, community, and cultural maintenance, which for them is embedded in Christian values, rituals, and the habitus of resettlement contexts.

In Section 2, the analysis extends Appadurai's notion of the 'capacity to aspire' in combination with Anderson's imagined communities to understand the social function of this faith-infused creativity. Here I argue that this emerging creative capital is a gateway to what Appadurai calls a new imaginary, constructed and maintained by this new generation of diasporic youth through social mediascapes. For the Sudanese youth spotlighted in Section 2, religion and the Christian faith provide a framework for creating communities of practice in the business of resettlement, capitalist aspiration, and retaining links to an increasingly mythical 'back home'.

Both youth groups' empirical data has been gathered, created, or curated primarily by the Samoan and Sudanese young people themselves. As 'insider research', this multimodal content represents youth views on the digital creative work being done here, but also reflects the religious implications, bounded understandings, and cultural recreation/maintenance that runs parallel to the church-based work being done in their youth groups. As such, these empirical data are simultaneously ethnographic accounts of youth cultures, faith-based/religious cultures, raced and gendered cultures, and arts communities of practice, documented using visual and aural methods.

Highlighting a diversity of methods and approaches, these data highlight the ways in which these young people are thinking in new and diverse ways about their own identities as cultured, faithed, and creative communities. Their links, in some cases, are stronger with others like them across the globe in 'home' communities but also other diasporic locations, than are their bonds with more diverse local others. Drawing on a combination of Appadurai, Anderson, and Massumi's digital imaginaries, this book takes a diverse approach and embraces diverse methods to interrogate new ways of thinking about creative arts and performance as an emergent capital that is not bounded by geography, but is fluid and resilient in its culturally and digitally constitutive role. These communities of practice (or what Anderson calls imagined communities) hold important implications for nation-state, corporate, and other increasingly anachronistic cohesion principles.

'Cultural creativity' has often been linked to colonial and anthropological notions of the subaltern, and the creativity found in such locations as craft-based, 'traditional' (read simplistic) expressions of a 'dying race' or documentation of exotic cultural practices or beliefs. Today's creative and

12 Introduction

cultural industries are deeply imbued with the hybridity of culture, faith, and youth. From 'The Voice' to 'The X Factor', from New Zealand's 16-year-old recording sensation Lorde to gender variant models Andreja Pejic and Ruby Rose, from worldwide fashion icon and Melbourne local Ajak Deng to Sudanese Australian basketball star Thon Maker, southern hemisphere young people are showing new ways forward in combining culture, creativity, and aspirations. Such increasing material and cultural success may suggest a new way of considering Walter Benjamin's (1936) notion of 'the aura', the kind of re-coupling of the arts—not with re-essentialising limitations on artists-of-colour, but rather a re-integration of histories, rituals, reverberations, and what Benjamin called the work of art's 'totemic value' rather than the emaciated 'use-value' of today's endlessly reproducible arts practices and products. Indeed, as such diverse movements as the Peoples' Puppets of Occupy Wall Street are now showing, the arts have the power to transcend traditional political strategies and can also address the multiple subjectivities of race, gender, sexuality, and religion that play so deep a role in the contemporary call to action. For these young people invested in performing their faith through church-based youth groups, spiritually homogenous communities of practice are the most effective place to start. They are not without civic engagement agendas at all; they draw their power base through religious rather than activist practices, yet for them faith is wholly political.

Appadurai's (1996) notion of the imaginary and its field of five scapes provide a geography across which the playing out of ethnicity, performativity, and identity coincide in powerful ways. Such orienting principles can be seen from the praisesongs of the young people in the empirical data of this book, to Anderson's (2006) notion of post-nationhood. Such performance and its role in the maintenance of collective and individual memory is troubled between the works of Anderson (2006) and Appadurai (2004), and the nexus of these ideologies can be seen to represent both posthuman (Appiah 2010) and also post-nation-state orientations. Appiah's (2010) articulation of cosmopolitanism can be seen in the way these youth performances transcend discourses of commonality between the increasingly polarised ideologies and values systems emerging or re-asserting themselves across the globe today, and move toward more hybrid understandings of the culture/religion nexus. Whether or not Appiah's cosmopolitanism conflicts with Anderson's focus on the nation-state continues to be fertile ground for unpacking the ways and reasons why people are drawn toward and away from one another in ideological and performative ways.

I hope that this text will be of interest to researchers, artists, community workers, and teachers, but more importantly I hope it will be satisfying to those youth who are featured here, by their words, deeds, songs, and incredible creative practices and orientations in a world that does not always recognise them—as creative capital or creative inspiration. While I have written this book with an eye to the international landscape of youth cultures, faith, and creativity, I hope it will particularly speak to those of us who live and work in the Asia Pacific, who must too often make do with texts that are solely or solidly focused on the global north and either denigrate or just simply ignore the amazing work that goes on in this region—and I say that as an American Australian who is still creatively and ideologically devoted to my birthplace. I hope my fellow creatives in the Asia Pacific will find in this text a welcome celebration and critical analysis addressing communities and practices from our own region.

This book also sets out to document how we are changing our relationship with creativity in its role in how we learn, form, and perform community. This is an analysis of the everyday, situated practices of creativity and creative labour, creative communities, and also the more immeasurable forms of creativity like the kind of 'slow creativity' evident in these two communities, which function not as product but as everyday process and practice. This kind of creative practice functions not only as community-building but also as digital creative precursor—they work hand in hand. Only secondarily do these creativities act as a tool of aspiration, or capital, or as a ticket out, by the collectivities and individuals who hold them resiliently as core to their cultural and religious lives. Within these pages you will find not only the creative artefacts but the feelings they trail—feelings which, following Erin Manning, "are associated with facts in Whitehead's philosophy, with creativity as their conduit" (2009, 195). Creativity here is a dynamic conduit for many things, and truly "creativity is a social effort" (2009, 203), not an individual one for these productively and multiply networked young people. Certainly, the creativity evidenced here is both a social effort and a conduit for faith, relationship, and love, and we hope you find them all within these pages.

Note

1 Many Samoans, including several of those here, were born to Samoan parents who had migrated to New Zealand, while some were born in Australia but still identify strongly as Samoan culturally. That is, in one family there may be siblings who were born in one or two different countries on their way to life in Australia, and whose parents were born back in Samoa. For the South Sudanese, most of these youth were born in exile, in Kakuma refugee camp in Kenya, or in Ethiopia, two common resting places on the way to resettlement. None of the South Sudanese youth featured in this book were born in Australia, but many of them have younger siblings who were, thereby creating a 'culture gap' in their families in which the parents may have been born in South Sudan, then had first children in Ethiopia, subsequent children in Kenya, and additional children in Australia. The Australian-born children are considered 'Australian' in a way the others are not, but of course each family—whether South Sudanese or Samoan—defines these differences for themselves.

Section 1

Samoan Mediascapes and Faith-as-Performance

Section 1 Overview

Figure S1.1 Ana showing some digital love. Photo and copyright, Anne Harris.

Overview

The first section of this book is devoted to the Samoan young people who perform their creativity first and foremost through their youth group at the Wesleyan Methodist Samoan Church in Melbourne, and share those performances more widely through social media. This and the Section Two introduction offer a brief overview of the approach and conceptual framings that have helped me think through the work of each youth culture here, and to which I think their particular creative expressions contribute. They also importantly disrupt the way scholarly work in those particular cultural 'spaces' has been done. In this first section concerning the Samoan youth, I use their work to think newly about creativity scholarship (O'Connor and Gibson 2014; Runco 2014; Collins 2010; Manning 2009; Barone and

18 *Samoan Mediascapes and Faith-as-Performance*

Eisner 2011), youth and education studies (Anita Harris 2013; White and Wyn 2013; Youdell 2012; Weis, Fine and Dimitriadis 2009; Dolby and Rizvi 2008; Fine 2008, 2004), and feminist (Ringrose 2015; Braidotti 2013) and critical race scholarship (Singh and Doherty 2008). But each introductory section also shares a bit about my relationship with the young people, as this is intentionally a creative and personal narrative, as well as a scholarly one. Our mutual and sometimes-collaborative work demonstrates the conceptual complexity that can be at the heart of both popular creativity and of "writing-as-research, and the creativity of theorizing our own lives" (Harris and Gandolfo 2013, 3), by jointly exploring these narratives of culture, creativity, and faith through the young people's commentary, creative writings, images, utterances, and my own.

"Creativity", Erin Manning tells us, "folds out of thought even as it proposes thought to itself. Thought is an untimely proposition" (2009, 228), and the Samoan young people whose work is featured here are aware of the limits of time in their abilities to actualize the creative thoughts and intensities they experience and share with one another. Temporally overcommitted and under-resourced as so many young people are, these youth multi-task by partly combining their praise practices, cultural and friendship communities, and creative pursuits. The Samoan community in Melbourne, Australia is a sprawling, diverse, but tightly knit group. They are linked closely with other Pasifika peoples (Tongan, Fijian) also living diasporically, an affinity which grows out of many commonalities including cultural, geographic, and religious. Many have come to Australia by way of New Zealand, and many of the youth featured in this case study—like their peers—have been born to Samoan-born parents in New Zealand. So when they talk about culture, many of these young people talk about feeling Samoan, 'Kiwi' (vernacular for New Zealanders), and Australian, and indeed they are a mixture of all three in practical and abstract ways. Through their uses of social media, these youth are also building new and extending their communities, into what Appadurai has called 'communities of sentiment' (1990), as I discuss later in the book.

Scholarly literature about the Samoan experience is fairly limited. Even historically, much of the extant scholarship represents white colonial, postwar, or western perspectives, as Chi and Robinson (2012) have written about its contemporary history:

> Samoa is a group of Polynesian islands in the South Pacific that came under western political control in 1899, when Germany and the United States divided up the islands for themselves. While the German-controlled half gained independence in 1962, the U.S. retained control of the eastern islands.
>
> (61)

As with still so many western narratives, the history begins from European contact. Apart from economic or anthropological studies, of which there are still quite few, works that document contemporary Samoan life are rare. For a general picture of the ill-effects of colonisation in the region, Giuffre is helpful overall; yet it is worth noting that—like so much other literature on Pasifika youth—this work is still generalising, even with the salient cultural analyses here that contribute to readers understanding the Samoan youth in this book and their family histories:

> As in the Cooks, annexation and/or colonization often negatively affected the traditional culture. The loss of indigenous language, for example, occurred throughout Polynesia and continues today. The Maori Language Commission poll conducted in 1995 found that only eight percent of Maoris speak a Maori language (Crocombe 2001, 107). Under conditions of colonial rule, it was often advantageous for indigenous people—especially those who could claim mixed ethnic heritage—to identify with the dominant colonial group. With the wave of independence movements that began in the 1960s, the situation throughout Polynesia reversed and those who had formerly identified with the colonial powers now made the most of their indigenous identifiers. . . . [cultural] fluidity is indicative of a pan-Polynesian indigenous cultural revival that began in the second half of the twentieth century and really gained steam with the first South Pacific Festival of the arts, held in Suva, Fiji, in 1972.
>
> (Giuffre 2009, 72)

Yet a new generation of Samoan-New Zealander and Samoan-American scholars are emerging, among them Samoan-American scholar, activist, and writer Tafea Polamalu, who puts it very differently using a poetic lens that critiques the colonial and anthropological legacy of Margaret Mead and scholarly analyses that have until now been the primary framers of his culture. His poem 'Diasporic Dream' (2009) succinctly asserts,

> I know all about Samoa:
> Population
> Climate
> Average life expectancy
> Margaret Mead
> I am the vision
> I am progress
> I am a masterpiece of assimilation.
>
> (2009, 62)

Like Polamalu and other young Samoans, assimilation and cultural maintenance have been an area of great concern for the Samoan youth and their families and church community, as have the material conditions of their diasporic resettlements. Contemporary Samoan stories often tell of frequent exploitative economic, tax, and legislative acts and trends that have left

20 *Samoan Mediascapes and Faith-as-Performance*

Samoans under-paid and under-employed. Not only in countries of resettlement like Australia, but as Faleomavaega's discussion of minimum wage in American Samoa and on the American mainland shows, financial inequities are common in Samoan life on a global scale:

> Today, most of the estimated 130,000 Samoans or part Samoans residing in the United States live in Hawai'i, California, and Washington. In general, Samoans have higher levels of poverty, and lower rates of home ownership, educational levels, and employment than the general population.
>
> (Faleomavaega 2012, 58)

If there is very little scholarly literature on Samoan lives in general, the experiences of Samoan young women have been almost completely ignored. Important new Samoan scholars are emerging (including Iosefo 2014; Faleomavaega 2012; Polamalu 2009; Tupuola 2004, 2000), highlighting the diversity of this community and the need for more Pasifika scholarship, especially from the global south. I have noted previously,

> Like the Samoan American and New Zealander young women of Tupuola's study, the young women [of *Culture Shack*] share certain socio-political attributes with some recent feminist and pop culture scholars (Fine 2004) who would have us consider aspects of girl culture more seriously. What Michelle Fine calls 'empirical archives of social reproduction and struggle' (in Anita Harris 2004, xiii) show scholars a way forward into new feminist (and pedagogical) geographies, and offer some possibilities for connecting 'the global ribs that sculpt bodies through gender, race, ethnicity, class, age and geography' (2004, xiii).
>
> (Harris and Lemon 2012, 429)

Approach to These Collaborations

As O'Connor and Gibson note, Australian cities "are now connected as never before to the emergent horizon of the Asian cities. . . . However, their ambitions, their vision and their priorities are very far from engaging" (2014, 63) with our Asian neighbours, refusing resolutely to see ourselves as an Asia Pacific country, always culturally gazing toward the west. This disconnect between the strongly Asian population of Australia and its western vision of itself and cultural and economic alliances is evident in the hybrid lives and work of the Samoan youth with whom I have been collaborating since 2005.

The young people who participated in these conversations, interviews, artworks, and filming sessions were all in the end female, although their youth group involves many males and they draw on their shared experiences in this integrated group. The youth featured here and I have been working together in one form or another since I was the drama teacher for some of them, including Vineta, who is my primary Samoan collaborator in this book. The process of self-reflexively and dialogically collaborating through creative and faith-based projects thus began in those classrooms at that all-girls Catholic school in Melbourne's western suburbs, and to a large extent it is still my primary approach in this project. Pivotal members of both the Samoan and South Sudanese groups of young women and I met this way and have continued through a familiarity that is both educative (certainly not one-way) and mutually enquiring. Coming from a theatre background, I ran my classes as collaboratively as possible, and the works created here were made in this same manner, through a practice-led approach. We have worked across several sites and projects over the years, and I consider them friends as well as collaborators. But this book is specifically about the religious and faith orientations and assemblages of which these young people are participants and practitioners, and much as they have welcomed me into those church and family communities, I am not a member, and I willingly and critically acknowledge that. We have learned much about one another, and others, along these travels, and I expect to continue doing so. But, like Gallagher, I recognise that, "I had to work hard to uncover the taken-for-granted assumptions of my own practice . . . what I had been was a witness of their telling" (2000, 17).

The young women self-documented their experiences by engaging a range of tools, including video (using phones, flipcams, and approached in a range of ways including ethnocinematic, diaristic, and ethnographic, including filming me) and visual digital tools like Photoshop, Sketch-up, and Flash animation. They are creatively literate with online tools like Vimeo, YouTube, and social media platforms like Snapchat, Instagram, and Facebook, and with their growing literacy, they are circulating their particular creative works in more sophisticated and multi-purposeful ways.

I share their methodology not to artificially decouple their tools from their way of living everyday life, their own doing of things, and the conceptual (and religious and cultural) framework from within which they curate these activities and outputs, but rather to highlight that their tools may be fairly standard in research terms (this could be considered an example of Participant Action Research (PAR) or a visual or multi-sited ethnographic or autoethnographic study), but our collaborative and longitudinal engagement with one another and these explorations of the intersection of cultural, spiritual, and creative aspects of ourselves is a rare privilege and goes beyond any one methodological approach. Like Jean Rouch and his innovations in *cine-ethnography*, creative and research expansion is possible only through long-term engagement of this kind, and I value our work highly, of which this book is only a snapshot focused mainly around religion. Many researchers (and artists too) never get the opportunity to continue working over a span of many years with the same group of collaborators, particularly with members of fast-moving, over-committed and easily distracted

22 Samoan Mediascapes and Faith-as-Performance

youth communities. Having for many years run community-based arts programs and projects, I know how hard it is to get a group of young people together more than once or twice, given the number of other things going on in their lives, so the logistics of conducting long-term research or creative enquiry together is challenging. However the logistics of this work and these relationships has relaxed over time, and I attribute that to our ability to move into more organic relationships which resemble intentional friendship with arts and documentation as only one part of it, rather than a formal 'research project' relationship.

But back when we first were getting to know one another, Vineta was in Year Seven, and she and her sister, cousins, and fellow church members were remarkable students if not always the most academically successful. They stood out in many ways: through their generally good nature when many high schoolers are surly or withdrawn; through their great skill and enthusiasm for drama as a subject; and through their willingness to engage in the social justice aspects of our school more quickly and passionately than most others. However, they were also outstanding performers, utterly unparalleled in confidence, skill, and pleasure, and this is how they first came to my attention and entered my heart and mind as gifted creatives. It can be typified by one particular summer lunch period when I was coordinating a well-intentioned cultural diversity week which became a bit of a forum for discussing the failure of multicultural policies, in schools and the 'outside world'. However this particular year, many different individuals and groups were participating, including myself as an 'American'. The cultural shares included food, artworks, stories, dance, and guests to the school from many different backgrounds. One day that week we were having the live performances during lunch, and students had signed up to dance, sing, share their food, or perform in other ways.

The Samoan and Tongan girls had been practicing, but I had not seen them do their dances. I knew they had been practicing mash-ups of traditional dances and more contemporary hip hop and R&B dance too. At our girls-only school the students all wore uniforms and had to tie very long hair back, no make-up, no nail polish (a practice I did and still do find misdirected and ideologically offensive), so when about fifteen Samoan girls—many of whom I thought I knew well through drama class—came out in single file and took their positions on the lawn, I (and everyone else present) literally gasped out loud. They were dressed in gloriously brilliants reds, greens, golden yellows, and oranges. They all had their long black hair down, their faces beaming, arms in the air, eyes fixed, and the graceful dance began. I had goosebumps. The girls danced for probably twenty minutes, barefoot, with crowns of grass on their heads, and (plastic) flower leis around their necks. It was the most graceful dance performance I had ever seen. It moved many to tears, and many to loud screams and hoots.

Many teachers will know the shock of seeing another side to the students they spend each day with in class, only to see them transform through arts performances, sporting events, or public speaking. I was well used to this experience as a teacher and in the theatre. Yet these students who day-by-day I knew to be respectful but cheeky, irreverent, sometimes shy, often hilarious, or real tomboys shocked me profoundly. I have thought about this shock response of mine many times, and seen it echoed in the faces and postures of my teaching colleagues at that school, and in multiple communities since then, as I've continued to be friends with and work with these young women and other Samoan youth elsewhere in Melbourne. It is a profound transformation that I think goes far beyond a question of stage presence and which these young people describe as 'doing it for God'. Section One discusses this relationship between performance and faith in detail, sometimes in my words and sometimes in their own.

Vineta is in her early twenties, now ten years on from this experience. So when we discussed the idea for this book, and the ways in which Vineta and her peers make sense of the world and continue to move out into the world while maintaining strong, faith-filled and family-centred lives and relationships, I knew it was important for the young people to record their own lives—so in this section (the first three chapters of this book) you will see a number of beautiful artefacts and digital documents and fragments that these young people have made either solely or partially themselves, and surely this is the power of creative methods—to bring an audience close into another's experience and to immerse us in an affective encounter with their own. But first I want to return to the moment of Otherness, which we laughingly call my 'Margaret Mead moment' with these girls whom I thought I already, all those years ago, knew so well but didn't. What was it exactly that caused me to stop and exoticise them in the way that I did?

My 'Margaret Mead Moment'

There are a number of aspects of that moment that make me feel uncomfortable: their dance, which was partly shocking because of its sensuality; their costumes, which were exotically beautiful; their particular performance style, which rendered them affectively and performatively different than they seemed to me in class.

As mentioned, many teacher and theatre folks can attest to the experience of seeing otherwise ordinary students take to the stage and be variously transformed. I had similar jarring shifts of perception in university when I'd see my drama professors take to the stage. I had in fact performed this transformation myself as a singer, actor, and performance maker for my whole life. But I had also seen it in my creative friends and family members during their performances, so it was not in itself something reserved for people who were unknown to me, or people who were brown or otherwise racially or culturally different from me, even as a migrant for the past seventeen years. Otherness is not very foreign to me, in its range of guises.

24 *Samoan Mediascapes and Faith-as-Performance*

However, the discomfort I felt in this context was primarily twofold:

- One aspect was the fact that I was their teacher and found their beauty almost disconcerting.
- The other was the fact that they came from a racially and ethnically different but also previously exoticised culture, and one that continues at times to be fetishised by white western people.

But perhaps I came to think of this particular moment as my Margaret Mead moment primarily because it made me want to *know them* or understand them, or what I have written about elsewhere as "both the desire and tension of educative contexts in which intercultural sharing can be productive, disruptive and mis/understood—all at the same time" (Harris and Lemon 2012, 414). This mesmerising effect has been critically interrogated by myself and others (Mageo 2008), and postcolonial literature certainly addresses the topic. Performatively, I felt they were successfully creating what Mageo has called 'zones of ambiguity' in their performances, in which these young people understood the intercultural complexities and were navigating them masterfully, but my attraction to their *difference* still made me enormously uncomfortable. In fact, I was not attached to their traditional dances and songs at all—I love their work at least as much or more when they are performing gospel or R&B harmonies and dances, which they often do as well. But the performative style is so different, and it made me want to understand why a particular transcendent look comes over their faces when they are performing traditional songs and dances. I asked them about the look a lot. The look for me is typified by their unwavering purposeful yet relaxed and focused gaze, radiant huge smiles that never falter, as their hands make complex, graceful, and expressive movements. I had never seen anything like it.

Many of my colleagues—drama teachers and performing artists and arts workers—have over time commented on the power of Samoan performance styles, and these performances are rightly praised. But the look on the faces of the young women in particular went far beyond expert 'performance focus'. It's more than a typical 'pick a spot at the back of the theatre' technique. When I first started to watch them perform, I'd look to where they were looking. When I asked them about it, they told me it's because they are trained from such a young age to perform, for the glory of God, not themselves, and He is their audience. Their joy in performing, as Vineta and her peers describe it to me, is a joy of sharing their faith and culture, not necessarily their individual performance abilities as in western culture. It remains a solidly collectivist experience, even when individual performers are featured. Wherever it comes from, it is a powerful performative presence that is seemingly without self-consciousness, a kind of glowing *here-ness*[1] that is both performative and also reminiscent of the 'luminous' countenances of those visited by the 'holy spirit', or who believe they see God or possess a kind of sacred vision that others simply cannot enter into but can only observe from without. Such affective performance is, in the words of Brian Massumi, "the *manifestation* of a concept . . . because they only come into being through the performance" (2002, 89); in other words, their dances are a fleeting enmeshment of the cultural and religious body, a now-here place that is completely ephemeral yet a nowhere utopia that is not accessible from without. This enmeshment drew me into trying to understand how Vineta and her peers *thought about* what they were doing. And that path led me in very short order to their faith practices and values, which led inextricably to their communities—both faith communities and cultural communities. For them, I believed I saw, there was an interweaving of faith, creativity, and culture—expressed in a particular way by what they call 'the Youth' (that is, their church-based youth groups, who are the ones who primarily perform each Sunday at service, and who dominate the annual White Sunday[2] celebrations).

Since that first performance, now already a long time ago, I have remained friends with Vineta and continue to meet more of her extended and church family. I have attended family celebrations, church services, and special holiday celebrations like White Sunday and the major holidays. I have seen them perform in a number of different contexts, and more importantly the youth themselves have documented their performances in these and other national and international youth church gatherings. But in those early years of our teacher-student relationship and in our co-participant experience in another arts education community research project, *Culture Shack*, a couple of years later, we were still getting to know one another and those differences included prominent differences in our respective intersectional subjectivities, most especially for me that I was gay and American, and for them that they were Samoan and Christian. What we all agreed on was that our gifts to share were a creative combination of our cultural, gendered, and spiritual ways of being. As I have written elsewhere, the Samoan young women's sense of place, culture, and self that was evident from their first dance at our high school, and remained in evidence in their public dance of thanks for their drama facilitator in *Culture Shack*, suggested a new way of thinking about cultural dance and "other forms of creative cultural expression" as "productive pedagogical portals for both academic and intercultural learning" (Harris and Lemon 2012, 413). In that essay, I highlighted how trends in "cultural and arts education policy" suggested a powerful turn toward "space and place-based learning that draws productively on cultural, gender and creative interventions" (413). So my relationship with these young people and their community/ies has progressed along creative, intercultural, and pedagogical lines for many years now, and this book is one coordinate in that map.

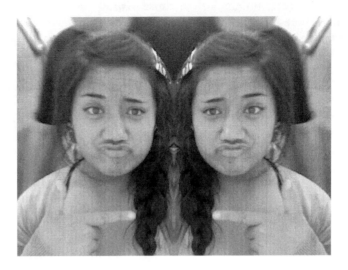

Figure S1.2 Rosada, double-selfie. Photo and copyright, Anne Harris.

The Public Body

Many scholars, including Dolby and Rizvi (2008), have argued that contemporary society and its global flows remain distinguished between those who 'flow' and those who 'do not', between the global class and the local class. Yet these Samoan and South Sudanese youth offer another way of storying global flows that transcends class and geography, in their expert uses of social media and online/offline networks and communities. They challenge Dolby's and Rizvi's claim that global flows are "contradictory: capital moves easily, bodies which control capital move easily, but bodies which are more expendable or peripheral are still largely constrained" (2008, 2). For them, their creative faith performances and artefacts offer a way of moving beyond corporeal constraint, offering "another kind of embodied resistance, that of cultural dance" (Harris and Lemon 2012, 414). I have highlighted and foregrounded "some creative expressions of both the mobility and boundedness" (Harris and Lemon 2012, 414) of these young women, in an effort to turn a critical lens on our own boundedness, in gendered, cultural, and discursive ways as artists and as collaborator-researchers.

Rizvi has claimed that "globalisation carries intercultural tensions and anxieties for both those who move, and those who do not appear to move" (Harris and Lemon 2012, 414), and I experienced such tensions and wrote about the discomfiting "anxiety produced in myself, my fellow teachers, and administrators by the sensual beauty of some of the rhythmic dance moves" (Harris and Lemon 2012, 415). What I did not mention were scenes like our high school's 'multicultural day' performance evenings, when I was sitting next to our principal as many grown male family members of the girl dancers mounted the stage, stripped off their shirts, and lay down on the stage under the feet of the girl dancers, while women and other family members also mounting the stage pushed dollar bills into their bras and skirts, whooping loudly, as part of their dance custom encourages. Such testosterone intensities in an all-girls school create excitement in many, and sometimes dread in administrators. At one such performance, the principal next to me audibly moaned when the Samoan men (in traditional fashion) pounded this all-girls school stage with their bare feet, baring their chests and more, their tattoos, in sensual and loud collaboration with the young girls on the stage of this normally fairly sedate girls' school. While it was not a sensual dance—culturally speaking—the sheer gendered power of these kinds of dances seemed to at least overwhelm this sexually repressed environment in which control of even sensuality is part of the day-to-day business of schooling. So I was used to the discomfort caused by these young women and the disruptive power of their cultural performances.

However, when we conducted the *Culture Shack* program at a community arts facility near to the school, somewhat different dynamics emerged. The caucasian academics and youth workers who attended this public day who were relatively unfamiliar with Samoan culture were shocked by the dance, which in itself was no surprise to me or the young women. But what was more interesting was the 'culture clash' of the Samoan traditional gift with the gay sexuality of Brett, the American drama facilitator who had never been in collaboration with youth from a Samoan background before, and against which the caucasian academics and youth workers in attendance implored me to police the dance on the grounds of the lascivious sensuality of it—which I knew to be completely misunderstood.

So what to make of the 'public bodies' of a contemporary Samoan performance (of culture and gender) that may be misinterpreted by many non-Samoan audience members? And how does this intersect with these young people's youth, faith, and religious orientations in the world, as Australian and not solely Samoan who are living in a culturally diverse western culture while maintaining and celebrating traditional ways of being and knowing and making? The role of creativity in such complex maneuverings cannot be overstated.

Others have written on aspects of Samoan youth culture, and the intersection of creativity, faith, and youth practices, but not often together. For understanding the important role of creativity in Samoan and other Pasifika cultures, Chi and Robinson (2012) and Giuffre (2009) have been helpful, as I will explore in more depth across the three chapters in this section. Lubart (1999, 1990) has written about cross-cultural variations of creativity, but not specific to Samoan culture, or to youth. On some ways in which creativity is socially functioning far beyond a so-called creative industries model, O'Connor and Gibson (2014), Collins (2010), and Runco (2010; 1999) have suggested a more culturally situated and place-making approach, but

28   *Samoan Mediascapes and Faith-as-Performance*

have not explored them in sufficient depth, certainly not from outside of the northern states or western culture paradigm. So there is still work to be done. And certainly at a time like this, when creativity is ubiquitous in economic, workplace, cultural, and educational contexts, it has never been more timely to remind readers of the still-diverse ways in which creativity continues to rhizomatically break its boundaries, and no better way to experience this boundary-breaking than through the eyes of the next generation.

Youdell (2012) has pointed out the ways in which all racialised identities, but particularly the imagined identity of 'Pacific Islander', can be understood as a subject position that is "performative as well as a site of identification and recognition and misrecognition" (2012, 144), in educational and wider contexts. In this book I make an effort to paint a longitudinal picture of the relationship between myself and these young people which began when I taught most of them in high school, extended through community arts projects like *Culture Shack*, and now into their young adulthood. As I have argued in Harris and Lemon (2012), these particularly Samoan forms of creativity make an offer to educators, creative collaborators, and non-Samoan others that we often decline, deny, or miss noticing completely, and it is one that is only partially about Samoan-ness, but additionally about providing an "opportunity for unlearning whiteness that Youdell suggests" (Harris and Lemon 2012, 417).

I acknowledge, as does Youdell, that "dances like these are received as "the exotic object of the White gaze" (2012, 150), but I go further in suggesting that while cultural dances like these in predominantly 'White' contexts do exoticise the culturally Other, they do more than just this. Their intercultural complexity is far more rich and also more unwieldy for both the Samoan youth and their non-Samoan others. In other words, more than Youdell suggests, the problem in the *Culture Shack* context was a shared problem, but the exoticisation (or 'otherness') was not.

These young women share their uniquely Samoan dances from an inextricably cultural and religious knowingness. Yet I want to suggest that they also understand the Australian non-Samoan superstructures of racism, euro-centrism, and sexism in which they live and perform. Their enculturation and cultural resilience does not erase their western knowing. This code-switching and 'trans-languaging' can certainly be seen as intercultural border-crossing, but can it also be functioning as a kind of cultural-to-social capital currency conversion? Might it be an example of how these Samoan youth are enacting creative capital that has value in multiple and proliferating ways? This is not to suggest that I am interpreting these embodiments as 'self-exoticising', but rather retaining their Otherness as a conscious act, as a resistance to White assimilation or the hegemonising influence of living 'in the west'. They may be doing both simultaneously, and expertly mining the power of online/offline literacies to do so. Perhaps Youdell may be over-essentialising, not by claiming that the white west does indeed 'Other' brown and global south peoples like the Samoans (as indeed they/we do), but rather that a contemporary Samoan subjectivity as performed by these young women at least some of the time makes conscious choices about the 'exoticising gaze' and the value of using it to benefit themselves. Even if these young people have only partially self-reflexively considered such possibilities in conversation for this book, it bears acknowledging here.

As I concluded in a decidedly inconclusive manner by asking

> Whether we can ever unpack exactly what the dance *is*, or understand who the Samoan girls are/were at that performative moment, or who I for that matter was to 'let' them present the dance, we might more productively ask what is its place in pedagogical space?
>
> (Harris and Lemon 2012, 419)

Here I use the term 'pedagogical space' broadly to denote public and other interrelational spaces in which we are co-creating, particularly as feminist subjects, "new connections to place, and community, transforming our sense of refugeity into one of belonging" in which "we—like our research products and processes—are in a constant state of re- or co-construction" (Harris and Gandolfo 2013, 13). Like Youdell, I have problematised my position as a researcher, teacher, and also as an artist. I have critiqued multiculturalism, and have positioned myself as a good "anti-racist ethnographer" (2012, 151 in Harris and Lemon 2012, 419), yet at other times have rejected the terms 'ethnographer', 'ethnography', and 'culture' completely. I'm not alone: in recent scholarship, "numerous ethnographers have pointed out, for example, that in the emerging global context, both the ideas of 'ethno' and 'graphic' have become problematic" (Rizvi 2014, 190). I actively seek my own conscientisation regarding cultural appropriation and white privilege. So why, then, have I returned to a place like the one I seem to hold here, a position some may consider as a fairly traditional 'outsider' ethnographer, fellow-traveller, not even immersed in their Samoan world as traditionally ethnographers do? As I have noted, "it is painful to cast a harsh and demanding light on the so often well-intentioned but misguided things we do as teachers and as researchers, in our hopes to make things better for our students (and sometimes ourselves) who are marginalised" (Harris and Lemon 2012, 419). As the years progress, I find that the creative collaborative process is an iterative one, that includes both outward and inward gazing. It feels good to be able and willing to admit it in scholarly contexts, for it informs the research work and the relationships both. There is strength in this transparency, for myself and my collaborators. It is a crucial component of creative becoming-capital. And I might argue, as Youdell has done, that "if they fail . . . even imperfect agendas to change the 'business-as-usual' of education are desperately needed" (2012, 419).

So as a migrant myself, and a practice-led and feminist scholar, I continue to seek ways of disrupting the business as usual of positivist paradigms and hierarchical research relationships, particularly in education. Together with my Samoan and South Sudanese collaborators, and like Vacchelli (2011), we see our "co-constructed narrative as the enactment of a feminist 'spatial practice,' in which 'performativity of identity in and through language' allows us to explore our scholarship in relation to another" (Harris and Gandolfo 2013, 2). Vacchelli's 'narratable self' (2011, 768) demands to be told in relation to another in which "we can narrate our own lives, but it is a co-constitutive act, dependent on 'exposure to others' for this collaborative self-portrait" (Harris and Gandolfo 2013, 2). With a commitment to creative co-construction in the research relationship, and following Weis, Fine, and Dimitriadis (2009), I seek to establish and maintain conditions in which we can

> argue through our interwoven narrative(s) our agreement with Dillard's call for 'research as responsibility,' but one that recognizes creative endeavour as deeply responsible, deeply invested, lived discourses that address the complexity and fluidity of being and belonging. This work is already being done in theatres, performance spaces, bookstores, between the covers of novels and short stories, blogs, and oral histories, a continuing testament to the affective power of narrative. . . . We and our colleagues and fellow artists recognize the power of the creative contribution, but understand the need to challenge the academy as a space of performance in motion, drawing on contemporary ways of being and knowing that are truly flexible and allow for a new imaginary.
> (Harris and Gandolfo 2013, 12)

I have noted the ways in which these multimodal research artefacts and relationships are also autoethnographic (for both the young people and myself), and Singh and Doherty (2008) resonate with the ways in which these youth (particularly the Samoan youth) have used their autoethnographic[3] accounts and performances to 'self-orientalize' their Samoan identities, parodied through the supposed eyes of the white western majoritarian culture in which they find themselves:

> Pratt (1998, 1992) highlights the strategy of auto-ethnography in the contact zone. By contact zone, she is referring to spaces where disparate cultures meet and through their contact play out various strategies of power and resistance. The internationalized university could be considered a current example of such a site of intercultural interface . . . [and auto-ethnographic texts are those] in which people undertake to describe themselves in ways that engage with representations others have made of them . . . autoethnographic texts are representations that the so-defined others construct *in response to* or in dialogue with those (ethnographic) texts . . . they involve a selective collaboration with and appropriation of idioms of the metropolis or the conqueror.
> (Singh & Doherty 2008, 122)

Autoethnographies thus construct accounts with the resources for representation at hand, that is, from the 'contingent order' forged in the politics of cultural contact. This resonates with Stuart Hall's (1996, 1991) concept of rearticulation as the identity process of reassembling elements of discursive representations to negotiate new positions. As one such strategy of auto-ethnography, the term 'self-orientalization' has been coined by Aihwa Ong (1997) to highlight the opportunistic take-up of triumphal Orientalism by Chinese diaspora capitalists and Asian leaders to produce transnational solidarity. Ong argues that such self-orientalizing is a strategic discursive response to certain settings, deployed by the transnational capitalist to further their ends opportunistically, rather than a claim to some intrinsic cultural truth.

"Similarly, Gayatri Spivak (1990) uses the term 'strategic use of essentialism' to signal two ways of representation—representation as delegation in the political sense and representation as portrait or depiction. Crucially, Spivak suggests that it is "not possible to be non-essentialist" (109). Rather, she suggests that we should consider the ways in which individuals represent themselves (depict, portray), and in the process represent members of particular social groups (delegation). In other words, it is important to engage in the cultural politics of representation—who is being represented, where, how, when, and to what tactical or strategic ends?" (Doherty & Singh 2008, 122).

One representational tension around the broad category of 'Asian' cultural identity, in which the Samoan youth here are sometimes included, confronts two persistent views that continue to marginalise and misunderstand some of the ways in which Samoan and broadly Pasifika actors are accumulating social capital, tied to creative capital and its global flows. Asians—especially lower-middle class or working class—continue to be 'orientalized' by majoritarian tropes, often (as in the case of educational contexts) in unconscious ways that maintain binaries of Asians as driving a globally mobile consumer class or Asians as passive subjects incapable of enacting change or agency within postcolonial contexts. In the case of the Samoan young people here, they are almost always positioned in the latter category, compliant and charming reminders of musicals and early Asia Pacific anthropologists. Their co-construction and circulation of very different and evolving hybrid identities through social and other media platforms confounds in different ways the feminist, education, youth, and Pasifika scholarship that exists. Over the next three chapters I will highlight some of these disruptions in different areas of engagement, and weave them with these other areas of focus including creativity, religion, and gender. In Chapter One, I start with Appadurai's cultural anthropological approach to considering minoritarian youth, and the use and functions of the cultural imaginary.

Acknowledgments

The excerpt from Polamalu, Tafea 2009. "Diasporic Dream: Letter to Grandfather." In *The Space Between: Negotiating Culture, Place, and Identity in the Pacific*, edited by A. Marata Tamaira, 62–63. Occasional Paper Series 44. Honolulu, Hawai'i: Center for Pacific Islands Studies, School of

32 *Samoan Mediascapes and Faith-as-Performance*

Pacific and Asian Studies, University of Hawai'i at Mānoa appears courtesy of UHM Center for Pacific Islands Studies (CPIS) and the author.

Notes

1 What Deleuze and Guattari have called 'now-here', a utopian spacetime that transcends both place and time, one that is creatively disruptive while noting the risks of utopia and utopian projections themselves.

2 White Sunday is an annual all-day church celebration which features the youth as they lead the hymns, performances, and prayers. I was somewhat taken aback when I attended my first White Sunday to realise that many of the church-goers do dress in white outfits, and most of the women wear wide-brimmed Victorian-style hats that looked to me disconcertingly colonial, and to hear them singing Christian hymns in Samoan language in these dresses. Perhaps another Margaret Mead moment of a different type, but I felt uncomfortable and guilty for that discomfort, all at the same time.

3 Note that this methodology is alternately written as 'auto-ethnography' and sometimes auto/ethnography, but most commonly 'autoethnography'. Although some scholars have differentiated between them, readers should consider them interchangeable here as the methodology that links autobiography (personal narrative) and ethnography (cultural analysis) and ideally relies upon a critical framework for its theoretical lens(es). For further clarification, see Holman Jones, S., T. Adams, and C. Ellis. 2014. *Handbook of Autoethnography*. Oxford University Press.

1 Education and the Creative Imaginary

View the 'Creativity and Faith Cultures' Samoan video here:
http://www.creativeresearchhub.com/#!cryc/h95tt

"Are We an Example of the 'Glocal'?"

Appadurai has told us that "the diasporic public spheres" that increasingly accelerate global migratory and cross-cultural encounters "are no longer small, marginal or exceptional" but rather have become "part of the cultural dynamic of urban life in most countries and continents, in which migration and mass mediation coconstitute a new sense of the global as modern and the modern as global" (1996, 10).

The Samoan and South Sudanese young people in this book are inheritors and creators of this dynamic, despite their frequent framing as 'local' subjects in opposition to their more 'global' peers. For Samoans, it is often difficult to retain a distinct identity in the eyes of white westerners or others from outside Pasifika cultures. As Pollock documents in the Californian context, Pasifika peoples often humourously distinguish between themselves, or not at all, as in this exchange about Tongans and Fijians: "There's Tongans, and Fijians . . . Tongans [are] different . . . we don't eat horses! We eat the pig, and chicken . . . and Tongans have big noses" (Maira and Soep 2005, 53). The Samoan youth in this book also see themselves as distinct but culturally related to other Pasifika peoples. In similar hegemonising fashion, these South Sudanese youth are similarly often conflated into all 'African Australians' or simply Africans. Pollock, like Michelle Fine (in Fine, Weis, and Powell 1997, and elsewhere), has documented the ways in which schools are sites of racial performances but also co-constitutive racialising sites, and schools are never far from the words and relationships documented here. While Pollock's focus remains firmly on "everyday race talk for analyzing everyday practices of racialization" (Pollock in Maira and Soep 2005, 46), this book is mainly concerned with the ways these youth use their creative practices to praise God in everyday ways—yet admittedly these are practices that are always infused with 'race talk' of their own, and racialising practices of those around them. While Samoans may be more familiar neighbours and friends to those living in the Asia Pacific region than those living elsewhere, globally Samoan are still regularly relegated to the historic past or the quaint, exotic, or brute sidelines. These voices

34 *Samoan Mediascapes and Faith-as-Performance*

and co-constructed creative works of and by Samoan youth aim to offer a counter-narrative to that, in sharing part of their 'creative counterpublics'.

Pollock has noted, by looking at "'multicultural' assemblies, one could notice that racial categorizations were actually leaking all over the place. Although performances often involved Samoan students in grass skirts performing traditional dances . . . Samoan students routinely sang rhythm and blues tunes" (2005, 59), very like Vineta and her peers who speak in these pages. They speak of creative and cultural mash-ups as business as usual even back home on an island that favours country music (in the old-timers generation) and borrows fashion and other influences from Europe. Yet readers should not imagine that this hybridity equals a loss of culture, or cultural confusion. As Pollock notes regarding American Samoan youth, "The students kept returning over the course of the conversation to expose race group memberships as infinitely malleable and multiple, yet somehow through all this contestation the single category 'Samoan' survived" (Pollock 2005, 53), and these Australian Samoan youth are similar. This chapter seeks to contextualise some of the publics in which these youth find themselves and speak back to.

Youth culture in some ways transcends the discursive discomforts and failures of the previous generation, particularly in policy and community programming. For example, "multiculturalism is now commonly criticised or retreated from on the grounds that it has inappropriately supported separatism and failed to foster shared community values" (Anita Harris 2013, 20). Vertovec and Wessendorf (2010, 1) too have noted a backlash against multiculturalism in the European and British contexts, highlighting the consistency of these critiques. Some of the Samoan youth here joke about using the term 'glocal' to describe their hybrid local/global communities and relationships, and speak eloquently of the ways in which they are performing on multiple stages and within multiple cultures at once, yet do not identify with the term multicultural.

When Vineta and her friends asked if they are an example of the glocal, I laughed but agreed. They laughed too; it's a funny word. But while they don't often think of their work as global labour at a local level, in many ways it is perfectly representative. Glocal has been used as "a catchphrase for projects and methodologies that address global concerns while staying firmly grounded in local contexts" (Harris and Lemon 2012, 419), and I have previously asserted that the demand for global mobility and local specificity as "a marketplace rhetoric which defends the value of creativity as an adaptive employee attribute" (419) does not draw sufficiently on the border-crossing work that culturally and ethnically minoritarian youth do as part of everyday life. So what do terms like 'glocal' and 'creativity' mean for these Samoan young people?

Is there a way in which these global concerns are taking shape in local spaces and practices which has not been fully recognised or valued yet, not unlike the culturally situated dance and misunderstanding that occurred in the *Culture Shack* project? These Samoan young people tell us how they wish to be perceived, commodified (and they do in some ways wish to be commodified), and how they wish to spread the glory of God and their Christian faith, none of which they see as mutually exclusive. In this chapter their words and artefacts begin to form a lens through which readers may consider Appadurai's notion of the imaginary in new ways, based in their hybrid perspectives, through their own multi-focal views of faith, gender, culture, and creativity. Their goals, and in some cases their strategies too, are not so different from a Floridian creative class and the ways in which *those* creative practices seem to offer mobility, freedom, and agency to their actors. These Samoan youth are using their co-constructed creative imaginary as a new social space that allows them to transcend the limits of their bounded embodied lives, and they are doing so in unique ways.

Dolby and Rizvi (2008) extend the notion of a 'new research imaginary' in ways that bridge the 'new geographies of modernity' (5) for youth who seek both global and local roles and capital, like many in the global south. Anita Harris (2013), in writing about intercultural cohesion and conflict in Australia, states,

> Young people personify the hybrid form of new kinds of mixed cultural identities. That is, third-, second- and 1.5-generation youth complicate multicultural policy that requires categorical ethnic identifications, because of the complexity of their cultural connections. . . . Their identity experiences also force broader thinking beyond the management of immigration and settlement because they radically alter assumptions about national belonging, citizenship and community membership in cultural diversity. Many young people of immigrant backgrounds take for granted the hybrid nature of citizenship in contemporary multicultural societies. This may mean that they seek inclusion not as a reward for assimilation or as adjunct minority citizens, but on their own terms, as entitled hybrid subjects.
>
> (22)

While evidence demonstrates that "young people are the most culturally diverse grouping in Australia and are those who most frequently and routinely interact across diversity" (Anita Harris 2013, 22), some in this Samoan youth group feel that "Samoa still bears the weight of Margaret Mead's famous research, and the stereotypes of sensuous Polynesian women" (Harris and Lemon 2012, 422), which influence the ways young Samoans are perceived as either sexy exotic women or (mostly male) dangerous thugs. While research from within the Samoan community is increasing, often the little existing contemporary research specific to Samoan youth

36 *Samoan Mediascapes and Faith-as-Performance*

and particularly Samoan young women focuses on their weight (McDowell and Bond 2006; Littlewood 2004; Tupuloa 2004), bodies, and health practices. As I have noted,

> Through dance, Samoan young women can participate in 'making new meanings and creating new discourses of self' in order to challenge hegemonic systems (Georgina 2007, 93). The Samoan participants did this masterfully in dancing their own manner of thanks—but also of self—to their arts tutor. In a powerful display of expert creative knowledge and performance skill, the students reversed roles and became teachers.
> (Harris and Lemon 2012, 423)

While these Samoan young women also focus in part on their bodies and weight, it is partly in relation to the publics they move within, including social media, school, and work contexts. McRobbie (2009) has noted how "young women are now in part constrained by the story of their enablement" (in Harris and Dobson 2015, 148), and these young women demonstrate that complexity. While white western girlhood is in some sense predominantly performed as digitally and sexually liberated and confident, the South Sudanese and Samoan young women in this book offer quite a different representation of 'western girlhood'. Where Harris and Dobson use three pivotal concepts for exploring agentic girlhood, including choice, empowerment, and voice, these same three concepts resonate very differently for the young women represented here. So-called 'free choice', empowerment, and voice are understood and practiced differently for these youth within their self-identified collectivist cultures. Free choice suggests independence, and for these youth, independence also represents solitude, loneliness, and isolation. The liberatory nature of being able to choose for 'one's self' is rooted in western ideals of individual identity and mobility. In that narrative, children pass through an articulate stage of adolescence in order to practice and then achieve an intangible but necessary notion of 'independence', by which in the west we mean adulthood and successful extrication from the childhood home. It is in fact seen as not just a desirable but a necessary stage of individual growth toward maturity, in which "it is a key requirement of contemporary self-identity that we are good choice-makers" (Harris and Dobson 2015, 148). This is not equally evident in all cultures, and to some degree not in the South Sudanese and Samoan youth cultures here, although these youth are simultaneously members of both their Australian and originary cultures which demand, in some cases, contradictory requirements for adolescent personhood.

Throughout the book I include or reference interviews or projects we have collaborated on, including the use of still images, video, audio, and social media screengrabs, all artefacts that have been self- and collaboratively generated over several years. Together, these are meant to provide a comprehensive picture of a collaborative working relationship but also an insider or autoethnographic account of their lived experiences as religiously creative young people. In this section, the Samoan youth culture is narrated for readers, mainly by Vineta and her family or church relations, through which we meet or hear narrated stories of the creative activities of others in their church-based youth group.

Tupuola is one of the few researchers who has explored the diversity and fluidity of Samoan young women in intercultural contexts. She reminds us that "generalisations cannot be claimed" (2004, 120), yet "cultural norms can be seen interweaving with global media influences in gender roles within diasporic Samoan communities" (Harris and Lemon 2012, 424). Such interweaving is evident in this first conversation excerpt with Vineta, Ana, and Newjoy, which is—like many of these collaboration artefacts—presented without interpretation from me, allowing the views and voices of these young women to stand on their own as powerful and valid knowledge creation for and within the academy. The link to this video interview at the beginning of this chapter provided readers with a chance to see some of this dialogue with the added bodily expressions and interrelationship between the three speakers, as video research allows us (Harris 2016). The following excerpt however allows something different; it brings readers in for a closer encounter with their words, a practice that text-based research products differently facilitate:

Figure 1.1 Still image from *Samoan Youth Creativity and Religion*, 2016, Alta Truden/Anne Harris. Photo/video still photographer: Alta Truden; copyright, Anne Harris.

38   *Samoan Mediascapes and Faith-as-Performance*

Anne: So what kinds of different performances or types of performances do you do? In the context of your church youth groups, and in community with the other youth?

Vineta: Okay so, so basically we have cultural performances, and then we have spiritual performances and then we have family performances. For, you know, special occasions—

Ana: There's a mix of two. Even though they're all sort of the same. Like for cultural performances we're like, we are performing more of our traditions and our cultural heritages and all of that but then—it's [similar] but for cultural performances it's more of our, you know, Samoan culture. For our spiritual performances it's more of the Bible and then family . . . Sometimes we have the same tunes of the Samoan songs but we will put . . . sometimes it's more informal than our cultural performances.

Vineta: [There are] birthdays where we have everything but mostly cultural and family performances. Yeah and then we have like for church conferences there's a lot of, what's it called—?

Ana: Mini conference.

Vineta: Mini conference because we have like a conference of countries and then we have a conference just within Australia with all the other churches in New Zealand and Samoa. So we have our church, our church is Methodist, Wesleyan Methodist. There's Methodist Samoan which is completely different and then they have Catholic. Also Mormons, Seventh Day Adventists, so it's all different. So we all have different branches, say for us so the Wesleyan branch we like, because it's new—it's only in New Zealand and Australia. But with the Samoan Methodist you have one in America and Samoa, especially Samoa we have one in New Zealand. So it all depends on what kind of church we come from, but all in all it's the same.

Anne: So would you be in touch with youth from the Samoan Mormons in the United States, for example?

Ana: No.

Vineta: Yeah if it were like to just cultural based I think we would—

Ana: We would—

Vineta: Be like in touch because it's spiritually different. Like we're Methodist and they're Mormons we won't, because they worship differently to how we do it. They have different versions of how they praise God and we do it differently.

Anne: Okay so you're primarily affiliated along religious lines and then would you say like secondarily along cultural? In other words, that the Samoan aspect is not then the primary organising principle, it's the spiritual?

Vineta: Yeah, okay but I think 99.8% of Samoans are Christians and we have that 0.2% which is completely weird because we—we

Education and the Creative Imaginary   39

> all don't know anyone any Samoans who are Muslims or—. But apparently there's a temple in Samoa. And it expanded when the tsunami thing happened in Samoa [in 2009] and everyone was like, they're in need and they needed help and stuff.

Anne: *Of course okay so it's like almost everyone's Christian, so just to recap, almost everyone's Christian, why? Because of colonialism?*

Vineta: *Colonialism.*

Anne: *So the Christians came, is that like the white Christian missionaries, the Europeans, came in the, what? Early 1800s?*

Vineta: *Yeah. We ate them.*

Anne: *Okay. Well, yeah. Really? Or are you just messing around?*

Vineta: *Can I tell a story. The guy who came, John Wesley, we ate him.*

Anne: *And now you do him, his teachings?*

Vineta: *That's it.*

Ana: *Our church is—*

Vineta: *Yeah this where our branch comes from.*

Ana: *John Wesley.*

Anne: *How's that work? You eat the guy and you still follow him.*

Vineta: *Yeah. We used to eat people. We really did used to eat people.*

Anne: *Okay I get that.*

Ana: *Back in like—*

Vineta: *Not like last year. Not like right now! [laughing] No, but—*

Joy: *Oh my God, stop talking about that!*

Anne: *Wow, that's really interesting though. Like I get eating people but how do you eat a missionary and then still follow his thing? That's kind of like—*

Vineta: *I have no idea, I think we have to rely on Wikipedia on that one [laughing]. But this is what our nanna told us and you know she's history so you know [laughing].*

After clarifying that cannibalism, according to their family stories, was an acceptable part of pre-colonial Samoan culture, and was present at times in the early years of contact with white Europeans, we returned to the topic of creativity in Samoan culture, which was in fact related to the cannibalism discussion through the role of storytelling. As we returned to a discussion of the roots of their church-based creativity, however, Vineta clarified:

Vineta: *Like because basically we grew up in church so that's sort of how we started performing and that's what sort of put us into that creative lane of going and getting in touch with our cultural side and performing through church. I think that's where it all starts.*

Ana: *Yeah, our performing starts from a very early age. Like for example White Sunday.*

40   *Samoan Mediascapes and Faith-as-Performance*

Anne: *Can you please clarify what White Sunday is for the readers?*

Vineta: *White Sunday is basically for kids. It's an all-day Sunday mass where we celebrate children and how they're going to be the future of our—like the next generation, and how they're going to build our ministry. So, yeah we start performing from baby, like as soon as they come, 'Okay your turn on the stage'! Our parents they don't really perform, like that's mostly us kids. Then they go on to talking and all the traditional like prayers and priests and the orators in Samoa, that's when they start learning and developing their understanding of that whole—*

Ana: *Traditional side.*

Vineta: *—traditional side of Samoa, like have you heard of cava?*

Anne: *No I don't think so. Cava?*

Ana: *The cava ceremony.*

Vineta: *The cava ceremony like there's so much more to it, but basically even though we're Samoan growing up in a full Samoan house we're still learning all of that. So we don't even know how that all goes, we only see it at church. . . . So as kids we grow up we have White Sunday and then we do Samoan dances at birthdays. And we maintain these things because you know it's our parents who tell us to do this. So we don't do it by choice, but we learn to love it and then we learn to sort of adapt to that kind of lifestyle where you just—where you perform when you're asked to, or you know we begin to associate the performance stuff with culture and also with our faith.*

Ana: *We learn to love it as well but sometimes you know—*

Joy: *Sometimes it's too much.*

Anne: *So basically do you perform because you like it or because you feel you have to?*

Ana: *Both. But everyone's different.*

Joy: *I'm not as shy anymore. Whereas before like it was—*

Vineta: *It's something like we grow up doing and then we have to learn to love it.*

Anne: *Yeah and do you think that it helps you break down ego stuff too? Because I know when I was teaching you guys . . . I would be like 'Wow, you're so confident on stage' and I think it might have been you Vineta, you explained to me: 'It's not about me, it's about, you know praising God or the collective, the group'. So there's not the usual western 'Look at me, look at me' kind of thing about it. Do you think practice breaks that down, that self-consciousness of look at me or everyone's looking at me? That it breaks down some of the fear around it?*

Vineta: *Yeah okay first of all I think I've learnt to say that. That's what we learnt, like that's what we learned to say. Like my nanna every time we perform she would be like, 'You know you're performing for God, not for yourselves.' Every like beginning of before we*

Education and the Creative Imaginary   41

would perform everywhere, no matter where we are, that's the thing that they say. Like when they encourage us, and they give us words of wisdom before we're up on stage.

Ana: *Yeah I think when we first started like just say from a youth perspective, when we first started we were are all so shy because we didn't want that kind of attention on us, like we didn't know if we were going to make the church look bad or embarrass ourselves. But like I think from doing this over and over again, it built our confidence. And performing in front of others, and because we do it with people we know, and because we've done this so many times, that we've been able to build on how we perform up til now.*

Vineta: *Right, like you know Anne how you asked us a question about what comes 'first', whether we can think of them separately, whether it's our religion and then it's our culture? I think it's different everywhere. Like even in Samoa we have the dances, we have the same language, but still it's different, like it's performed differently wherever you are, even over there. So I think it's partly because we're in Australia that it's like that. Like in New Zealand where I got my culture, like it was there that I got to know the language and everything from home, and all the stories and the legends from home, back in Samoa, I got all of that from my nanna. But the dancing I learned from my primary school in New Zealand. So my parents didn't really teach me that, it was more when I was in New Zealand.*

Ana: *Yeah, and so I learned my culture from different places too, like the first Samoan dance I learned was in church from our older youth people.*

Vineta: *And it's more because a lot of parents who moved away from Samoa they take culture with them in different ways. Like some parents they teach their kids the Samoan way, other parents modernise it, like they westernise—*

Ana: *They are like almost a different Samoan culture—*

Vineta: *Yeah they only like to—not like to, but because the kids are growing up in schools in Australia or in New Zealand or in America wherever they are, it's like it's not the same as the way it was in New Zealand or in Samoa.*

Ana: *Yeah I will say our performances at White Sunday are like a good example of that kind of thing—in Samoa we don't do that, but we live in Australia and we're accustomed to the whole hip hop culture and like all the other Polynesian cultures—and so those creative influences find their way into our White Sunday performances—*

Joy: *The new, like we bring new styles to influence our culture.*

Ana: *Even from Samoa to New Zealand, like it gets modernised and then when you move from New Zealand to Australia it gets even more, like—*

42 Samoan Mediascapes and Faith-as-Performance

Vineta: *Yeah it's different. And that's what I realised in Australia, we're not the same in Australia, this is our home but a lot of the kids who were born here who are Samoan they're not as in touch with like our culture as we are (who came from New Zealand), because there's so many Islanders everywhere, especially Samoans. They're like next door, you see one across the road or next door, you know? And the churches are way bigger too and we touch base with our culture more in New Zealand. Like even in New Zealand in our church we have church Monday, Wednesday, Friday, Saturday, Sunday. But here in Australia, we only have church Saturday and Sunday. Saturday for one hour and then Sunday for two hours, you know what I mean? So what about those kids who never knew how it was back home, or even New Zealand? They are totally different from us, everything is different, and they are not as creative as us either. So it's so different.*

Ana: *I think too because there's more Samoans in New Zealand than there is here, so you also have that bigger amount of culture. It's more common, it's richer.*

Anne: *What do you think is the biggest influence on your performance styles or singing styles here in Australia, besides home culture?*

Ana: *Like R&B, hip hop.*

Anne: *American R&B?*

Ana: *Yeah.*

Anne: *Do you listen to any Australian hip hop?*

Vineta: *No. Is there such a thing?*

Anne: *Yes!*

Vineta: *No we have more like old school, you know I listen to musical influences like old school R&B, like the nineties, and the sixties as well.*

Ana: *And reggae, that's another thing.*

Vineta: *Right! Because we have island reggae. So you know how you have when people think of reggae they think Jamaica, but in Samoa like how you have the famous Samoan singers, their genre is island reggae.*

Joy: *Yeah Bob Marley, and Stir it Up did 'Praise the Lord' something,*

Vineta: *Yeah we do 'Valerie'. We sing our songs, we plagiarise. [laughter]*

Anne: *I love it it's like a mash up. Like doing religious mashups.*

Vineta: *Exactly! Yeah we just get the soundtracks and then we change the words. And I am like thinking because we're not really known I think, oh, my gosh, if people knew that we were copying their songs our whole country might be fined. [laughter] Oh my gosh, the copyright people are going to put Samoa in jail! All of Samoa for plagiarising! [laughter]*

Ana: *Okay well I guess that means we have a lot of influences in our performing style. I guess they are just all jumbled up together in a way.*

Education and the Creative Imaginary 43

Figure 1.2 Vineta and Ana, Samoan style, October 2014. Photo and copyright, Anne Harris.

These young Samoan women show in constantly humourous and evolving conversation how varied the influences on their creative practice and genres are. They draw from everything around them, and recognise their creativity as both culturally and religiously situated, a lifetime and intergenerational practice which began at birth. They also note how fictitious is the category of 'Samoan' creativity itself, evolved and evolving in a multitude of ways, as culture itself is. Yet they speak as agentic young women who see their creativity as both individual and collective, private and public. These practices they describe and enact (what Bourdieu would call 'habituated mediations') represent not only community-/family-based knowledge, but also forms of pedagogical and educative value that largely remain unrecognised in either marketplace or education contexts in the west.

While the gap between skilled and unskilled labour in a globalised emerging knowledge economy continues to widen, Bourdieu's (2000) notion of the role of 'habituated mediations' inherited from family, culture, and local contexts presents new possibilities of pursuable options, a new creative imaginary (Barrett 2011). In this chapter I lay the groundwork for a discussion of faith as performance, and performance as pedagogy, based in these Samoan young people's ability to use creative arts and popular culture to synthesise their religion, languages, and cultural diversity for making sense of their emerging identities in intercultural contexts.

Following this, in Chapters Two and Three, I apply Appadurai's theoretic of a 'capacity to aspire' (2004) against Bourdieu's notion of capital to explore the cultural and pedagogical imaginaries possible through their community and church-based arts practices. Combined, this section asks

44   Samoan Mediascapes and Faith-as-Performance

whether these aspirations represent vulnerable or resilient identities, and in what ways these practices might weave waves of aspiration into new identity formations and forms of capital, especially for young women (Allen 2014). By interrogating the social function and layers of meaning rather than just the cultural practices as artefacts, this section turns the reader's attention to the ways in which creativity can open new avenues of identity that merge existing notions of local versus global Samoan citizens.

In addition to drawing on the two years of ongoing conversation, self-documentation, and co-creation of artefacts that we conducted for this book project, I will draw on previous research experiences with both the Samoan and South Sudanese youth. Doing so highlights the longitudinal nature of my research, creative, and social relationships with them, beginning in a teacher-student relationship with key members of each group when they were in Year 7, now approximately ten years ago. Focusing on one stream of an earlier creative intercultural project as a critical site of emergent creative capital (Matthews 2008), I am able to explore the meta-context of the social and pedagogical landscape these young people navigate. While Vineta, Ana, and Newjoy spoke above about how they learned the important cultural stories and practices primarily from their grandmother, their Australian educational experiences have not been so rich. These sites of private versus public pedagogies are crucial in understanding their creativity labour as capital, in ways that both they and their Australian public contexts can value.

This discussion is intended to be neither an abstracted educational analysis, nor a solely cultural one. As Appadurai has shown the interconnectedness of scapes (spheres of practice) and imaginaries (spheres of conjuring), I too am attempting here to show the ways in which the Samoan youth scapes of 'culture', 'church', and 'performance' are interrelated with creativity and educational mastery. While these young people (like many other Samoan and non-Samoan youth) are resilient yet not always top students in formal Australian educational contexts, these same young people are youth leaders, teachers, and expert creative mentors within their own subcultural contexts. In this next section I address those connections and contradictions explicitly.

Intercultural Creative Imaginaries as Pedagogical Scape

I am not attempting to advocate for the public pedagogical value of creative practice in either their public and faith-based sites, nor its value as 'labour' or aspirational means for advancement, but rather what O'Sullivan (2002) calls 'integrated transformative learning', a kind of pedagogical intersectionality that ripples both linearly and laterally throughout their multiple lifeworlds.

O'Sullivan positions his work in contrast to Mezirow's famous definition of transformative learning as primarily a cognitive theory, for while

Mezirow tips his hat to emotion, relationships, and critical social change, his approach to transformative pedagogical practice remains largely individualistic. The recent creative collaborative project *Culture Shack*, in which several of these same Samoan young people were involved, offers a different approach to transformative learning and the role of creative imaginaries, one that is collectivist in both religious and youth-cultural ways. My discussion examines such creative and intercultural endeavour as offering links between creative capital, transformative collaboration, and social change.

Through intercultural creative collaboration, our ability to act and "think relationally" (Bourdieu and Wacquant 1992, 26) remains at the core of both creative agency and transformative education. If capital can be performed and accrued through creative practices, cross-sectoral arts partnerships and collaborative learning continue to extend what constitutes fields of practice. In the *Culture Shack* project, for example, we did not claim that transformation was the only purpose or educational outcome that our co-participants (including teacher-educators, pre-service teachers, and youth participants) pursued, but rather that collaborative creative enquiry can provide a firm base for a more transformative approach to learning overall, and that this learning can then be extended into a form of creative and social capital.

While creativity scholarship is proliferating, the remainder of this chapter will explore some ways in which the 'social creative' (Wilson 2010) can be enhanced to build young people's creative capital. One place in which this can and should be occurring more effectively is in the education sector, and these young people represent the contrast between successful public pedagogues and often under-performing school students. Through their creative labour, they can begin to impact education in Australia not just through new intercultural forms of capital, but by pointing toward new forms of pedagogical scapes that do not currently exist.

Despite an increasingly neoliberal cast to the development of curriculum and pedagogy, educators continue to take little of value from workplace contexts when considering questions of creative capital (Wilson 2010; Matthews 2008). For Bourdieu, capital (social, cultural, economic, human, and symbolic) can be understood newly in relation to shifting cultural attitudes and education policies regarding creativity. This suggests that through the measurement, commodification, and production of such a 'new creativity', both its symbolic- and use-value are changing. For young people like the Samoans and South Sudanese featured here, the cultural and educative function of creativity can be more transparent than for some others, by offering an alternative space (or scape) in which they can excel and escape from the relentlessly literacy-based academic demands of the formal education system.

Whether creativity can offer transformative potential to education or not remains context-specific. But within intercultural contexts, creative and collaborative artmaking presents opportunities for integration of both cultural and religious diversity, in educationally productive ways. Teachers, scholars,

46 Samoan Mediascapes and Faith-as-Performance

and students from all backgrounds can benefit from further consideration of collaborative, dialogic, and culturally embedded creative approaches to learning and teaching (Tisdell and Tolliver 2003), like those explored here.

This book in part revisits the *Culture Shack* project as a site of intercultural border-crossing to explore the notion of creative capital and suggest that rather than representing only a commodification of creativity that is hostile to inclusive and transformative learning, it might offer new perspectives on transformative education pathways in its effective world-linking. In doing so, I highlight the benefits of what Bresler calls the "intensified cross-fertilization" (2007, xvii) possible in interdisciplinary approaches to research and education. These productive models seek to soften "boundaries [to] allow border crossing" (Bresler 2007, xvii), a phenomenon both methodological in research spheres, and that which in creative practice "is manifested in the juxtaposition of artistic genres and styles" (Bresler 2007, xvii). In doing so, I highlight the value of multi-perspectival transformative education with a critical and social agenda, through creative "narratives of location and positionality" (Anthias 2002, 497).

Culture Shack as a Site of Creative Pedagogy

In order to make explicit the links between *Culture Shack* and the current relationships and creative practices of these youth, I offer a brief review of the *Culture Shack* project. *Culture Shack* was a program established as an arts-based education pathway for young people from migrant and refugee backgrounds in order to break down barriers between higher education, community college (known as TAFE in Australia), secondary schools, and community arts facilities for young people 'at risk of disengagement'. These are youth who were dynamically engaged in community arts activities and classes yet had low academic engagement or achievement, and were amongst the most at-risk for non-attendance post-Year 10. This program sought to bring together the education and community arts sectors to break down the barriers for these students, but also for teachers and workers in all these contexts, with a goal of transforming the educational pathways and relationships that for migrant and refugee-background youth were characterised by disconnection, deficit positioning, and feelings of hopelessness or lack of aspiration.

The project brought together over fifty pre-service teachers (i.e., teachers-in-training), teacher-educators (education scholars who train teachers in university programs), refugee- and migrant-background youth participants, and artists from three countries (Australia, Canada, and the United States) during 2010–2011. The *Culture Shack* artistic team included one international arts-education scholar (from New York), two artist-practitioners (from Montreal and New York), three local scholar-collaborators (from Melbourne), an Australian Indigenous artist (from Central Australia), four local artists, three community arts facilities and their staff, and the twenty-four young people who participated. The broadness of the collaborative team was deliberate, but not without methodological challenges explored in depth in other publications (Harris 2013a, 2013c, 2012). The participants were sourced through personal and professional networks (including several Samoan and South Sudanese ex-students of Anne's), and public advertising through local schools and the primary community arts facility in Melbourne's western suburbs.

Central to the project's goals of reflexive, relational, and transformative pedagogies, and to its arts-based methods, were its 'peered and tiered' knowledge-sharing model (Harris 2013b) in building an emergent creative capital for these youth participants. By fostering peer-to-peer creative knowledge-sharing through horizontal structures, combined with a vertical tiered structure of scholar/artist-student-teacher-youth participant, co-participants were able to learn from one another and share knowledge in a multi-directional way. This process of building creative capital offers transformative potential for education contexts, but artistic ones as well.

Culture Shack's structure flowed along three 'streams': drama, media, and hip hop, an arts-based approach increasingly common in critical approaches across a wide range of disciplines and contexts (MacDonnell and Macdonald 2011). The *Culture Shack* workshop period ran for two weeks, culminating in a public forum and performance attended by approximately fifty-five people. The average participant number per day of the workshops was sixteen, and the ages of the participants ranged from fourteen to twenty-three.

Creative Capital in the School and Community

As explored in greater detail in the introduction, creative capital is a nascent but already variously defined form of capital in Bourdieuian terms, and creativity in industrial terms. Matthews defines creative capital as "the ability and potential of individuals and groups to generate ideas or to apply old ideas in new ways" (2008, 1), whilst I have problematised it in more economic terms through a discussion of commodification (Harris 2014). In an extension which highlights individual versus social aspects of this new creativity, Wilson (2010) calls for a "move from an individualistic conception of creativity to one that is inherently inclusive and social in nature, whilst not denying the creative individual" (378). For the purposes of understanding *Culture Shack's* goals, I draw primarily on Wilson's focus on the individual.

The wide diversity of *Culture Shack* co-participants set the context for an effective form of social creativity that suggested not only pedagogical value, but potentially a creative form of capital as well. Situating this work within discursive framings of capital does not alienate it from its transformative educational potential; rather, it may provide a link between the social capital of creativity as a tool of reconciliation between cultures, with a new exchange-value in economic terms, which recognises that the "primary commerce of art, after all, is a gift exchange" (Wilson 2010, 378). Bourdieu's acts of resistance move against the relative autonomy of these kinds

48   *Samoan Mediascapes and Faith-as-Performance*

of economic and cultural 'restrictive fields', which are now being rapidly erased (or at least significantly altered) by interdisciplinarity and neoliberalism. A critique of Bourdieuian reflexivity can be seen in a call to behave ethically as educators, to develop an ethics of care (Fine 2008; Peters and Besley 2008) and a real responsibility to all co-participants, inside and outside of our fields, which must be decided in conditions of unknowing. Critical teachers and our so-called innovations come "out of a meta-analysis, a deeper study of the ideological and epistemological assumptions on which the framework supporting knowledge production and the academic curriculum is grounded" (Kincheloe 2005, 94). However, the links between an emergent creative capital and future-focused transformative learning are clear: increasingly neoliberal education contexts demand a range of new strategies for accessing learning and educational degrees. That creativity itself can now be considered 'capital' in education economies can work to the advantage of students who would previously have been considered 'unacademic', or academically unsuccessful. But what kind of creativity are we talking about?

Creative capital might point educators productively toward the further development of a transformative learning and arts-based pedagogy. As Mezirow has said, "To take the perspective of another involves an intrapersonal process" (2003, 59), a process that is intrinsic to creative collaboration. A transformative approach to creative capital theory extends the value of arts-based education and socially inclusive education sites like the arts centre and community locations we used in *Culture Shack*. By moving from an individualist to a collectivist notion of arts and education (which both creative capital and transformative learning advocate), the *Culture Shack* project exemplified the ways in which transformative education is changing, even in these neoliberal times.

Culture Shack's Unique Methodology

The drama stream from which this chapter primarily draws attracted a total of eleven girls over the two-week intensive, five of whom were Samoan (four of whom are centrally involved in the current collaboration for this book). There were also six South Sudanese participants who attended mainly through the hip hop stream, and which I will discuss in greater detail in Section Two of this book. At the public showcase, which was the final culmination of the *Culture Shack* workshops, three Samoan playwriting participants presented works in progress, each including a monologue.

The *Culture Shack* project, like much of my ongoing research with young people from these two communities, featured almost all female participants, despite considerable outreach to South Sudanese and Samoan young men. While there are certainly a good number of these young men involved in creative arts scenes, activities, and arts education programs, they are generally more heavily involved in sports than in the arts when it comes to

Education and the Creative Imaginary 49

community or outside-of-school programs, although certainly not always. Snowball sampling amongst young women may account for some of the preponderance of girls versus boys, as my doctoral work focused solely on South Sudanese young women, and the South Sudanese youth comment on why their male counterparts felt too uncomfortable to attend these workshops. For whatever reason, the workshops and the collaboration for this book remained very unbalanced in favour of the female.

Culture Shack's drama stream was facilitated by Brett,[1] a New York-based professional playwriting instructor, and Kate, a local professional physical theatre performer. The workshops ran from 9am to 5pm, and consisted of practical activities, improvisational and writing tasks, and both small- and large-group collaborative work. The combination of group and individual activities enabled critical reflection, intercultural sharing, and interdisciplinary arts knowledge-building, as noted in my analysis of its unique 'peered and tiered' learning model (Harris 2013b). Reflexive practices enrich both their pedagogical and collaborative potential (Kumashiro 2009; Velde, Wittman and Mott 2007), and the drama workshop stream provided considerable opportunity for reflexive practice. On the last two days of the program, focus groups and interviews were conducted by the researchers (who were also teacher-educators), the pre-service teachers, and by the youth participants themselves, interviewing their peers using both audio and video technologies, sometimes ethnocinematic and at other times self-documenting.

Programs like *Culture Shack*, which offer diverse entry and exit points for young people who do want to be in school but sometimes don't know how, serve an important role as innovative models in providing improved educational pathways and interrelationships for teachers and students (Harris 2012b; Tisdell 2008; Cassity and Gow 2006). In our model, pre-service teachers served as workshop co-facilitators and also co-researchers, thereby reflecting on their own emerging teaching practices and the relationship between arts and education for the youth participants.

Wilson (2010) encourages scholars, teachers, and economists to move beyond the "dominant individualistic model of creativity [that] perpetuates the notion that creativity is the exclusive property of a particular type of talented person" (371). In the *Culture Shack* model that combines community arts organisations, professional artists, teachers, and universities, the youth participants were able to move beyond notions of 'giftedness' and mastery, while at the same time valuing creative skill in their peers. Pedagogically, the refusal to foreclose any level of expertise in collaborative enterprise of this kind offers teachers new avenues for exploring aspiration and productive risk-taking, a point in teaching creativity noted by Netzer and Rowe (2010).

According to Lather, "that is precisely the task [of education]: to situate the experience of impossibility as an enabling site for working through aporias" (2007, 16), in supported and perhaps even joyful ways (Montuori 2008). Creative collaboration confronts the im/possibility of arts and cultural multiplicity together as a tool for new kinds of education. In the spirit

50 Samoan Mediascapes and Faith-as-Performance

of Ellsworth and Lather, *Culture Shack*'s failures as well as successes were equally celebrated, "in order to produce and learn from ruptures, failures, breaks, refusals" (Lather 2007, 16), and to reinforce the value of productive risk as a pedagogical venture.

Many of the co-participants, including the South Sudanese and Samoan youth here, are creatively active in their church, school, and community groups, as well as in arts initiatives run by local government and community organisations. They have learned valuable skills in drama, media, and dance, but despite satisfying skills development, they were still encountering difficulty in gaining university entrance or job opportunities, lacking the kind of creative capital that holds more value in the creative industries and digital technology discourses in which these youth seldom enroll. Many of the migrant co-participants of *Culture Shack* expressed disappointment that as future pathways remain scarce, they would not be able to continue pursuing their artistic passions but instead will have to look for the kinds of unskilled or unsatisfying jobs to which their (lack of) education relegates them.

In establishing the *Culture Shack* program, I recognised a pathway opportunity: while many of these young people might not become professional artists or fulltime creative arts students, they might be interested in becoming arts teachers given pathway assistance by mapping community arts-based workshops, through community college certificates, into university entrance requirements—a 'creative industry' not included in the highly digital, design and production oriented jobs which characterise creative industries training programs. These young people's views suggested that a radical rethinking of education must happen within institutional education as well as within the youth participants themselves, as research on 'transformative' interventions so often advises and celebrates. Instead, *Culture Shack* exemplified what Korn-Bursztyn calls the "questions and creative tensions that a meeting of institutional cultures calls forth" (2005, 46).

In Australian, American, and British contexts since the turn into this century, interdisciplinary partnerships for arts education have been well documented (Donelan 2010; Peters and Besley 2008; DeMoss 2005; Burnaford, Aprill and Weiss 2001). Yet questions remain about sustainability: the national Australian Curriculum (while including an arts curriculum) mirrors an international move toward standardization, ranking, and outsourcing arts engagement to arts partnerships external to the schools. By actively engaging teachers in the *Culture Shack* arts collaborations, creative and pedagogical training (at least in the way this pre-service teacher thought about the potential of his students and his teaching ability) were productively intertwined:

> It [*Culture Shack*] made me realise that you can't have predetermined notions about the students. Like I remember at the start of last week, some of the things that I wrote in here [journal] were like 'how will we do this [drama]'? There's just no way—they just don't want to. But then

Education and the Creative Imaginary 51

halfway through last week, the [CS] approach worked for them, and now they are just full of artistic potential. And for whatever reason at the start of last week—and I feel horrible—I just couldn't see it.

(pre-service teacher Nick)

Britzman (like Nick above) reminds us how difficult it is for a pre-service teacher to feel confident in his "own power to explore with students the dangerous territory of the unknown" (2003, 224), and perhaps all the more so for established teachers or teacher-educators.

The *Culture Shack* staff/scholars were well aware of some significant challenges when it was first conceptualised in 2010, but the complex nature of schooling for migrant and refugee-background students demands an equally complex approach from teachers. To work across disciplines, sectors, and countries was tricky, but the international scope was important to the ethos of the project: part of what we were trying to say to these young people was that the international community is smaller than you think, that the values, skills, and perspectives you as students (and artists) bring from your own countries are very welcome here, and are pedagogically and artistically valuable. By employing artists (and scholars) from other parts of the world, the young people could find solidarity in other intercultural (and transcultural) perspectives and methods, but also begin to develop artistic mentoring relationships with these artists that may inspire or assist them in their globally mobile artistic and educational journeys later. By building multiple forms of capital together, and rejecting traditional hierarchical pedagogical structures, both teachers and students were liberated from reproductive learning (Mezirow 2003) patterns and allowed to emerge into self-regulating and creative ones:

I found that the groups moderate themselves. . . . somehow or other mediation seems to happen and it seems to get moderated from within the group. Almost like the teacher doesn't need to get involved. Equally effective is the idea of mirroring in terms of the tiered and peered learning model, that somehow you are kind of instinctively copying behaviour and appropriating things from different disciplines, or different levels of experience. And even watching [the program coordinator] do logistics, I've been learning a lot from that as an artist and teacher.

(Sarah, pre-service teacher)

By incorporating creative practice as a kind of levelling agent that allowed for two-way learning, *Culture Shack* acknowledged the ways in which such collaborations can encourage both youth and the adults with whom they collaborate (teachers, artists) to critically interrogate their practices and motivations. By combining drama and hip hop with educational pathways, *Culture Shack* aimed to create space for both participatory and immersive collaboration toward concepts of further education, especially for too-often

52   *Samoan Mediascapes and Faith-as-Performance*

deficit-framed learners like these. This intergenerational and interdisciplinary creative approach to learning is not so different from the faith and family experiences of many of the Samoan and South Sudanese youth in this book—indeed, they commented upon it as a familiar learning model when they participated in the *Culture Shack* program.

Culture Shack worked hard also to ensure that this deeply immersive experience was not seen as some kind of education panacea in itself, but rather another step in a sustained and deliberate journey in which 'education' can include a range of both familiar and unfamiliar practices:

> but it wasn't like school [where] you have to write it down . . . it was a fun way of learning new things . . . when we needed help they just told us to get up and act it out and we'd just go from there.
>
> (Eseta, Samoan, 15)

Vineta and other *Culture Shack* participants experienced creative and evolving self-concepts as learners, young people, and cultural actors. Creative capital, and its impact on other forms of capital, suggested the powerful pedagogical potential of combining creativity, culture, and community sites of collaboration.

Culture-Based Creative Collaboration

Culture Shack used creative collaboration as an approach to transformative education in order to "listen empathically, 'bracketing' premature judgment, and seeking common ground" (Mezirow 2003, 60). The Samoan youth came to the drama stream initially solely as actors, comfortable with improvisation and (school- and church-based) performance. Language matters, as we found out, and 'playwriting' as a way to create performance was, Vineta and her peers reported, completely unknown, and consequently almost none of them wanted to jump into the drama stream. Both Kate's and Brett's skills as teaching artists were effective. Their many years of experience were on display when these skilled Samoan youth performers continually returned to improvisation as the only way to begin and develop narrative. Brett's specialty is character; all playscripts, for him, grow out of well-developed character, and this is how these young women who entered as performers were able to leave as playwrights.

Kate's skills as a performer supported this work as she brought the physical theatre component to Brett's Young Playwrights' Festival skills with text. Words and movement combined to allow the Samoan young women to expand their drama skills, and to develop new literacy-based skills as they crafted and then revised their playscripts. That the drama and other streams were interculturally delivered by both local and international artists underlined the fact that creative collaboration translates well across geographical and cultural space and place, and the Samoan youth coached their non-Samoan peers in what they had learned.

As Matthews (2008) has noted, creative teaching, learning, and collaboration "usually includes some training in techniques which promote divergent thinking" (4), and *Culture Shack* certainly encouraged this. One way to build creative capital is through "bringing groups of people together to facilitate the exchange of ideas and stimulate innovation, in both structured and informal ways" (Matthews 2008, 4), an approach we used effectively in *Culture Shack*, but one which would make a welcome and significant change in the approach and design of formal education institutions. Non-hierarchical teaching and learning practices, which thrived in the peered and tiered model of *Culture Shack*, enhance opportunities for this cross-pollination. The Samoan youth were already well-versed in acting as peer mentors and youth leaders through their church youth group roles, but other youth participants were not so comfortable or experienced, and praised the Samoan peer educators for their generous, committed, and skilled approach to this aspect of the program.

Another way in which the creative capital of public pedagogical events and sites like this one may be understood is through aesthetic experience. Kokkos (2010) articulates an approach to aesthetic education that focuses on its affective qualities (158), and certainly the experiences of those involved in *Culture Shack* reinforced Kokkos' notion that creative collaboration is a highly affective proposition. It is impossible to 'do arts' without personally investing oneself, an endeavor which in itself can be risky business. But Kokkos also highlights the inherently critically reflective function of creative teaching and learning. He draws on Kant in challenging sweeping claims of transformation in studies of aesthetics, an area of enquiry now almost wholly extinct in schools. The recognition of a distinct 'field' or critical mode of thought made possible by aesthetic enquiry points to another kind of creative capital that may not often enough be included in marketplace definitions. Contact with art and aesthetics, Kokkos argues, importantly "functions as a field where critical consciousness is cultivated" (162), in ways that may not be present elsewhere in contemporary education. Furthermore, it would be difficult to imagine the ways in which standardized curricula can fulfill the critical theoretical function of arts. As he sees it, "Works of great art, due to their anticonventional character, their holistic dimension, the authentic meaning of life that they display and the multiple interpretations that they are susceptible to, are in contrast to the instrumental rationality" (Kokkos 2010, 162) offered by conventional education and socialisation.

The *Culture Shack* project did not claim to offer or create great works of art, but rather argued that pedagogy through creative collaboration is similar to Kokkos' articulation of aesthetic education. Further, these are not characteristic of typical creative industries' definitions and perhaps should not be—there is certainly room for divergent thinking, defining, and training within the creative industries sector. Yet these value sets seem to be narrowing rather than expanding, and in the next section, I suggest some ways in which creative capital can represent a middle ground between transformative education and Bourdieu's notion of cultural capital, building on Kokkos' understanding of aesthetic education.

Figure 1.3 Vineta's first *Culture Shack* poster, theatrical wizard. Photo and copyright, Anne Harris.

Creative Enquiry as Culturally Transformative Learning

Vineta and the Samoan young women with whom I have been collaborating now for ten years speak powerfully about their many creative and cultural border-crossings, but they sometimes speak about class-based and gendered ones as well. Such discussions were central to the *Culture Shack* project and arose in parallel to one another. Post-Bourdieusian articulations of capital have proposed some ways in which fields might intersect and not, as he claimed, remain distinct. Field theory argues that reality is socially constructed, in which all endeavor is relationally defined and experienced.

Certainly in creative collaboration, power differences are constantly under negotiation in ways that are more fluid than within classrooms and more

Education and the Creative Imaginary 55

traditional student/teacher relationships. In the culminating days of *Culture Shack*, similar boundary crossing and field-switching was evident, as co-participants struggled to articulate their experiences, and to finalise creative products for sharing publicly. Nick—a student-teacher/drama intern and a professional actor—was facilitating the 'drama group' focus group discussion with some of the (mostly) Samoan participants. A conversation centred on cultural reasons for enrolling in the same workshop quickly shifted to questions of gender. One of the workshop participants took over the questioning role:

Vineta:	*(asking her peers) Would you feel comfortable performing and acting what we've been doing these past days in front of guys? I mean guys our age?*
Ana:	*I'd be more nervous. (pause) If they were ugly I wouldn't care.*
Rosalba:	*Boys are too immature.*
Nick to Ana:	*So you're playing a male rap artist, would you have done that if there were guys in the room?*
Ana:	*(laughing hard, shaking head) No way.*
Rosalba:	*Even if it was the hip hop girls or the girls from animation, I wouldn't have done it. Cuz I only like performing in front of people that I'm close to.*
Aluel (South Sudanese):	*If there were boys in this drama class, let's say mixed, we'd actually learn some different things, cuz now we actually learn girl things. But in front of boy or mixed we learn something different. . . .*
Eseta:	*If there were good looking boys I'd be like (silent). I'm just saying—this is honesty!*
Rosalba:	*I wouldn't let my character be a 10-year-old girl, I would be like a 17-year-old person.*
Vineta:	*—it'd change things.*

This exchange during the focus group discussion offers insights not only into the gendered nature of creative processes, but a marked contrast between the sole South Sudanese co-participant's perspective and the Samoan ones. While the Samoan participants all felt they would be inhibited by the presence of boys, Aluel (who was admittedly a little older at twenty-three) felt it would signal simply a 'different kind of learning'.

Ellsworth cautions against ignoring the ways in which power and agency in pedagogical relationships are always problematic and unstable, intersubjectively multiple and contradictory. The work of collaborative creative pedagogies like *Culture Shack* always references the personal (Grumet 1990), and points us in new directions for understanding relationality within the pedagogical exchange. These participants also indicate ways in which family, society, and peers influence decision-making:

> *last year, I was like 'oh, I love drama, I want to act'. But then this year—year 12—I should get serious, do something better, like something that will help my family . . . not exactly something that I would like. And then as we were doing the workshop I was like 'Yeah, I'm thinking of doing drama'. Like, as another option.*
>
> (Vineta, 18)

Such influences also demonstrate the ways in which applied learning in community settings can have ongoing pedagogical value. Montuori (2008) has articulated a range of ways in which academic enquiry can be a joyful and creative enterprise. He recognises the central role of personal narrative, a storytelling in which the self can look critically at the self. For students and teachers navigating intercultural roles often in tension with one another, "the process of navigating these cultures with their different customs" leaves students in "constant inquiry" (2008, 12). This heightened awareness of difference becomes pedagogically and artistically productive when creatively collaborating in a peered and tiered or collaborative model of knowledge sharing, such as *Culture Shack* was, and as the ongoing collaboration between myself and these Samoan and South Sudanese young people is also.

Figure 1.4 White Sunday goofing, 2015. Photo and copyright, Anne Harris.

Cultural and Creative Border-Crossing as Wide-Awakeness

The 'wide-awakeness' that Maxine Greene has celebrated as necessary to transformative education is what the arts do best: to release the imagination is an act that requires both practice and intention (Greene 2000). When Vineta and her Samoan peers participated in the *Culture Shack* program, our individual and collective experiences at times showed the strain and the pleasure of maintaining Greene's brand of openness. For those like Vineta, with family and community obligations, *Culture Shack* opened up educational aspirations, but also collectivist loyalties, obligations, and alternative family structures to many of their non-Samoan peers. Vineta described to her drama tutor-collaborator Nick that deep cultural crossings were also happening, which unsettled old assumptions:

Nick: *Do you think Culture Shack has other important values besides educational pathways?*
Vineta: *Definitely. Because at Culture Shack there's people from different backgrounds coming together and they're not only learning about the arts, they're also learning about each other and their backgrounds as well. So, even that first week when we started off it was like the Asians were in animation and the Islanders in drama, and the Africans in hip hop; now the relationship between the kids are together . . . we've changed completely.*

While Vineta may not have employed the language of pedagogical discourse, she describes clearly *Culture Shack*'s goal of creatively addressing the dual project of intercultural exchange and creative experimentation. The participants and interns rightly imagined that more intercultural conversation would lead to more bonding in the beginning, and to avoiding what we called the 'cultural segregation' which dominated the first few days (most visible during lunches and other whole-group times). While the participants had interests and affiliations across cultural and genre boundaries, they were asked or opted into a singular choice, which—as Vineta says—almost always broke out along cultural lines. The *Culture Shack* team did not intervene, and the young people became more interculturally interactive as time went by. Some enlightening discussions, artworks, and improvised ethnocinematic videos attest to the very active cultural interrogations of self and other that were occurring throughout this period, including during the student-teacher focus group on the last day:

Anne: *So has Culture Shack impacted on your thinking about race and culture? I've been thinking about race and culture and we [have] talked about the 'cultural segregation' that's happened in this project. . . . But [then there were] what I call 'border-crossers'—*
         (general agreement from student-teachers)

58 Samoan Mediascapes and Faith-as-Performance

Nick: —There did emerge some border-crossers, gender-wise and also culture-wise, and some of those were articulated, like 'My sister Newjoy decided to go to animation to break through the culture thing'. So who does that? And who doesn't do that? And why?

We knew that the participants maintained different narratives representing competing identities, which—like Appadurai's "disjunct global flows, [that] produce local contradictions and tensions of many kinds" (2006, 30)—are intrinsically linked to intercultural exchange. Here the pre-service teachers saw clearly that cultural and creative border-crossings were linked:

Patrick: I think it [cultural mingling in workshop groups] could have happened in time.

(hubbub of agreement)

Liz: It did start to—
Patrick: I found that Rania, for instance, started to join the continental dance that I was doing with the Islander girls—
Liz: . . . these are the questions that come up in classrooms, right?
Sarah: . . . there were a couple of border-crossers. And they were a little bit older . . . entering into new territory—certainly I think our entire group were aware that this was an issue . . . do we need to actually talk about culture? I don't know.
Demian: I kinda got the impression that there were certain things that if we didn't—They probably wouldn't have tried it.
Kate: I think if we had more time—they're all going with what they're comfortable with—and the first thing they're comfortable with is the culture. And then, later on they would have mixed themselves up and actually gone for the art form that suited them better.

These student-teachers continued to productively grapple with the impact of place and pedagogical relationship throughout the program, as did the youth participants. The engagement the student-teachers saw happening was in many ways completely different from much of what they experienced in their placement schools—both in teacher/student relationships, and also in the quickness with which these young people were learning. As artists enrolled in a teacher-education training program, these student-teachers prided themselves on the 'expert knowledge' they were bringing to their secondary school students; after *Culture Shack* they began to think much more about the pedagogical value of collaboration and interdisciplinary work, for they recognised the ways in which these 'students' (in some cases) carried just as much creative and educational expert knowledge as they did.

The student-teachers and youth participants also began to consider new ways of partnering with community arts facilities, a well-recognised and more holistic approach to effectively engaging creatively with students (Netzer and Rowe 2010). While their class work required the student-teachers to consider ways of bringing these types of programs *into* schools, they spontaneously considered and debated ways of moving educational work *outside* of schools and of building coalitions *between* schools and other organisations. The constant desire for more interdisciplinary swapping time between streams during the workshops mirrored the student-teachers' desire for more cross-curricular collaboration in their placement schools. Teaching about and across cultural difference using creativity does not attempt to erase differences; rather it highlights the value of engaging in the ongoing production of culture in a way that returns our shared focus to the value of "yet another difference" (Ellsworth 1997, 139) in creative intercultural endeavour, rather than the neoliberalizing move toward hegemonising both creativity and education.

Conclusion to Chapter One

In this chapter I have laid the groundwork for a discussion of faith-as-performance, and performance as pedagogy, based on commentary from these Samoan young peoples in two different contexts—an earlier project, *Culture Shack*, and their current self-documentation for this book. I have argued for both its transformative educational potential and also for its powerful ability to suggest a new creative imaginary, in the youths' abilities to use creative arts and popular culture for synthesising their religion, languages, and cultural diversity. This potential I also suggest has material and symbolic value as an emergent creative capital, but it also usefully expands current creative interrogations of the social imaginary (Pimpa and Rojana-panich 2011).

I have purposely examined in such great detail the *Culture Shack* program's ability to celebrate multi-directional creative collaboration that builds emergent creative capital based solidly in creative and cultural subjectivities and practices for a very specific reason. It exemplified the benefits of creative partnerships between community arts organisations, professional artists (local and international), and vocational and higher education to address both short- and long-term needs of the Samoan and other youth participants. But it also shows readers an example of something else: that is, the skills of these young people represent a kind of capital which positively impacts on their social habitus as students, artists, and peers. While the origins of their collective cultural creativity may be embedded in a context of birth-to-death performative participation in their church, and while they might not always love it throughout adolescence, its impact is evident. Their ability to mentor their non-Samoan peers in the *Culture Shack* program shows how transferable these skills are, and how the integration of their religious, creative, and cultural values and practices make room for other successes and citizen-participation.

60   *Samoan Mediascapes and Faith-as-Performance*

Finally, I have included this extended discussion of the *Culture Shack* project to argue the links between creative capital and transformative learning, extending Mezirow's largely cognitive theory of transformative learning, by examining its interface with O'Sullivan's focus on emotion and the potential of the notion of creative capital. Sometimes those engaged in creative approaches to education can feel marginalised in ways not so different from the marginalisation experienced by minoritarian students in schools, such as Samoans and other students from migrant backgrounds. This marginalisation can create a similar kind of 'impossible project' for artists, students, and teachers.

In this chapter I have tried to suggest a different view. Creative collaboration and our ability to act and "think relationally" (Bourdieu and Wacquant 1992, 26) remain at the core of both intercultural labour and transformative education. This is one reason why cross-sectoral arts partnerships and collaborative learning continue to remain so popular, even in these economically conservative times. Yet a dynamic creative dialogue does not, in itself, constitute a transformative education that offers students and teachers from diverse backgrounds and cultural/ethnic identities a way forward; it does suggest proliferating possibilities for the ways in which intercultural work can assist the transformative potential of creative pedagogies, with the potential for building creative capital. Creative educators and scholars agree that learning must begin with the context and create opportunities for exchange in multi-directional ways.

I am not suggesting that such exchanges can be perfect or always comfortable. Creativity in education requires a "direct intervention by the educator to foster the development of the skills, insights, and especially dispositions essential for critical reflection" (Mezirow 2003, 62), and in this chapter I have attempted to show that creative collaboration with both public and educational goals can provide fertile ground for such work. Transformative education discourses sometimes fall prey to unproductively essentialising notions of a homogeneous underprivileged in classrooms and in communities, and our imagined work to empower 'them' or to transform them beyond their current circumstances. Creative collaborations, on the other hand, provide opportunities in which together we can make the most of what's good about those circumstances. Programs like *Culture Shack* have pointed some ways forward—based in the words, creative views, and collaborative practices of the Samoan young people.

In the next chapter, I will extend this discussion by drawing on Appadurai's theoretic of a 'capacity to aspire' (2004) and combining this with Bourdieu's notion of capital to explore the cultural and pedagogical imaginaries possible through the Samoans' community and church-based arts practices. If this chapter has asked whether these aspirations represent vulnerable or resilient identities, it has also asked of the education system what can be changed to better incorporate these expert knowledges and practices. By examining these multiple social functions and layers of meaning rather than just the cultural or creative practices as artefacts, this chapter has directed readers' attention to the ways in which creativity can perform multiple social and educational functions. In Chapter Two, I ask in what ways these practices might weave creative subjectivities into hybrid cultural work for these young people as they move into and out of their church communities, with the complex layers of religious, cultural, and creative work that typifies their lived experience.

Note

1 All names have been anonymised for privacy of the co-participants. This project was conducted with the approval of the lead university's human research ethics committee.

2 God Culture and the Capacity to In/Aspire

Figure 2.1 Getting real with the spirit, at White Sunday, 2014. Photo and copyright, Anne Harris.

Chapter Two details how this Samoan Christian youth group's self-representations of their faith experiences represents a new kind of agentic subjectivity for them and is representative of a growing youth culture centred on 'faith communities'. Yet these young people and their relationship

God Culture and the Capacity to In/Aspire 63

to music in particular go beyond an expression of their faith and become an enactment of what Appadurai calls a 'capacity to aspire', a strategy by which they partially bypass the many constraints of their material conditions. By documenting their experiences of developing and sharing new work, both religious and secular, these young people's voices are foregrounded as providing a more complex interweaving of the usually binarised notions of secular and spiritual in contemporary culture (including their intersections with hybrid musical genres like hip hop and R&B). This chapter traces the ways in which this faith-infused music scene in Samoan youth culture provides a type of global citizenship for these otherwise locally embedded young people that links them to global communities of culture, faith, and creativity.

The Samoan youth perspective recognises the ways in which "the incorporation of the creative arts . . . also allows us to access other ways of knowing and understanding" (Harris and Gandolfo 2013, 2), for both faith sharing and scholarly knowledge sharing as a collaborative creative research endeavour. Because we share an interest in creating a pedagogical imaginary that invites readers to enter into our experience as intercultural creative collaborators, into the Samoan youth experience of Wesleyan Methodists, and into their cultural subjectivities as Samoan young people, we value

> ways of knowing that are much more experiential, attached to feelings and emotions, and that generate empathetic responses from readers (Eisner 2003, 11). We acknowledge that with this form of writing, it is more likely to elicit alternative and multiple interpretations and understandings than more traditional scholarly forms.
>
> (Harris and Gandolfo 2013, 2)

In this chapter I examine both our shared aspirations for this work but also the Samoan youths' aspirations as citizens, artists, and intercultural and interfaith border-crossers. While these young people remain largely framed as vulnerable (or at-risk) subjects, in this collaboration they speak from their own perspectives as they see themselves, and like most young people reflect a mixture of hopeful, agentic, and emergent. In this chapter I focus more closely on the ways in which the intersection of their religious and creative practices might offer them a kind of global mobility through Appadurai's notion of mediascapes.

In this next excerpt from a group discussion on the affective experience of performing in and through their church youth group, Ana, Vineta, and Joy talk about the ways in which social media allow them to 'spread the word' but also at times become zones of surveillance—a double-edged sword that provides encouragement for creative experimentation and risk-taking, but can also inhibit their free expression in order to avoid negative reflection on their church and families.

64   Samoan Mediascapes and Faith-as-Performance

Joy: *I like singing in the choir because there's heaps of people.*
Anne: *But you really don't like the one alone thing?*
Joy: *No.*
Anne: *Why is that?*
Joy: *I don't know, it's just not me.*
Anne: *But you guys have had lots of followers, thousands of followers on social media. Doesn't that give you confidence?*
Vineta: *Well that is only some of the time, and it also brings problems with it! You have to be strong to deal with that.*
Anne: *What do you mean? Can you tell us a story about that?*
Vineta: *Okay well I'm going to talk about that first video that we made then. A lot of people added me and it was mostly the Samoan people that I had become—like this was, when was it 2013, two years ago, it was this time two years ago. So people that added me that day now it's the same Facebook page I feel like I know them from seeing their stuff on news feed and they see my stuff. Sometimes we message as well and say 'Oh, my gosh, you've got an awesome voice'. So they are like 'Oh, my gosh, you have an awesome voice'. And you know sometimes we've even been talking about collaborating. So yeah like social media and the computer, it goes a long way. It all depends on how much you dedicate your time to it because we have other commitments as well. So sometimes it dies down and then we upload our video and it goes viral. But we are always talking to people on Facebook, yeah. It's a good way to get out there and be connected, be visible. I think it [social media] works for like church stuff too because for church, we have so many branches, like the ones in New Zealand, and here we have a Facebook page for our church. So that kind of keeps us like connected with our other youth members and it keeps us updated with what's going on and because sometimes we don't go to conference which is like always held in New Zealand and we don't get that chance to go. So sometimes through social media they always keep us updated of what happened, what's new and like what's been going on and what's going to happen next year.*
Anne: *Okay and so and in a way, if time or money or distance prevents you from gathering physically you feel like it's a pretty good alternative?*
Ana: *Yeah that's right.*
Anne: *And so with your songs, your performances, do you just upload it from your phone or whatever?*
Ana: *Yeah.*
Anne: *So if you closed down your account or something what happens to those videos they're just gone?*

God Culture and the Capacity to In/Aspire 65

Ana:	*Yeah, they're gone.*
Vineta:	*I reopened it because of—you know the reason why I went off that one?*
Anne:	*No.*
Vineta:	*[Laughing] Because I think I was, I felt like I was too open.*
Anne:	*Do you want to talk about that?*
Vineta:	*And you notice how I don't upload as much selfies as I did before, I don't do it anymore, right? I've become more self-conscious.*
Anne:	*Why is that?*
Vineta:	*I don't know. Like because I see other people do it, and it frustrates me sometimes so I'm thinking what if I'm frustrating people with my selfies. Like no more. Like I do, but. There's so much hate in the media and for me I'm really, really, really sensitive with that kind of stuff. So like even one word, that can make me cry my eyes out. Because I hated it when some of my own family were getting bullied as well, or having that kind of, what? Experience on Facebook. I'm thinking it's hurting me watching my family go through this or my friends go thought this. Imagine if I'm actually going through it you know, like no I don't want to.*
Anne:	*That sounds really painful. And stressful too.*
Vineta:	*I'm back on my old page now but I deleted a lot of my other stuff that I wrote. Yeah I deleted some things because I was pretty open. Yeah I was open. But people found it hilarious which is why I kept doing it because people were like, oh, my gosh, I love your statuses. But then now thinking of my 18-year-old self I'm thinking, oh, my gosh, I can't believe I wrote that. Delete, delete, delete.*
Anne:	*Right. Yes they were very open. And you have such a wonderful way with words that simply as stories, they were very compelling, right? So you got a lot of feedback, a lot of praise, I remember. And so like, one thing I noticed at times was that while you got lots of encouragement and praise, some of them were quite painful or quite revealing and how did it feel to have people regard that as funny? You felt like they thought you were funny.*
Vineta:	*It made me feel better. Actually it made—it didn't offend me in any way. In a way, to me Facebook was real. But when I'm saying that Facebook is real, it's like a kind of real that when people were commenting on my stuff they were pretty, you know—Okay so there was this one time, I think you have seen my status about this, this one time when I went for an interview and the people saw me, like took one look at me, and then they just didn't—they were like, 'Sorry, we don't need you', when like a moment ago they were like, 'Hurry you have to be here quickly! You know you can have your trial right*

> *now because we're really busy, so we need you to work'! So that was ten minutes before I got there, but then when I arrived, they took one look at me and they're like, 'Sorry we don't need anyone anymore'. And it's like, 'Okay it's pretty obvious it's because I'm big', and like I know that. But because I've been big my whole life, I know how it feels when I get that kind of response. But having Facebook and all the people who supported me out there, it was really like it really made me feel better about myself, and I think that's the other reason why I started to love myself more. . .. It's hard [to lose weight] you know, because the food we eat at home, it's mostly fattening food. A lot of fried food. And the other thing is we have to do what our nanna wants first. Like we have to just feed her what she wants and then we have to work around that. And it's not very healthy. I mean she likes to put taro and bananas.*

Here Vineta has veered from the narrative of faith-based performer into the ways in which social media create new relationalities and identity borders. While all three young women started out talking about individual versus collective creativity, Vineta quickly recalled how easily her Facebook identity shifted from (not irrevocably, but fluidly and at times unexpectedly) the musical performer with a great voice to the over-sharing teen girl who has weight issues and uses humour to win over fans and deliver social critique about the 'big girl' bias she encounters regularly in society at large. As Riggs suggests, "bodies are dynamically always under construction, or 'constructed as being material (i.e., stereotypes about bodily makers)' (2007, para. 3), but also as self-constructed and repetitively performed (as in Butler 1993)" (in Harris and Lemon 2012, 423), and Vineta's commentary about the pain of over-exposure is her reflexivity about not only her material body-under-construction, but her online body as well, her performed body, which constitutes both virtual embodiments and a flesh body. Interestingly, she disrupts her narrative to identify the social media world as 'real', yet is ultimately unable to define that realness further than a comparison with the painful and partly 'unreal' nature of the offline flesh world.

Her care for her younger self, and the contradictions about how hurtful or supportive was the social media commentary regarding her status updates, highlights the risky terrain that social media presents for youth, including those like Vineta who may begin using it only for specific goals such as for proselytising, but soon begin to live in those landscapes in a multitude of ways, both individual and collective. Vineta's status updates, which were essentially like blogs or mini reality-show-narratives, have become famous amongst all who know her online, and these 'friends' amount to several thousand people. Yet Vineta makes it clear that while her ersatz reason for being online is to share her youth group and family faith-based creative activities, she is also calling her audience to attention in ways that are powerfully feminist, anti-ageist, and anti-racist.

God Culture and the Capacity to In/Aspire   67

As Hickey-Moody has written about migrant youth arts in Australia, "Through calling an audience to attention, youth performances create 'affective and emergent *publics*' . . . which are 'structured by affect as much as by rational-critical debate. Such engagement can occur in and through popular culture . . . and everyday communication'" (2013, 25). But above, Vineta also identifies herself as marginalised by her weight, not by racist or other social structures. Scholars have noted the ways in which both community- and school-based youth arts often speak to marginalised bodies (Hickey-Moody 2013; O'Brien and Donelan 2008), and the sanctuary of youth arts extends into social media and the sympathetic audiences found there, as Vineta describes. Such audiences may not be so numerous or so readily available in offline worlds, especially largely localised ones like those that Vineta and her peers inhabit. She goes on:

Vineta: *The other reasons why I love myself is if people on Facebook like me like this, you know then I can be like, 'Oh, there's nothing wrong with me'. So right now with the whole weight losing thing that I want to do, it's more to help myself get better and healthier, because I notice that that's why my leg is taking ages to heal. Because you know I think I've got diabetes and I say I think because I didn't really go back to know the results because I already know. So yeah I just signed myself because I know if my parent saw that it was confirmed that I have diabetes, they would be strict on the food and I won't have the food that I want to eat. Yeah, so. That's the good thing about Facebook. You know you have to have your friends on there and random people as well. I think getting that response from random people makes me feel so much better than having it from my friends and family, because of course you're thinking, 'You're just saying that because you're my friend or you're my family'. But then when other people say it, I'm like, 'Okay, that's true, I'm pretty'! [laughing]*

Glenn Savage helps me to consider how Vineta's deeply personal journey intersects with her public ones, and her creative and religious aspirations with pedagogical ones. For Savage, inhabiting public spaces (both online and offline) represents some of "the significance of informal pedagogies, their interactions with globalisation and corporatisation as a core means through which young people connect to, and participate in, social imaginations. These social imaginations are part of multiple and disparate publics, rubbing against each other" (Savage 2010, 104). But why is, in this case, Vineta's experience of online acceptance more resonant for her than the offline rejection she encounters from her job interviewers, for example?

Appadurai's global imaginary offers one way of thinking about realness for young people like Vineta for whom "social innovation and creativity are contributing to more autonomous learners. . . . in diverse contexts including

68 Samoan Mediascapes and Faith-as-Performance

at-risk learners, [in] elite schools, [and] community arts interventions in public pedagogies" (Harris and Lemon 2012, 426). For many young people, online worlds are increasingly real and certainly more accessible. For Vineta, the anonymity of many of her online admirers is a plus—she believes them simply because they are *not* known to one another, and therefore, she seems to suggest, they would have no incentive for lying when they praise her (like her family does). This kind of 'schooling' into what 'works' in the expanded publics of online worlds is what I have elsewhere called a new pedagogical imaginary, one which is both virtual and local, extending Rizvi and Appadurai:

> Dolby and Rizvi (2008) and Rizvi (2006) calls on the potential of social imaginary to assist global flows to create new opportunities not just for capital, but for intercultural ways of being. The globalisation of knowledge creates potential dangers for new methods of exclusion, but simultaneously new creative innovation in social visions (Appadurai 1999) for transcultural endeavour and education. . . . [Here Samoan creative youth culture in collaboration with others] shows how creative global flows can embody both the discomfort, miscommunication and cultural capital for transcultural bodies and collaboration, by highlighting both the differences (as gendered, sexualised, moral and geographical subjects) and the similarities (as artists, collaborators and co-participants).
> (Harris and Lemon 2012, 427–428)

This sense of an expanded social imaginary (Pimpa and Rojanapanich 2011) for Samoan young people like Vineta hints at ways in which she can move beyond her localised physical embodiment into a broader (and more famous) virtual one, even when at times it proves to be uncomfortable, or one in which she at times feels over-exposed. Even as an emergent virtual subject, she has noted with confidence that when it becomes too much she simply de-activates that/those account/s, literate as she is in the rules of that world, and the terms of those publics in which she engages. This is quite a different picture than the vulnerable and at-risk young people that youth literature often portrays Samoan youth and young women of colour to be. Vineta continues her narration about the risky emotional landscape of online praise and attack:

Vineta: *Our video, our Harlem Shake video, there was so many mean comments about me. But the thing is it was—sure it was hard for me, but the thing I loved about it was, there was so many mean comments about me, but there were more comments defending me and I was like, 'Thank you so much'. Because people were calling me a whale and the big girl with the pink hair but I had more comments people saying, 'Oh my God, she's so hilarious'. So like I think that was a learning because it was the very first comment that really hurt me. But then when I started getting other comments I was like, 'Whatever'. Because I got over it . . .*

God Culture and the Capacity to In/Aspire   69

Anne: That sounds really painful.

Vineta: Not really. It's nothing I haven't heard to my face all my life. At least online you have people sticking up for you more.

Anne: Well I hear you. But that doesn't mean that it's not painful. Especially when there are so many attacks too, possibly more than in real life right?

Vineta: Maybe. But the main thing is about my responsibility to my family and the church. That's the other reason why I'm self-conscious about what I post.

Anne: Because of church people?

Vineta: Yeah, especially church people but family as well. Because you know, before I was all right because it was just me and my cousins and my sisters and you know just us. But now I have my uncles and my aunty on Facebook and they're like once you write something they are going to go, 'Oh, my gosh, she—', so that's why I block a lot of my uncle and aunties.

Anne: You don't want them to be hurt, or you don't want them to judge you?

Vineta: . . . I'm like a totally different person on Facebook, because I'm more open, and people like it.

Ana: And then when you have family they sort of take out of context and they spread it differently to what you—like, to what you're trying to say. Like that time on your birthday—

Vineta: I got home from school—I got home and it was on my birthday my 18th birthday and I'm home and my Mum was like, 'What did you write on Ana's page'? and I was like, 'What'? and she was like, 'You wrote something mean on Ana's page', and I went like, 'No I didn't'. And then I showed her and was like, 'See'?, and she was like, 'Oh', and I was like, 'Oh'. I think that's the main reasons why I'm not friends with most of my uncles and stuff because they take it out of context and I'm just like—

Ana: They don't know how we roll. [laughter]

Vineta: I think because like for Samoans, because you know Dwayne [Dwayne Johnson, also known as 'The Rock']? Like he's this famous Samoan, he's making it big for us Samoans, but like I think most people view Samoans as very—how do you say it—like, not so good people. Like they view us as like people who are scary and they don't—

Joy: Yeah tough!

Vineta: That we're like so tough, yeah they don't realise that we're not.

Ana: We're nice.

Joy: We're really nice.

Ana: There's people who are saying don't mess with Samoans because they're scary and then I was like, 'No we're not'. There's only one person (Dwayne) and that person ruins it for all of us Samoans. And then I was just like, 'Oh my God'!

70   Samoan Mediascapes and Faith-as-Performance

Vineta: Yeah like it doesn't help when a lot of our kids act like—you know, when they get in a lot of trouble and so of course—Hey, were we trouble for you in high school?

Anne: No!

Vineta: We were just really loud hey. [laughter]

Anne: Okay but going back, do you think that there's some kind of prejudice or bias about size there? And by that I mean bigness: tall, broad, big boned-ness, apart from weight issues, because is it something similar to say brown-skinned people like Sudanese who can barely walk down the street. They could be the nicest person in the world but the darkness of their skin scares a lot of white people. So do you think that there's something, that it's additionally just wouldn't matter what you do, but that people are scared of you because you're big or something like that?

Ana: Yeah but that's us. There is something.

A: Yeah we're all big people.

A: Oh yeah we're pretty big. Like people are scared of Maori people.

A: Yeah because they're like scary—! [long laughter]

Building upon the discussion of *Culture Shack* in the previous chapter, and the above commentary which spans family, bodies, popular culture, and social media, I will pause to unpack the part of Vineta and her peers' identity-formation work that is interwoven with their creative labour and its dissemination in hybrid online/offline worlds. To begin, however, I will return to a discussion of culture-specific learning in formal and informal educational contexts, an experience shared by both the Samoan and South Sudanese youth in this book.

Education in Recognisable Cultural Contexts

Gray and Beresford (2008) have noted that previous analyses of educational standardization has demonstrated that by increasing the cultural context of education for Australian Indigenous students, they are more likely to complete schooling. Like migrant and refugee-background students, Indigenous students also infrequently benefit from learning from Indigenous teachers or teachers from their own cultural backgrounds. Indigenous and other traditional knowledge systems often take different forms than that of western knowledge (Nash 2009), which impacts on education, enculturation, and capital. For migrant and refugee-background learners and young people, as well as for Indigenous and other youth growing up with other or more than only western knowledge, the impact of these different knowledge systems is profound, from a lack of culturally appropriate pedagogy and curriculum, to social structures in schools and society. Simpson warns that while some acknowledgement of these differences has been addressed by curricular adaptations, and has been largely welcomed, culturally minoritarian communities and community members are cautious:

> Eurocentric analysis is unfortunate because it fails to recognize how and why Traditional Indigenous Knowledge systems became threatened in the first place, it undermines the inherently Indigenous processes involved in transmitting TK, and it devalues the rigor Traditional Indigenous Knowledge systems employed for millennia to transfer knowledge to younger generations.
>
> (Simpson 2004, 374)

In the case of Indigenous knowledge and the evolution of Australian education, research into the links between Indigenous knowledge, language, and culture have been widely noted (Ma Rhea 2012; Nash 2009; Reynolds 2005). Gale (2011) stresses that in early Australian European settlement, missionary education included the Indigenous languages as a tool for Christian conversion, followed by schools' inclusion of a bilingual approach to language-learning. However, scholars continue to stress the importance of a focus on Indigenous languages (and we might extrapolate here to other non-English languages, such as Dinka, Arabic, and Samoan), "not just because of the social benefits to be gained by its students, but also because of the schools' recognition of each language's intrinsic cultural value and linguistic complexity and uniqueness" (Gale 2011, 284).

Reynolds (2005) describes how the 1993 Australian of the Year, Manday Yunupingu, hoped to improve ways of assimilating aspects of Indigenous culture into a western curriculum, by linking to his theory of 'Ganma'. This approach represents a merge of western and Indigenous cultures in a way that they "mutually engulf one other, washing away white hegemonic control" (35). The national Australian Curriculum does address Indigenous cultural relevance, yet the research literature indicates there is limited training of non-Indigenous teachers in how to apply cultural relevance in the classroom to students. Scholars continue to note how the western model of schooling based on a standardized approach to the English language, for example, negatively affects the engagement, success, and satisfaction of minoritarian students including Samoan, South Sudanese, Indigenous, and other students (Wigglesworth, Simpson, and Loakes, 2011; de Plevitz 2007; Reynolds 2005).

Such formal educational contexts and conditions impact these young people's approach to work and further education. When Vineta speaks about her negative experience interviewing for a job and the bias she encountered, which she interpreted was based on her weight, she describes this kind of rejection with a disturbing sense of equanimity. She and her peers have encountered the challenges of literally and figuratively fitting themselves to non-Samoan contexts for so long, learned in part through their formal education, that they have to some degree come to expect this kind of treatment.

72 *Samoan Mediascapes and Faith-as-Performance*

Creative and religious belonging and success, then, can provide not only personal satisfaction, but a kind of overcoming of themselves as minoritarian subjects who are less than desired by mainstream culture and markets.

Capacity to Aspire and Samoan Subjectivity

These young people demonstrate various forms of aspiration, or what Appadurai calls a 'capacity to aspire' through their religious, creative, and cultural labour. They hope to have an impact on the wider society in which they live, and to be recognised for their expert knowledge and skills. As noted by McRobbie (2011), young people in this increasingly commodified creative global culture, like the Samoans here, can be considered young creatives (even if unconventionally so) for whom creative labour provides them with a "motivation by the hope of making it in the star and celebrity system" (88), where "dreams merge with the new meritocracy . . . and the power of the visual media which further bury the social democratic vocabularies of workplace protection, job security" (88), and other forms of security. Even if Vineta and her peers do not use the language of the creative industries, or recognise the global direction of the dissemination of creative products and impulses, their narratives and artefacts continue to show the ways in which a globalising trend is infiltrating everywhere, including the culture-specific religious and creative work they do.

McRobbie references *The Green Paper*[1] (which I discuss in more depth in Section Two), which she says produces

> the categories of talent and creativity as disciplinary regimes, whose subjects are taught and told (apparently from birth onwards through primary, secondary and tertiary education) to inspect themselves, look deep inside themselves for capacities that will then serve them well in the future. If culture is thought of as a 'complex strategic situation', then the brilliant move in this new discursive formation is that it simultaneously appears to do away with older forms of reliance on labour markets, on the dull compulsion of labour, and on routine, mindless activities. . . . *The Green Paper* celebrates the importance of creativity and its encouragement in schools, nurseries, at home and in other cultural institutions. Children and young people will have to do more than routine tasks. They will now be expected to be creative. Even if they do not go on to earn a living in the cultural sector, thinking creatively is now at the heart of the new knowledge economy. . . . Thus there is social rupture as the political order conforms to economic global rationalities to tax the young with being its new subjects.
>
> (McRobbie 2011, 88)

Such new global rationalities do tax the young, sometimes in ways that are not yet apparent. For the Samoan youth, their church-based communities

God Culture and the Capacity to In/Aspire   73

offer some insulation but also some constraints in the demands of this new creative 'labour compulsion'.

Samoan youth culture, global in its performativity if not its outlook, represents a form of Appadurai's social imaginary and a counter-narrative, a creative landscape. Appadurai sees the imagination as a social practice, no longer just a fantasy, a simple escape, or an elite pasttime, but rather an important (indeed requisite) "organized field of social practices" (1996, 31). It is also

> a form of work (in the sense of both labour and culturally organized practice), and a form of negotiation between sites of agency (individuals) and globally defined fields of possibility. . . . The imagination is now central to all forms of agency, is itself a social fact, and is the key component of the new global order.
>
> (Appadurai 1996, 31)

This role of imagination (and, I would argue, creativity as its performative extension) as a social practice is a powerful reframing device for Vineta and her peers. If it is work, it is also a form of community, the kind of 'culturally organized practice' that provides both community in their worlds but also commodity for negotiation with larger publics.

Appadurai's (2004) capacity to aspire offers a way of reconsidering mobility and in some cases resistance (or at least transversal agency) for young people of colour and non-western cultural affiliations. It is, as has been suggested, a tool for conceptualising "a way out of constraining preferences or cultures of apathy" (Rao and Walton 2004, 24). In the labour of developing social agency, Appadurai's theoretic of a capacity to aspire can offer some minoritarian community members like Vineta and her peers a way of levelling the different modes of transcending class constraints, and the socially embedded views and beliefs that go along with them. When Vineta talks about the ways in which she (and her family members and peers) are perceived by 'strangers', she always does so in relation to those within her own community. This comparative approach, however, does not always reflect most positively on her own community members, as in her commentary about the weight issue or feedback more generally on her 'beauty': despite the many valuable forms of support she receives from her strong community and family context, she believes strangers more readily than her own family, as a more unbiased (and somehow therefore more reliable) assessment. But within this economy of capitals, Vineta and her peers do recognise that if their Samoan cultural identifications and subjectivities are in some ways a constraint to their aspirations, they are also a form of capital that has value to outsiders who want to know more about them. For example, in the next excerpt, the discussion centres around the interconnection between Samoan cultural knowledge and religious practices, not only as home culture but as a site of interconnection with non-Samoans:

74   Samoan Mediascapes and Faith-as-Performance

Anne: What do you think that they don't know about Samoans?

Vineta: A lot of church gossiping [laughing].

Anne: Do you think people know about your spirituality like people your age generally now would think of you guys as spiritual or is that something that's kind of private for you?

Vineta: Actually that is. That's true. A lot of people view us as religious people.

Ana: Yeah they do.

Anne: And is that comfortable for you? Is that what you want them to know, or do you want to keep that kind of a private thing?

Vineta: We want them to know about our culture I guess. Because we're like there's so much to the Samoan tradition that nobody really knows. There's a lot of people that I know that just get to Samoa because like it's pretty and stuff, and they are like probably three out of ten people that I know that go to Samoa to experience the culture.

Ana: But you know, it's funny. It's more so the tourists that want to go there and learn the culture more so than us. Like we don't even know much about Samoa any more, but we only go there to boast about what we have, and the things that we have in Australia! Like, 'I'm from Australia, I've got an iPad, I've got an iPhone', you know what I mean? And when we do go to Samoa, we're so busy talking about the things that we have, instead of really diving into where—

Vineta: Where we all came from.

Ana: That's so true.

What followed on this and other occasions when we gathered to film or talk or sing was a discussion of how cultural knowledge gets passed down, their close relationship with their nanna and other elders, and whether that kind of traditional knowledge is a form of capital that should remain somehow sacred within the family/church/culture, or whether it is appropriate or available for outsiders to consume. We spoke about Indigenous knowledge and the notion that in Australian Indigenous culture, some of the sacred stories are not appropriate for sharing with non-Indigenous others, and whether Samoan knowledge too was regarded in this way. Mostly, according to these young people, knowledge is a powerful capital within their communities/families that is only enhanced by sharing with outside others, a big reason why they and their parents and pastor of their church agreed to participate in a book project like this one. Ultimately, they want people to know about their culture, their faith, and their creativity, and they see in it not only a chance to do faith work, but also its links with aspiration and their own (differently expressed) capacity to aspire in these multiple ways.

The cultural capital of their traditional, creative, and religious knowledges offers them a tool for Appadurai's notion of 'terms of recognition' (from Charles Taylor 1992), which he defines as poor recognition of minoritarian

God Culture and the Capacity to In/Aspire   75

groups by dominant ones, and the site or constituents of that recognition (or lack thereof). Appadurai defines Taylor's notion as a "path-breaking concept [and a] key contribution to the debate on the ethical foundations of multiculturalism" which acknowledges "the idea of aspiration as a cultural capacity" (Appadurai 2004, 62). While such terms of recognition offer potent ways forward for aspirational young people like Vineta, Ana, and Joy, such terms don't come without ambivalence, which is often based in intergenerational sets or clashes of values.

Anne: *Okay is there any kind of anxiety that it's going to be lost? That it's only the old people who know all those stories, and grew up there, and that they are going, and it's going to be lost at some point. Is there anxiety about that or not really?*

Vineta: *Yes.*

Joy: *There is.*

Ana: *Big yes.*

Vineta: *Because none of these Samoans know anything! There's like this generation—they have no clue of what it's like, I mean we were sort of still learning as we were growing up, but like this generation, now they're lost. When you try and explain to them some cultural stories, they don't care. They don't want to speak Samoan, or they want to—*

Joy: *Yeah, they say, 'What happens in Samoa, stays in Samoa'!*

Ana: *Yeah.*

Vineta: *But you know, I'm honestly speaking for myself, like for me I know that when I grow up I'm not going to a Samoan church. That's what I've said.*

Anne: *Why?*

Vineta: *Because. Too many politics. It's too intense, you know? I have to live my life. A lot of people don't even go back to Samoa because it's too much money. But me, it's emotionally draining. You know what I mean? I feel that with my—for me as a person, like not my church or anything, but me as a person, I go to church and I'm stressing about performances and other stuff when I should be, when I'm going to church for God, you know? And I realise when I go to church it's because that's mostly what I know about our culture. When we have meetings, church meetings, it's all about money. A lot about money and roles and all of that stuff and it's not only in my church, it's every church. Actually my church is pretty good. But I know that from the church growing up it's all about money and things like that. I'm not dissing my culture or anything, because we have beautiful performances and I love the history behind our culture and everything. But for church, like it's not about the congregation it's more about like praise. I have this quote, 'You go to church to praise God, not to praise the*

76 *Samoan Mediascapes and Faith-as-Performance*

church'. Yeah, go to church for God not for the church. Like the congregation, do you know what I mean? We focus so much on our congregation and how peaceful we are, like as people of God, and you know it's true but too much energy goes on the operation of the church rather than the purpose of church.

Ana: *I got you. I got you, sis.*

Vineta: *Yeah and like I feel bad for saying that because my nanna taught me—because I listen to my nanna, like everything she tells me, I do listen to her. But with this thing, I said like I'm just going to go to church on Sunday, you know, find my spiritual connections with God and then go home and just leave it at that.*

Ana: *Well that's so true. That's like the biggest problem for Samoan community, like churches like that is—*

Vineta: *We're going to get—if you put this online we're going to get probably a lot of hate, hey.*

Ana: *But it's true.*

Vineta: *Everyone will be like 'Yeah', and then it will be, 'Did you see what she said about us'?! [laughing].*

Ana: *But that's why a lot of churches—a lot of people from Samoa are not connected to the Samoan side because they know that thing, they know that it's always about money.*

Anne: *But how can it not be about money when people are struggling?*

Vineta: *Because we go to a Balangi church, I don't want to say white, what's another word for white.*

Ana: *White. Gringo. Anglo. Honkies. [laughing]*

Vineta: *Yeah, white churches are so straightforward, you just go to church and like I feel it—*

Anne: *Maybe it just looks straightforward to you because you're an outsider in a way, right?*

Vineta: *True.*

Anne: *I mean, probably all churches have their politics right? Like all families do.*

Vineta: *Yeah but there's just so much things that go into building our church, but it's still the fixed purpose of going to church like we still have to pay rent, we still have to have all these Samoan customs that go into church, which is like it doesn't really go with what going to church IS, and it just ruins the purpose, I guess. For me. I think I'm just happy that the little kids don't understand what's happening yet because its—*

Joy: *It's too much.*

Vineta: *Yeah I think it's because the people they bring the culture into the church.*

Ana: *Into the church, yeah.*

Anne: *So no matter where people gather, God is there but also messiness is there?*

Ana: Yeah.
Vineta: They bring their stuff there—
Anne: Their stuff right, you can't not bring your stuff.
Vineta: And they call it culture.
Anne: That's human nature.
Vineta: They call it culture and then it's just them. [laughter]
Vineta: Like it's nice, but church is church and culture is culture.

Figure 2.2 Spoofing Samoans. Photo and copyright, Anne Harris.

Cultural Loyalty

In Appaduraian terms, Vineta is expressing a tension between her sense of cultural loyalty and her ability to give voice to her position of 'dissensus'. For Appadurai, "we have tended to see cultural affiliations almost entirely in terms of loyalty (total attachment) but have paid little attention to exit and voice. Voice is a critical matter for my purposes since it engages the question of dissensus" (2004, 63). For him (as for Vineta above), "loyalty is clearly no longer generally clearcut" (63). If these young people's capacity to aspire to more than their family's current circumstances in a multitude of ways—economically, interculturally, virtually—is to become what Appadurai would call a capability instead, the mediascape in which they are partially finding their autonomy is a major part of that expansion.

78   *Samoan Mediascapes and Faith-as-Performance*

But a second subtext of the commentary above is their recognition of the commodity value (in multiple ways) of their culture and cultural affiliation. As Vineta, Ana, and Joy commented upon, their cultural affiliation and knowledges have become commodities, both outside of their community but also inside of their church constellations. Appadurai (1986) has claimed that when goods become tools for exchange, they become commodities, and these objects (and the sticky practices and affiliations they are attached to) have a life, and this life has changing value depending on its cultural situatedness and its social function. For these Samoan youth, their cultural knowledge as well as their creative abilities have value, and they recognise that in some way their church participation is the object through which those practices are performed. While Vineta may be frustrated with the political enmeshment of their church community's focus on money, they (even as a group of young people) acknowledge that while they may wish a clean separation articulable as 'culture is culture and church is church', they recognise the interconnectedness of all these things. That is, church is where performing happens, which can be exhausting and stressful; church is tied to the cultural knowledge that nanna has passed on to them, and they do not want to disappoint her even though Vineta may wish at times to stop going to church; church is not only a cultural and performative community but has its own economy and economic/exchange needs which at times overshadow the faith practices that draw them all back. But, as Appadurai reminds us, "we do not need one more omnibus definition of culture any more than we need one of the market" (2004, 59), and this goes for religion too. Anthropology and economics have, of course, always been intertwined, and the Samoan church in Melbourne to which Vineta, Ana, and Newjoy and their families belong is just one example of this interconnectedness and at times messiness.

Appadurai's articulation of a capacity to aspire focuses on just one aspect of culture, "its orientation to the future—that is almost never discussed explicitly" (60). Culture, he claims, has almost always been theorised as a 'kind of pastness', and this is no longer (or was never) sufficient for understanding the dynamic life of cultural formations, and the commodifications which accompany them: "the keywords here are habit, custom, heritage, tradition. On the other hand, development is always seen in terms of the future—plans, hopes, goals, targets. This opposition is an artifact of our definitions and has been crippling" (60). Economics too, he claims, has "become the science of the future" (60). In other words, Appadurai makes plain the opposition between cultural actors, who are always seen as "a person of and from the past, and the economic actor, a person of the future. Thus, from the start, culture is opposed to development, as tradition is opposed to newness, and habit to calculation" (60). Sarah Ahmed has expanded this analysis in her commentary on 'melancholic migrants' (2010) and other false oppositions implied within Appadurai's analysis. If, for example,

> by not elaborating the implications of norms for futurity as a cultural capacity, these definitions tend to allow the sense of culture as pastness to dominate, [e]ven the most interesting recent attempts, notably

God Culture and the Capacity to In/Aspire   79

associated with the name of Pierre Bourdieu (1977), to bring practice, strategy, calculation, and a strong agonistic dimension to cultural action have been attacked for being too structuralist (that is, too formal and static) on the one hand, and too economistic on the other.

(Appadurai 2004, 61)

In Vineta, Ana, and Newjoy's discussion, readers can hear considerations of exactly that which Appadurai calls "the recovery of the future as a cultural capacity" (2004, 62) and a rejection of anthropological (and largely popular cultural) framing of culturally identified or traditionally active subjects as imbued with 'pastness', or somehow out of touch, out of date, or on the road to extinction. These Samoan young people are completely modern and their tasks in juggling hybrid lives are in many ways more representative of contemporary global subjects and coming-of-age challenges than many of their peers. That is why in this book I am suggesting that their 'young adult journey' can be considered real cosmopolitan and creative industrial labour, representative of the kinds of global flows that increasingly typify mainstream society, not—as they are so often still represented—as a kind of charming anachronism, a Margaret Mead leftover to be exoticised. Yet to be sure, they straddle many worlds, and not all these worlds have equal capital value in an accelerating world.

Conclusion

I have begun an engagement in this chapter with Appadurai's notion of the capacity to aspire that I will continue later, in Section Two, to expand this discussion as one aspect of a lens for looking at the South Sudanese youth and their creative cultural work. Appadurai's purpose in theorising his notion of capacity to aspire is firmly focused on the improvement of the material conditions of minoritarian communities, as is all his work, and for this reason he continues to be a useful interlocutor in my collaborative work with these young people. While I believe that in many ways the question of their developing 'voice' from the margins is partly aided by social and digital media and partly reproduces social inequities, overall I feel that their ability to leverage the capital they have is not incidental, not without agency, and for this reason I reject a deficit framing of them and their places in their countries of resettlement.

This is not to ignore the very real material challenges they face that far exceed most of their non-migrant and non-refugee-background peers. It does, however, recognise that their capital—including creative capital—has a place which is perhaps of increasing value in the commodified landscape of cultural and creative economies, and that their generation fuses religious, cultural, and creative subjectivities to great effect and satisfaction. Where that will lead remains to be seen, but I assert their agency as already evident in their works, lives, and self-documented and collaboratively-documented commentary about those lived experiences a multi-faceted cultural study but not a nostalgic, objectifying, or backward-looking one.

80 *Samoan Mediascapes and Faith-as-Performance*

In the next chapter, which is the last chapter in the 'Samoan' section of the book, I will integrate some of my own reflexive commentary from my role in this collaboration and my intercultural or border-crossing experiences as a migrant myself and as an insider-outsider in this community. While I am largely an outsider (that is, non-member) to the Samoan Wesleyan Methodist church community of these Samoan youth, they welcome me as an insider due to my long relationship with some of the families initially through school and now through community and personal connections. How does this connection with these members of the Melbourne Samoan community represent my own capacity to aspire, and how does it impact on my interwoven creative, spiritual, and cultural lives?

Therefore, I will bring together the Appaduraian notion of the mediascape with creativity theory in order to highlight the ways in which these youth simultaneously use their (semi)localised church and cultural community, as well as the digital mediascape, in order to develop a sophisticated and contemporary creativity that is personal yet commodified for outside others. By combining Appadurai's theoretic of a capacity to aspire, especially his notions of 'loyalty' and 'voice', and combining this with a deep examination of his well-known notion of the mediascape, I try to highlight some ways in which these youth are building new cultural imaginaries through an amalgam of online/offline worlds, namely online community and church-based arts practices. If this chapter has asked whether their aspirations (creative and cultural) represent 'pastness' or futurity, it hopefully has also directed readers' attention to the ways in which creativity can perform multiple social and educational functions, and offer a kind of voice that is both honouring of cultural loyalties while still suggesting new pathways for cultural integration. In the final 'Samoan' chapter, I ask what ways these practices might weave creative cultural mastery into creative capabilities through the lens of Appadurai's mediascapes and joint personal narrative.

Note

1 A Green Paper in the UK is a government report that is the initial stage toward changing legislation. Here McRobbie is discussing the Green Paper *Culture and Creativity: The next 10 years* (DCMS, London 2001).

3 Semblance and Praisesong

Figure 3.1 White Sunday, 2014. Photographer: Alta Truden; copyright Anne Harris.

God-Botherers and Hangers-On

Sunday, October 6th 2013
  Today I went to the Samoan church for the first time.
  I took notes and tried to record everything about the service. It was meant to be 'White Sunday', which they assure me is about white as cleansing the soul, not white as in White people come to gawk. So I showed up at the little church in St. Albans (not far from where I used to work) at 10am, and noticed there were no Samoan people around. I checked my phone again and realised that I had made a mistake and it was scheduled

82   *Samoan Mediascapes and Faith-as-Performance*

for 11am rather than 10am. So, dismayed, I drove onto the 'strip' where people were in St. Albans proper, parked, and started walking up and down looking for coffee. I looked like a real wanker—lost white person, that kind of thing. No seriously. I was walking around white as snow, wearing Ray Bans, with a trendy Crumpler bag on my back, out of my Peugeot, asking for a latte.

"You got a latte?"

"Vietnamese coffee."

"No, I'm looking for a latte. Do you do lattes?"

"Vietnamese coffee."

"No latte?"

"Vietnamese coffee."

I would leave, and every time as I was walking out the door I heard laughter behind me. Well, yeah.

I'd laugh at me too.

So finally I spotted the Golden Arches. Don't think about it, I told myself. I went in and got my latte, sat down and pulled out my MacBook Air and did some work to pass the time. Like wankers do.

11am came and I went back to the church, feeling a bit less desperate.

They were all there—the Samoan men out in front, smoking, in their sarongs and flower design cotton shirts. I went in, deciding to leave the camera, tripod, etc. in the car (thank God).

Newjoy was in the entryway to the church, dear old Joy who is really growing up I thought to myself, who I had met when she was such a little girl when she came into Year Seven at Marian College and who was a participant in Culture Shack in 2010 and 2011.

"HI!" I practically screamed.

She looked at me dubiously, walked back into the church. I thought I'd got the girl wrong, maybe it wasn't Joy after all. I tried to mill around with the men, but they looked even more dubious. One of Joy's family members I'd met before smiled and said hello but then looked away. Was it her father? I couldn't recall. What was his name? Some time passed, and I stuck my head into the church proper. It was tiny—kind of like the size of a living room.

I saw Joy lean over a young woman in a wide brimmed hat—in fact, all the females were in wide-brimmed hats.

"Anne's out front", Joy said to Vineta.

Vineta got up and walked toward me, laughing nervously.

When she got near me we hugged but she was laughing uncontrollably, kind of alarmingly.

"Should I go?" I asked in her ear when we hugged. "Have I embarrassed you by coming?"

"No!", she said, but kept laughing and looking scared and embarrassed. "No, but it's not actually White Sunday—that's next week!"

Semblance and Praisesong   83

That was fine with me, I was just glad to know someone who would talk to me. She brought me in, sat me down in the back row next to a lady who had come from New Zealand only about a year earlier.

"My husband is Methodist (like this church) but I'm Catholic", she said very seriously.

"Ah", I tried to nod, knowingly. Dead silence. "Well, you know what they say, opposites attract".

I laughed nervously now.

She didn't.

"Methodists and Catholics aren't opposites", she said.

"No, that's true", I said and looked at the ceiling.

What bodily and emotional impressions do I have from that first visit, what affective intensities have stayed with me? I am going back tomorrow for this year's 'White Sunday' (hopefully) and so I want to get my first impressions down before they are changed by new impressions tomorrow. But to be honest, the main thing I worry about is what I worried about with the Sudanese community too—that I'm gay.

I seriously worry about this.

I wear a wedding ring on my wedding finger, since my partner and I got married in New York last year. This is usually fine, but I'm automatically dreading The Question tomorrow.

This is heteronormativity. When you meet new people, especially interculturally, you just steel yourself and wait for it. You feel your difference like a bright glaring interrogation lightbulb, and you wait for The Question, and you wonder if you're actually going to deny yourself, your true self, yet again.

You swear you won't, but you do. It's always a quandary, after all these years. It never gets easier, and the worst of it comes in religious environments.

*

So last Sunday I sat there and participated as best I could in the service. It was over two hours even though it wasn't a special service like White Sunday. I was the only female over ten years old without a hat. I also was the only female not wearing white, and pretty much the only female not wearing a dress. One of the men gave me his song book, which I tried to follow along although everything written and spoken was in Samoan. I tried my best to sing and chant along phonetically, and it was mostly enjoyable. It was good to be out of my comfort zone again—made me remember all the gifts and pleasures of intercultural stretching, including those times of traveling, teaching in multicultural schools, and celebrating the benefit of being reminded of humility—it is important.

I held a song book (black) and the red prayer book, which was totally incomprehensible, both in Samoan. For the first three quarters of the service

84   Samoan Mediascapes and Faith-as-Performance

I just sang along with vowel sounds. It was nice. But by the end of the service I could follow the song book phonetically and enjoyed the singing.

The church we were in was a Methodist church that their community rents from a larger Methodist community. The Samoans all drive up from Hoppers Crossing, nearly an hour away, but rent this one far from home because—according to Vineta—it was the cheapest, although I have my doubts about this reason. The church has a painted message at the front of the room, in German, which translates roughly to something like 'love God'. A simple altar, about thirty attendees sitting in pews.

The choir sits together on the front right side. The men sit behind them. The children and general women seem to sit on the left.

The hierarchies are: men run the service. Intermittently a woman will join in, but only to administer communion. All share the caretaking of the fussy children.

Age ruled: oldies go to communion first, followed down by age.

I was strongly encouraged to go. At first I declined, as I didn't have a head covering and I thought that would be disrespectful, but my friend Tessa said it didn't matter and she'd go up with me which basically meant 'move your ass' so I went. In this church you had to pick up the communion wafer and put it in your mouth; the priest didn't administer it directly, like in the Catholic church that I'm more accustomed to. Then the lady came past with a tray of small cups with fruit juice or sugar water to simulate wine. This all while we were kneeling at the altar. It reminded me of hot summer masses in Evansville, Indiana when I was a child so small that kneeling at the altar railing I couldn't see over it, and I closed my eyes and tilted my head back and waited for my uncle, Father Sylvester, who would come along the rail and pass out the wafers with his repetitive refrain: 'Body of Christ, Body of Christ, Body of Christ' . . . and my other uncle Father Richard who was home on leave from the church in Kenya would follow him with the chalise and give wine (the blood of Jesus) to the grownups and I remember the smell of their cassocks and the look of the stitching on the white linen and the light falling across the altar while my cousins played folk mass guitars and sang.

I snap back to the present. The entire service is in Samoan. There were only two sentences in English. I can't remember the second one—something about prayer or God—but the first one was "On behalf of the pastor, the community and all of us, we welcome Professor Anna Harris to the church and thank you for joining us today". Very embarrassing.

Then after the service, the pastor, his wife, and then pretty much everyone else, shook my hand and some of the women kissed me.

Vineta assured me it wasn't a humiliation (which it still seemed like it was) to have me there as her guest, and that I should keep the following Sunday full day free, as her mother had told her that I WILL come back for lunch after White Sunday the next week.

Semblance and Praisesong 85

"But I don't have a big white hat", I said to her.

"It doesn't matter. I'll get you one", she said. Then, like Vineta, she made some joke about it and we laughed, and I left. Everyone staring at me, me waving frantically like most white people do when we are nervous.

Driving home from that first mass, I recalled vividly another intercultural Christian encounter since my emigration to Australia: not long after I arrived from New York, in the late 1990s, I drove the hour or so out of the Central Australian town of Alice Springs to a place called Hermannsburg, which started its European incarnation as a Lutheran mission but became famous in part due to its most illustrious son, the incomparable Indigenous painter Albert Namatjira (1902–1959). On this trip I was driving out the Western MacDonnell ranges to attend an Arrente mass at the old Hermannsburg Mission, which was—similarly—settled by more German missionaries.

I loved being there, and seeing all those beautiful older Arrente women gather to sing, but as soon as they started in on the first hymn, I realised they were all Christian missionary hymns and I felt sick to my stomach. It felt like a living breathing not-postcolonial moment. Similarly, last Sunday at the Samoan service, I felt really weird to be singing along in a Samoan language I didn't understand, to "This little light of mine" and "Glory be to God on High". I looked around from the back of this church, and all these women were very big, very heavy women. And they were singing these mission songs. And they were dressed in what appeared to me as archaic, almost Victorian, dresses. And I remembered the way some of the Sudanese women dress when they go to church, and it reminded me of the old-fashioned feeling, and I wondered how much this had to do with colonialism and missionaries and yet I didn't want to relegate their own adaptation of their own experience of these Christian songs to some kind of event in which they were not in charge and not all-powerful and weren't making active contemporary and thoughtful choices. Of course they were. Another moment of alienation, like the school dancing moment, when this great gulf of difference opened up between us and I read some of their performance of selves as an outsider and am shocked.

It's not like I refuse to sing English songs because they were the colonisers of the United States, or refuse to eat borscht or bratwurst because Russians and Germans slaughtered my Polish ancestors. But nevertheless, it felt kind of shocking. And I really do respect these women and their white frilly dresses and their wide brimmed hats (as though they were still in Samoa) and so many of them were barefooted or wearing thongs on their feet, and some women were wearing those flowers (both real and ceramic) in their hair, and it just felt really weird on a cold winter's day in Melbourne. It all felt so misplaced. Displaced. And then it just felt like I was working so hard to let go of my internal voice: both my objectifying exoticising observational voice, and also my critical postcolonial voice. And then my completely

86 Samoan Mediascapes and Faith-as-Performance

self-conscious (white and queer) voice that said that actually everyone was looking at me and thinking how funny I look, because I don't have a big hat or a white dress or a companion. And just when I thought I couldn't get any more meta or in my head about this amazing in-the-moment experience, the predictable happened:

The choir started singing, and it was absolutely beautiful. Breathtaking. And the men had roles and the women had different (vocal) roles, and it was beautiful. And there were a lot of young people there—way more than when you go to typical Catholic masses in Catholic churches these days. And it was moving. And I saw that there was something there for these young people. And Ana was playing the organ and she looked so beautiful and the music was awesome and I remembered all that Vineta and Ana shared with me about how hard they work on and for this youth group, this choir I was hearing so casually, and it moved me. And I felt 'there is no easy way to understand what is happening here. This is a performance of many things, many relationships, many beliefs, and many temporal and geographic realities, all at once, and I would be very foolish to dismiss or try to easily categorise it'.

That's what I remember.

And I was relieved to leave, as an outsider, and as a gay woman, because I could relax. And while I was so busy surveilling them in their otherness, I felt stressed out at being surveilled BY them, in my otherness, as I was of course surveilling myself. And so I was happy, and I was exhausted, and somewhere in there I did have the great privilege of attending their church service and being warmly welcomed by these generous and faithful people.

That's what I remember.

And now I will return, tomorrow morning. And hopefully I will find something white to wear.

Queer Times and Places

One example of Vineta's ability to walk the insider/outsider line in her multiple lifeworlds is the ways in which she has taken a lot of heat from family and community members when she defends the gay people in her life. She has never said whether she has had occasion to defend me, but she has described how she defends her cousin Sam after Sam was excommunicated for being gay. Sam used to be the leader of the Youth Group. Then one night Vineta's parents and the pastor and other church leaders met in her living room and decided that Sam has to be out. They told him and he accepted it. I was outraged, but Vineta and Sam too by her account saw it as just the way things are. It's not nice, but it's how things are. Sam is still very much a member of their family and extended community but no longer attends church. I asked how he must feel about

Semblance and Praisesong 87

this after being so integral to the youth and the community at large, for so long. He is, by all accounts, also a breathtaking performer and singer. Vineta reported that she had no idea how it made him feel, and it's not something they talk about, it just being the way it is and that is accepted by all, including Sam.

However, a few months later, the following exchange happened on Facebook. I have included a short excerpt of exchanges that Vineta had with others in June 2015 when the U.S. Supreme Court ruled in favour of the right to same-sex marriage, and so many Facebook users chose to use the 'rainbow wash' on their profile pictures in a show of support, including Vineta. Her post in part reads:

> As the devoted Christian my grandparents raised me to be, I felt pressured these past few days to change my profile picture because of videos and memes by fellow believers questioning my faith because of what I believe and support. I believe in Jesus. Jesus is love. So yes, I believe in love. Please don't tell me otherwise. My profile picture will remain as it is until I take another killer selfie that is 'profile picture worthy'. #lovewillalwayswin #becauseJesusislove #andJesusalwayswins

The post had seventy-one likes and more than thirty comments when I screen-shot it (after about two hours up), but many more followed. Her sister Newjoy wrote, "And this is why you are my inspiration and role model in life, always teaching me to smile and be kind to everyone even when my *gukus are faauu* lol!! Love you forever and ever—☺". Vineta's commentary that followed included this:

> Oh wow, I didn't expect these responses! Thank you for the different perspectives! I love and appreciate them all! I'm not going to rebut anyone because you have every right to your opinions and your beliefs!!!! That's the beauty of God's gift of freedom. And so yes, you have your beliefs, and I believe IN you. All I ask is that you respect mine whether you like it or not. DON'T tell me I'm not Christian for believing what I believe. That's basically all I was trying to say on this post. But this was very entertaining. PS: I'm still not going to change my profile picture, and I won't justify myself and my faith by explaining why, because I know myself and I know my beliefs. In high school, for Year 12 English, my best friend and I chose to do our oral speech on Gay Marriage: I was for, and she was against. We both had strong arguments and ended up getting full marks. And 4 years later, she's still my best friend. Moral of this totally unrelated story ☻ I hope we can all still be friends despite our very different beliefs and after this very heated debate. After all, we are Christian!

Performing God: Creative Youth/Faith Culture

Appadurai (1996) articulates a social imaginary that is generated by a collective imagination process, a tool for creating and accessing publics in which diasporic citizens can come together in new kinds of communities. Vineta and her peers are creating what I consider a new social imaginary that is Christian and creative in new ways from their parents' and grandparents' generations, but also distinct from other Christian youth cultures and other creative youth cultures. These and other Samoan young people who develop their creative skills through church- and culture-based creative communities are indeed the kind of cosmopolitan citizens about whom Appadurai is talking, who are finding ways to move beyond the limiting material (and at times doctrinaire) conditions of their primarily localised experiences. Through social media (Appadurai's mediascapes) and other online technologies, these Samoan youth are comfortable in cosmopolitan conversations with their Samoan and non-Samoan, youth- and non-youth counterparts in both local and far-flung publics, counteracting relentless discourses of marginalisation, disenfranchisement, voicelessness, and vulnerability. They are living different truths from these narratives about them.

Massumi (2011) and Appadurai (2004, 1996) both invite counter-narratives to the simplistic yet prevailing hegemonic stories of culture, religion, and identity regarding Pasifika Others, in which notions of embodiment no longer must represent 'pastness' and tradition in opposition to virtuality, futurity, and cosmopolitanism. Vineta and her peers are demonstrating some ways in which Pasifika youth—in particular Samoan youth who express themselves creatively and culturally through church communities—move beyond 'diversity' into 'semblance' (Massumi 2011) and possibility.

While Yip notes that the preponderance of scholarly literature on religion and youth studies remains focused on Christianity, there is also a growing body of work focusing on Islamophobia and the Muslim experiences of young people (see Noble 2016, for example). Yet there is very little from the youth perspective itself which highlights the positive motivations and effects of youth participation in church and faith-based scenes, communities, and activities. The Samoan youth featured here have done so, while also narrating some ways in which they combine local participation with global/digital community networking. Importantly, these online networks are not in opposition to the localised worlds in which they participate, as digital media scholarship and popular media so often seek to portray, but for Vineta and her youth peers, these two 'publics' are compatible and indeed seem to be interdependent. Justin O'Connor's scholarship on making new imaginaries is pertinent here, albeit that O'Connor's mediascape pivots on an unrealised notion of creative industries and its problematic relationship with the 'cultural industries dream'. Here I'm suggesting that these Samoan youth are creating just the kind of new imaginary we need, through the interrelationship between their mediascape/s and their ethnoscape, pointing to the kind of cultural/creative industries that O'Connor laments we may have already abandoned. These youth suggest that it may still be on its way, but perhaps found in other areas than the ones in which creative economists are looking. As Appadurai has explained his scapes to be fluid and mutable according to cultural shifts, I am suggesting that they have a kind of fluidity too, based in the creative shifts occurring within this Samoan youth culture.

The disjunction of Appadurai's global flows includes technoscapes as well as mediascapes. The ethnoscape of evolving and fluid cultures intersects with, and of course alters, both the mediascape and technoscape of those like Vineta and her peers. As impactors on global mobilities and exchanges, Appadurai's five scapes all work together and separately. For example, technoscape and ethnoscape certainly work together and cross-infiltrate on the mobilities of Samoan youth such as Vineta. If her Samoan cultural flows can be considered an example of Appadurai's ethnoscape, it is happening partly with and partly due to technology, which is inexorably tied to capitalism and the economy. Her ethnoscape has been moved, altered, and continues to flow in relation and response to financial flows. But mediascapes too cannot be considered significantly separately from technoscapes. If the Samoan youth group members use social media to circulate their ideas and creative performances, this technoscape is never totally removed from the mediascapes in which they live and to which they are responding. The 'mash-up' songs they regularly record, as they narrated, are a mixture of a kind of ethnoscape and mediascape that is generated within that field, and then become circulable due to the fluid technoscapes in which they live and thrive as contemporary youth. In fact, Vineta's narrative about her birthday conversation with her mother highlights the difference between the generations, where her generation feels very comfortable within the technoscape of social media, and her mother (as she describes her) does not 'get it'.

Following Nayar and Bhide (2008), I agree that a major challenge of—in this case—understanding the simultaneous labour of Vineta and her peers as individual but collective, local but global, and creative but tradition-bound can be described as unpacking "the seemingly contradictory but connected trends of globalization and localization and to unravel the disjunctures and differences in the global cultural economy" (329). These multiple labours lead Vineta and her peers toward Appadurai's notion of the social imagination, and toward an impact on the way localised and globalised labour is perceived and valued, especially imaginative or creative labour. Ito too claims a return here to

> creativity and the imagination. A notion of participation leads to a conceptualization of the imagination as collectively rather than individually experienced and produced. . . . I treat the imagination as a 'collective social fact', built on the spread of certain media technologies

90 *Samoan Mediascapes and Faith-as-Performance*

> at particular historical junctures [in which] . . . imagination is not an individualized cognitive property, but rather is the shared store of cultural referents, common cultural source material that exceeds individual experience. This collective imagination requires not only ongoing interpretation, performance and expression, but also media technologies for representing and circulating products of the imagination.
>
> (Ito 2008, 401)

This collective imagination (based in shared faith and cultural practices) becomes a collective creativity through these youth, and while Appadurai does not conceive of it as holding (or necessarily moving toward) a commodified form, in the acceleration of contemporary global flows I believe it does, and that this is an important and distinguishing feature of what the Samoan youth are doing (whether consciously or unconsciously). I'm not suggesting that every creative endeavour (whether individual or collective) must now be profitable (as some have misinterpreted from my previous work), but I am suggesting that there is a tenor to the 'scapes' or global flows—including creative ones—that now place them in a kind of market competition against one another, and against which so much creative labour is judged. This is not to say that I believe these two are mutually exclusive, regardless of the cultural context; I'm simply noting what I observe as an acceleration of this way of evaluating creative endeavour. As Abra and Abra (1999) have noted:

> It is well to remember what transpires when societies purportedly succeed in minimizing competition. Margaret Mead compared the cultures of Samoa, which stressed cooperation and togetherness, and Bali, wherein ruthless competition and antagonism reigned. Not surprisingly, mental health and happiness were more prevalent in the first case, but indicatively, Bali was far more productive in a creative sense, suggesting that competition, and the insecurities and unhappiness that oftentimes result, may be the price that must be paid.
>
> (292)

Such a binary is indeed a fairly laboured one to my mind, and the evidence here suggests that creativity and productivity do not pivot on competition—although I note that this is a core characteristic of the creative industries discourse.

But it's not only creative industries that revert to capitalist and eurocentric interpretations of these kinds of nuanced lived experiences and scapes. For example, in the same issue of the *Encyclopedia of Creativity*, as late as 1999, Raina uses standard traditional anthropological objectifications like 'primitive' to describe Samoan and other non-western cultures, especially in relation to culturally specific expressions of creativity:

Different cultures tend to foster their own distinctive intellectual styles, which, in turn, presumably influence the form that creative expression will take. Drawing on anthropological materials from different primitive cultures, Mead studied relationships between the forms provided by a culture and the creativity of the individuals within the culture, on which statements of regularities may be based. Studies of styles of thinking and learning, examined in two cultural contexts, have suggested a reexamination of Western reverence for logic and intellect over intuition and creativity.

(Raina 1999, 457)

While Raina is drawing on that old binary of science/art (or logic/intuition), readers will also note the cultural reductivism of researching cultural artefacts, or what Benjamin called the totemic value of certain artworks, neither of which is the goal, approach, nor the scholarly outlook of this text. Rather, I extend Appadurai's scapes as they offer ways of seeing the global movements of these different but interrelated practices of labour and thinking while acknowledging the cultural spheres in which they occur, but in the next section I'm going to look for a moment at the particularities of cross-cultural creativity, the ways in which these Samoan youth have demonstrated their unique approach, and what it might mean for others interested in creative global flows.

Cross-Cultural Creativity

Some of those who have approached creativity psychometrically, though within the framework of person-environment interactions, have used various instruments to measure creativity in different cultural settings, with of course widely diverse objectives. I have written about some of these in other publications, most notably *Creativity and Education* (2015) and some journal articles on creativity in education. A range of differences within these test tasks and the supposed universality of the stimuli within these creativity tests (for example the Torrance tests) highlight the ways in which they might *not* be readily adaptable to different cultures and subcultures, and remain euro-centric. Raina closely examines the ways in which such globally acknowledged tests claim to "bring out cultural differences, and a test task that would not elicit cultural differences would not be very useful in comparative studies" (Raina 1999, 457). Indeed, Torrance tests are widely used in cross-cultural studies of creativity, but questions remain. "To some it is difficult to determine whether creativity as embodied in the Torrance tests is congruent with the actual definitions of creativity in the cultures studied", says Raina, and indeed the 'actual definitions' of creativity in any cultures, I would argue, are very hard to come by. One of the primary difficulties of creativity studies today is the inconsistency with which creativity is defined

92 *Samoan Mediascapes and Faith-as-Performance*

even within western cultural contexts, and harder still is its measurement and implementation. For Raina, "Some hold the view that in applying a complete Western perspective to assess creativity in a traditional or indigenous context, there is a serious problem in seeing this context as an impediment to creativity" (1999, 457), and yet we have seen how some scholarship persists in representing traditional contexts and practices as impediments to futurity overall (Ahmed 2010). Indeed, the Samoan youth have commented on the way they are regularly framed as 'backward' if their commitment to tradition takes more traditional performative enactments as described in this book. Yet their spiritual approaches to everyday life as well as their creative ones continue to thoroughly merge contemporary and traditional life in new ways. Here the youth merge church and popular songs, using multiple digital media platforms to share that work:

Ana:	*We are just going to quickly sing.*
Anne:	*One of your church songs?*
Ana:	*Yeah, it's only like five seconds. Okay so this is a song that no matter where we go, every Samoan child knows this song. If you know the song join along [laughing]. [Singing] Five, six, seven, go. [Singing]. . .*
Anne:	*Beautiful! I love it, thank you.*
Vineta:	*What else should we do?*
Anne:	*Do Valerie. Do some of Valerie, do you remember that?*
Ana:	*What the Samoan version?*
Anne:	*Yeah whatever you did yeah.*
Joy:	*I forgot the lyrics.*
Vineta:	*You sing the riff part [singing] and then Valerie is like [singing] [laughing].*
Ana:	*I don't know the lyrics, that's enough. . . .*
Vineta:	*I think I have a video of it. Can we give you footage? (to Ana) Can you bring that old one that we were watching at your house the other day?*
Anne:	*Sure.*
Ana:	*Oh, my gosh, that's the best. I want you to share that one.*
Vineta:	*I will bring it. I will send it to you and then, yeah.*
Anne:	*We can Dropbox or something maybe.*
Vineta:	*Yeah my Dropbox. That's how we used to do it.*
Anne:	*Is that how we did it before?*
Joy:	*Yeah.*
Ana:	*Yeah cool I will put it in Dropbox.*
Vineta:	*Cuz that's how we roll. [all laugh]*

"Mead, in her discussion of innovation in traditional cultures, found that Samoan people were only allowed to change the details of their dance, not the basic form of it. In other words, the culture allows them to add details,

Semblance and Praisesong   93

not to invent" (Raina 1999, 456). When I asked Vineta about this claim, she laughed. "Of course we are allowed to invent, invention is my middle name!", she shouted. Is invention the same as creativity, and do Vineta and I mean the same thing when we talk about innovation? Innovation, like contemporary creativity, is a fluid notion that flows in both global and localised ways.

Mead (1959) believed that immersive anthropology could result in artefacts—be they studies, objects, scholarly writings, or audio recordings—that reflected a whole culture. Some anthropologists—particularly visual or video anthropologists—work quite differently today, and many non-western collaborators or participants might imagine that as a very good thing. When I asked Vineta and her peers about whether they knew who Margaret Mead was, they replied in the negative. When I described who she was and what she had done, perhaps ahead of her time but very much objectifying by today's standards of research and intercultural politics, they responded that she seemed 'like a cool lady'. Vineta and her fellow youth group members are always trying to find the good in every person, and despite her acerbic humour, her outlook is very hopeful, always seeing the presence of God in each person. When I pushed harder that Margaret Mead has been criticised by some as not only conducting rather shonky cultural research at times, but also doing active harm to Samoan people, these Samoan youth found it an outrageous suggestion that a stranger could harm them in representational terms. They wondered aloud what those Samoans thought of this strange woman, and how they represented Mead to their own community. "Everyone is judgmental", Vineta told me. "That's why our faith is so awesome, because it helps us bridge difference". Whether Vineta's claim is true for all is a matter of debate, but the power of (Mead's) representation of Samoa and Samoans is undeniable. Intercultural crossings are challenging, to be sure, but all border-crossers are not the same.

My own experience as a high school teacher involved in 'cultural diversity' initiatives and activism at both schools in which I taught (in Melbourne and in the Central Australian desert town of Alice Springs) over eleven years was that some students enjoy 'multicultural day' activities peppered throughout the year that seek to celebrate cultural difference, and some do not. At my school in Melbourne where I met the core members of both the South Sudanese and Samoan groups whose perspectives populate this book, I was told one year with extreme anger by one of the South Sudanese young women to 'take down' the murals about welcoming refugees, about the (admittedly tokenistic) strengths of multiculturalism at our school, and to do away with the Cultural Diversity Days each year for which we all toiled so hard (see more in Harris 2013). The South Sudanese students found them all patronising and alienating, despite a raft of research literature which celebrates the effectiveness of such strategies, including Anita Harris here, that "such activities have been recently re-animated . . . [and] were the kind of intercultural initiatives mentioned most often by young people. For example, James (Samoan background) reflected the views of many in referring

94   *Samoan Mediascapes and Faith-as-Performance*

to multicultural festivals as places where young people often mix" (Harris 2013, 62). Certainly it can be hard for researchers and teachers to understand what might be the best approach to thinking together about cultural diversity, especially in contexts where racism and inequality flourish (like schools). While collaborative creative projects can be a powerful meeting place for border-crossing, it can also be a re-objectifying site of alienation.

As Anita Harris points out, mixing it up in 'multi'-cultural events and school days can be more hegemonising than anything: "when people of different backgrounds are encouraged to come together it is often by performing cultural difference to each other. In the process, difference becomes reified and culture is stripped of its complexity as it is transformed into an object for consumption" (64). Such days, in the words of the youth, are 'fun', but don't necessarily demand that people "develop a deep understanding of culture beyond the consumable clichés . . . [and] multicultural festivals and other events do not place any obligation on white people or white culture to be an equal part of the diversity" (64). Once again, the border-crossing requires (more) labour from the non-white participants, and cultural representations devolve into stereotypes or snapshots. Within Australia, this demand may be higher than in some other western countries, with particular forms of moral panic concerning African and Pacific Islander youth. Anita Harris (2013) has claimed that

> Since the 2000s, anxieties about dangerous and anti-social 'Pacific Islander' and Sudanese youth have risen. Once again, minoritised young people are imagined as those who disrupt public order and fail to integrate into civilised and peaceable mainstream community values. . . . While front-line youth and community workers as well as youth researchers question the ethnic youth gang framework . . . this image has taken hold in the public imagination.
>
> (Anita Harris 2013, 68)

Indeed, even Vineta, Newjoy, and Ana mention in the last chapter the ways in which some Samoan young people (and also the very few visible Samoan celebrities) may be read as unsafe, dangerous, or embarrassing. These kinds of fears about negative associations are one example of the ways in which the contemporary mediascape influences the Samoan youth group's ethnoscape and intercultural self-perceptions, or what Appadurai would call part of their emergent social imaginary. "In Australia", Harris goes on, "media and political leaders routinely raise the spectre of the 'ethnic youth gang' in the context of youth integration into the mainstream", with " . . . Pacific Islander youth just some of those identified as problems (Collins et al 2000; White et al 1999). Most recently, it is Sudanese young people who have been scrutinised for a supposed failure to integrate" (Anita Harris 2013, 24).

While this focus is on youth as indicative of failure to integratealso attends to their creativity: not only do these youth (especially males) perform their masculinity by appearing in groups publically, they also seem to celebrate their cultural, ethnic, and racial differences in ways that are frequently read by mainstream Australia as failed White Westernness." Of course the language used to talk about integration—even in some 'sympathetic' youth studies literature—retains a clear subtextual implication that assimilation is only masquerading as integration, and the real goal is hegemony.

If, as Appadurai argues, culture is a dialogue between aspirations and sedimented traditions, then the kinds of culturally inflected creativity such as the Samoan youth group and their South Sudanese counterparts are central to poverty reduction and Appadurai's future-focused cultural capacity. Those who work in community arts recognise that these sites of creative cultural production are crucial for transecting class divisions and social exclusion, but that is still not enough in these conservative times, in which such programs that nurture these activities and pathways are being cut. If government strategists and policy makers could recognise this work as not only good for migrant, refugee-background, and culturally diverse youth, for example, but good for business (e.g., creative and cultural industries) and national economies, perhaps support would be different. As it stands, the kinds of programs that nurture this work remain in-community, such as church groups like Vineta's, or youth or community programs that too often continue to frame such youth as at-risk.

These youth do not see themselves as at-risk. They have clear ideas about how they contribute and how they would like to increase this contribution to Australian society, and the continual focus on their failure to do so ignores their powerful and agentic self-perceptions. Their faith communities provide a crucial 'critical mass' of like-minded others who support their visions of a successful future. In May 2015, Vineta and I talked again about the importance of voice, story, and faith in their youth community. Sharing a commitment to the need for and ability of these youth to speak for themselves, Vineta highlights the ways in which, for them, creativity and faith go hand-in-hand:

Creativity, Ethnoscapes, and the Word

Anne: *What is important about you and your youth peer creatives being able to tell your own story, or tell it in dialogue with others like me?*

Vineta: *It's not so much our story, but moreso God's story. That in itself is extremely important to us because we are spreading His word—a purpose that we as a youth pursue. There are many youth groups alike, with the same vision, same purpose, same mission. But what differentiates us all is the way we work our mission. Some have youth pastors that preach the word of God, using their creativity to motivate the young believers in ways that can relate to them. Others, including our youth, use culture, music, and performances.*

96 *Samoan Mediascapes and Faith-as-Performance*

> *Youth Rallies is where it all combines, and youths learn from each other. Being given this opportunity to tell it to you and other writers and researchers is a blessing that we embrace with utmost importance because not only are we telling and showing it to you, but also to all your audiences and readers, which spreads our work for God and our cultural identity well and beyond the walls of our church community. We want to spread our work as far as possible.*

Anne: *What don't the rest of the world understand about creative Samoan youth in your church?*

Vineta: *Our youth try to work our mission in creative ways that can relate to everyone because we reach out to all children of God—our brothers and sisters. Regardless, our Samoan culture, being our prime motivator in deliverance, is sometimes misunderstood by non-Samoans. E.g., Samoan church services and especially youth services take forever, and although we are used to it, it is understandable for someone new witnessing our services to get bored. Also, humour is our strongest form of deliverance in performances, and we love to use our typical Samoan lifestyle to deliver the bible skits—as it appeals to our elders' type of humour. That can sometimes be hard for non-Samoans to understand—nor find funny—because they don't live the Samoan life. But nevertheless, it is through these performances that we show our cultural identity whilst delivering God's message, and this is why we are so passionate about what we do! It's our life!*

Anne: *What aspect of your faith does your creativity let you express? What can you express through your art/singing/performing that you can't express any other way, even through prayer?*

Vineta: *In our youth, individuals express their faith differently. We are all different and passionate about different things. Some people love singing, and represent the youth by leading songs with solos, others dance and/or teach the group their input and passion, others are phenomenal actors that portray our Samoan life so hilariously well, and so on. Then there are those who play instruments or write our scripts/poems and bring the performances together with their passions. It is when we come together with our individuality that our faith is expressed with a force that allows us to share more than just our faith, but our spiritual connection with our awesome God. Expressing our faith in God is one thing, but syncing that faith with people of different talents and perspectives, but the exact same mission, is what makes us so sure of God's grace, and all the more motivated to share with people. Our overall performances are not taught by the leader of the youth, it's a group effort, which means so much more than one person's effort because, well, imagine one person's vision, compared to a whole group's vision combined. Creatively using our talents to express our faith is more meaningful than for example, praying, because it's what we do best, it's what we are passionate about. It's us using our gifts from God, to exalt God.*

When asked if her faith helps her make sense of the world, Vineta answered,

Yes, it truly does for me. The way I live my life as well as my perception of this world was hugely influenced by the Bible lessons and sermons I've learned and heard from my nanna, church and other religious functions. Where many children were read fairy tales, my nanna read stories within the chapters of the Holy Bible where I learned and understood that this world consists of bad, of sinners, of laws (10 commandments). It is also through Jesus' parables and lessons that I learned that we can redeem ourselves, that people can choose to be kind and there can be good if we choose to [take] that path. But this does not mean that I wholeheartedly see the world through the Bible's perception. The strong women in my life who taught me the contents of these parables and stories also taught me to believe and live by them, through my beliefs and understanding. I'm a feminist. So yes, my religion helps me to understand the world.

Vineta's perception of the foundational role of creativity and the ethnoscapes that have animated her childhood and ground her worldview are intricately linked together. Following Yip and Page (2013), Vineta makes it clear that her youth identity and social role is imbued with influences from both the ethnoscape and the mediascape, both of which are inflected with religion. Yet literature too often ignores the ways in which these intersections can be productive for the young people, claiming that "putting the words 'youth' and 'religion' in the same sentence warrants an explanation, as dominant academic and popular discourses continue to neglect their connection and emphasise their incompatibility" Yip and Page (2013, 41). Recognising the orientation of youth as experimental and religion as structured and hierarchical, they claim, "in these discourses, the relationship between religion and youth is at best tenuous and negligible" and that "research has incontrovertibly shown that religion and faith connections do matter for many young adults, significantly informing the construction of their biographical narratives and strategic life-planning" (2013, 173), or, in other words, affecting what Appadurai has called their capacity to aspire. Yip's and Page's extensive research certainly confirms what Vineta and her peers have reported, that:

Religion, alongside other factors such as youth culture and family, could constitute a significant 'field of existence' or 'biographical domain'

98   *Samoan Mediascapes and Faith-as-Performance*

(Thomson 2009) that is meaning-generating and subjectivity-producing. Thus, exploring how young adults understand and live out their religion can generate important insights into how they construct their personal and social identities by engaging with the broader social processes of individualisation, de-traditionalisation and subjectivisation.

(Yip and Page 2013, 4)

If, however, we look more holistically at the combination of creativity and religious participation together, their sociocultural functions can be mapped across how they are expressed within the ethnoscape of being Samoan in contemporary Australia for this particular group of young people. Here, too, the social function of creativity in this collective is clear, but we must keep in mind that its function—and indeed capital—for the individual is always distinct from its value to the collective. Sometimes this distinction seems characteristic of western notions of creativity, or, in other words, assists in the project of commodifying a kind of creativity in which as Margolis has said, "creativity is a function of the collective life of an entire society, though we tend (for good reason) to locate its proximate source in the productive work of particular persons" (Margolis 1985, 25).

Mitias and others have noted a similar tension at the intersection of creativity and religion, but set against a larger backdrop that challenges the ultimate -scape of human existence itself:

> Creativity in the laudatory sense is simply a special case of creativity in the categorically general or transcendental sense applicable to God and every creature (other than mere assemblages or swarms of creatures). If the human species is more Godlike than others we know, this means its members have more creative freedom. More than other creatures, they are co-creative with God. Our greater importance is that we add more to the definiteness of reality. Some of these additions are less fortunate than others. We can do more good than the lesser creatures, but obviously we can do more harm. Degree of creativity is not the sole criterion of value. At our worst we threaten all the life on the planet. The old idea of sin takes on a new and, alas, terrible form. It might become us to meditate now and then on this fact. It might do something to moderate our arrogance or conceit, or what the Greeks called *hubris*.
>
> (Hartshorne 1985, 7)

Like the proliferating fields of posthuman and new materialist research, Vineta and her contemporaries are far more focused on ecological sustainability and the interconnectedness of all living things than my generation was. Despite the constraints of their material conditions, they seem to know better than I did at their age that "living is an art, and any artist wishes to add to the world definite patterns that were not previously in anyone's mind, not because of ignorance but because there were no such patterns to

Semblance and Praisesong   99

know" (Hartshorne 1985, 8). The challenge of writing a book such as this one is to avoid the trap of generalising their choices and orientations as anthropologically 'Samoan' in a way that diminishes their other lifeworlds and subjectivities.

I know well enough that Vineta, her family and community members, and their South Sudanese peers too for that matter, are individuals as well as members of an assemblage, just as we all are, but that subaltern or minoritised communities and members are more readily over-generalised and stereotyped, especially in the academy, about the ways in which their decisions and behaviours are somehow representative rather than individual choices or characteristics. It is important to me to continue to engage in these collaborations and creative/research relationships which by their nature challenge categories of many kinds, but it is also important to continue working to avoid and dismantle essentialising discourses.

So too with creativity. While creativity may be a kind of zeitgeist for this sociocultural moment—and this in itself is fascinating and worthy of further study[1]—it is similarly at risk of being or becoming unintelligible to readers through our discursive over-ascribing of hopes, dreams, and pathologies to it as a practice and as a notion. While many have meandered through the relationship between creativity and intelligibility (what Ken Robinson calls 'value'), Hausman's (1985) is one of the best when distinguishing between a thing's relevance and its value to its users—that is, what the 'good of it' may be. Hausman claims that, "A more restricted kind of newness, which might be thought sufficient to justify the attribution of 'originality' in its weakest sense, is qualitative difference." (31). But creativity must go beyond originality, and Hausman describes why the creative contribution of the Samoan youth might be so necessary to the rest of us, why their creative endeavour is enhanced by the integration of their religious and cultural attachments. Hausman claims that

> a stronger kind of difference is needed, a 'relevant' difference or what may be called a 'difference of intelligibility'. What counts as relevance is not easy to make clear . . . [but is] crucial to the open-ended concept of creativity [and that] . . . the most appropriate kinds of examples for our purposes are created (and creative) metaphors. These articulate unfamiliar meanings and references; yet they somehow make sense. And they make sense immediately, before we interpret them and see how they offer possibilities for future implied meanings.
>
> (Hausman 1985, 31)

Might the kind of creativity that Vineta and her peers are engaged in, then, be considered something *beyond* Appadurai's capacity to aspire, for it addresses something far greater than the material conditions of lifting oneself out of poverty. It speaks, as it were, to these young people's vision of a new world, in which the creative technoscape plays an important role

100 *Samoan Mediascapes and Faith-as-Performance*

and is able to integrate the diversities of their multiple lifeworlds, including religion, age, ethnicity, and gender. It is, for Erin Manning, a space of the 'almost', in which "the elasticity of the almost is textured, its texture that of unbounded creativity [which] . . . produces conjunction, but not conjunction in a one-to-one relation. What is produced is the conjunction of the one-many, of the infinity of potential series coming together" (Manning 2009, 38), a new kind of collectivity.

Feminism and Samoan Ethnoscapes

Vineta and some of her fellow youth group members have highlighted the intersection of their faith- and gender-based values in both their creative work and interpersonally. As Harris and Dobson (2015) have argued, Vineta's views can be understood in light of a post-structuralist youth studies theoretic, in which "subjectivity and social structure [are] produced in concert" (145). In exploring what might typify 'feminist agency' and resistance in the west today, Harris and Dobson (from Gonick et al 2009) identify three pivotal concepts, which include "choice, empowerment and voice" (145). These are not unfettered concepts, however, and their contradictions can be seen in the young women here. For example, not only do Vineta and her peers represent a kind of hybrid Christian-creative-feminist subject, but they also express a generational skepticism or mediatised attachment to it, or what Harris and Dobson (from Egan) call a " 'feminist melancholia' over the loss of generational hope when they fail to live up to expectations of 'resistance'" (146), variously interpreted. So Vineta, for example, may be at times an ambivalent feminist or postfeminist subject, embodying what might be read as a restrained or almost 'failed' feminist subject, both culturally and religiously, in the secondary role that women play. However, as Vineta makes clear, they also embody a new kind of religious-creative and clearly gendered subject that is not just dismantling the sometimes-melancholic 'dangerous Samoan youth' narrative in mainstream mediascapes, but also represents racialised resistant bodies. In multiple ways, these young women demonstrate the kind of hybridisation required of all feminist or activist youth today, and in doing so are able to border-cross in effective ways, not just in offline but also in online worlds.

For Vineta, the distinctive role of youth in their church community is tied to hope, not failure, and cultural maintenance, not resistance. It highlights how not only she and her peers see the particularity of youth, but also how the elders see them, in which the youth specifically function to

> *enlighten the congregation with songs and performances. There have been some adults who started coming to church purely from the peace and passion and the Holy Spirit that they received through the youth performances. It's the inspiration they receive from young people—learning*

Semblance and Praisesong 101

that the faith is there, and that these young people have shown them what it's all about!

For Vineta and other migrant youth of colour, this leadership role in their religious and cultural community through church is a powerful antidote to the racist, ageist, and patriarchal messages they must weather every day. Vineta sees their intergenerational impact both with older community members and with younger ones:

> *It's also the influence and impact we have on the younger kids so they can aspire to be a part of a fellowship so dedicated and passionate, along with teaching them the stories and God's love through performance. Youth have been preachers through their performances, inspiring and reaching out to the wider community and giving faith to those inspired.*

Harris and Dobson (2015) call for an expansion of vocabulary as a 'material-discursive' project (from Barad 2003), as "important both for feminist theory and for girls themselves to develop accessible language and terms that enable an articulation of the complexity of girls' relationships to the structure/agency binary" (146). Often non-white, non-western girls and young women (and others) do not identify with feminist discourses in the same way that white western ones do. That is why, in this book, I take an intersectional approach, which recognises these young women as articulating their agency through a range of discursive and material-discursive means, including faith, religion, culture, and gender. For them, feminism cannot stand apart from their other subject positions, fluid as they all are, and how they are enacted in various scapes. Indeed, when asked how her faith affects her understanding of being a youth, Vineta answered:

> *My faith builds on my understanding as a youth in that it guides me into adulthood and teaches a lot about love. One story in particular that really taught me a lot during my adolescent years is the parable of the prodigal son. With an inexperienced young mind, youth are exposed to sins and doing things selfishly. This story embraces the love of parents and God's love that never dies, regardless of the sins committed.*

For her, faith stories, cultural and religious community membership, and adolescent development are inextricable. The youth, she explained, practice their faith through prayers in the morning and before bed, Bible lessons and family prayer time every night, attending church every Sunday, and "being righteous in everything we do". Yet Vineta acknowledges that things are not always as simple as they might seem:

> *Sometimes, unexpected turns of events on an ordinary day can test our faith. Like doing the right thing in difficult situations (sticking up for someone who is wrongly treated in public, or not being afraid to do good when it is required), are not so much practicing faith, but more like using common sense. How we respond reflects on our faith and all that we've learned from the Bible.*

These practices help construct a contemporary cosmopolitan youth subject that is flexible and capable, and according to Harris and Dobson reflects something more than a simple matter of agency or what Appadurai has called voice. Agency, from a post-structuralist perspective, is not seen solely as an "inherent, individual and separate internal force located within the individual that pushes back against social structures. Rather, it is a relational process" (Harris and Dobson 2015, 147). This relational process, for those like Harris and Dobson, and Karen Barad (2003), encompasses other material discursive forces including "cultural, psychic, economic, natural and physical" (Harris and Dobson 2015, 146). These theoretical explorations are embedded in white western sociocultural landscapes, reflective of both mainstream euro-centric perspectives and histories of resistance and citizenship within white western traditions. These remain highly individualist, rather than reflecting the collectivist orientations and perspectives typified by the young women here. For Vineta, her faith practices help make her part of a community that she describes in this way:

> *Relating to people who have the same beliefs creates a sense of understanding from one to another. Building that fellowship and learning from each other creates a togetherness that encourages the faith to spread not only within the community, but with everyone else, extending the community. It's magical!*

As she notes in her commentary about how she and her fellow youth use social media for posting creative and community-related videos and comments, for Vineta the collectivist 'togetherness' performs both expansive (as above), and constraining and surveilling functions (as in her commentary on getting in trouble for joking with Ana on Facebook). This tension 'between' the individual versus collective approach to faith and creativity is powerful:

> *There are [Samoan] churches everywhere around the world and each church and their creativity is what defines their individuality despite the same messages preached through their alters. [One example of] the role of creativity in my church is the decision on colour we choose as a community to make our church uniforms. It is our rendition of hymns that we change to suit our choir as we sing our praises. It is the combining of the ideas of individuals within our church community to build one unique congregation. It is making use of what we have, to build an*

empire for the one and only God whom we serve wholeheartedly. Creativity is the foundation of our church. It is using our talents to give all our glory to God, who gave us the talents.

Where Harris and Dobson note postfeminist claims that "feminism and the 'resistant' capacities it is seen to offer girls and women is deemed . . . only or primarily of relevance to girls and women in developing countries and outside of liberal democracies" (147), the young women in this book show some ways in which feminism remains necessary to young women (in this case, of colour) still within western democracies, but which are experienced differently by classed and racialised minorities. These distinctions between geographic differences are perhaps unnecessarily reductive and ignore the widely disparate experiences of the range of youth in liberal democracies. However, creativity here becomes a kind of scalpel that cuts through racialised and gendered subjectivities, and specifically in this community, the creativity of these youths' faith practices becomes not just the kind of aspirational tool that is most widely noted in the literature, but partially also a leveller. I am careful throughout this book, however, not to ascribe unrealistic value to the creative faith practices, but rather note it to suggest that 'agency' in youth studies terms (in particular for girls), is not only co-constructed in opposition to socio-cultural structures but also in relation to them, where religious practices and communities function as sites of humanist and more-than-human connection with the world around them.

The young women featured here might be understood as having 'voice', specifically a kind of creative voice evidenced in their faith-based activities and performances. Yet at the same time, their narratives also suggest a kind of contemporary voicelessness, one noted by McRobbie as a " 'new sexual contract' whereby young women must give up critical voice in order to gain social status and some forms of personal economic power as part of the constitution and maintenance of post-feminist social conditions" (in Anita Harris and Dobson 2015, 150). These faith-infused constructions of the young women in this book—their Facebook and other social media performances of their creative selves—not around sexualised agency, but as faith-based agency—marks them as different from many of their western girl-peers. Thus, through their creativity, which can be simultaneously sensual, cultural, and religious, "the [Samoan *Culture Shack* project] participants showed how cultural dance can change the signifying system within community arts in western contexts, contributing to what Georgina calls a gradual re-ordering of girls' and women's roles" (Harris and Lemon 2012, 423). In their dance and vocal performances, these young women can self-represent in ways that reject essentialising identity-constructions like sexualised versus agentic, or secular versus religious. Vineta and the other youth, who make themselves seen and heard through social media for the stated aim of glorifying God rather than their own glory or their sexual/sexualised

104 *Samoan Mediascapes and Faith-as-Performance*

agency, can in fact go 'unpunished' in postfeminist debates about good and bad girl-agency, girl-choices, and girl-power.

It is also important to note an increasing recognition of the classed and raced nature of the sexualisation of girls. In a postfeminist landscape of self-policing and surveillance of girls' sexuality in which girls must "be capable of taking care of themselves . . . of protecting themselves from injury", they tell us, "speaking up critically becomes a signal of such capacity" (Harris and Dobson 2015, 151). In other words, girls who are self-critical of female sexualisation rather than critiquing social structures are seen in contemporary culture as agentic, highlighting for us "how the work of eliciting girls' voices as a form of cultivating agency cannot be easily disentangled from the work of governmentality" (2015, 152). In contrast to Appadurai here, they assert that 'voice' cannot easily be held as a simple conceptual marker of agency in girls' power and self-determination. Girls' studies scholars, in this context, are usefully focusing more closely on the social contexts in which this intersubjective, interrelational agency-construction is performed (Kennelly 2009).

Surely Vineta and her peers represent the call for something beyond a victim/heroine binary as evidenced so often in girls' studies literature, and the kinds of youthful subjectivities go beyond the "impossible binary construction of young people as either the ideal reflexive subjects of late modernity (including post-feminism) or its passive victims" (Harris and Dobson 2015, 152). They acknowledge how "forms of struggle are still present, especially in attempts to not only name but to conflictualize through social and creative expression" (152). That kind of approach to social media visibility is present in the commentaries of both the South Sudanese and Samoan young women in this book: that is, they do not see themselves as overtly political subjects but rather as agentic, individual, or otherwise-motivated ones (i.e., in service to God), but certainly at times as involved in a struggle. This difference opens up new and fluid ways of understanding the self-representations of their social media and creative activities, made and circulated in "areas of life and culture that Berlant terms 'juxtapolitical' (Berlant 2008)—located next to, but not directly within political spheres" (Harris and Dobson 2015, 153).

Their stories and creative works stand as testaments to the different expressions of feminism as well as interculturalism, yet certainly both concepts are culturally context-specific. No longer measured by simplistic notions of "the capacity to make free choices" which has been "central to feminist definitions of girls' agency" (Harris and Dobson 2015, 148) in the past, these Samoan youth suggest additional (collectivist, non-western) ways of exploring choice and agency. While some youth and feminist scholars still define "autonomous choice" in differentiation from choiceless oppression "imposed by the patriarchy" (148), for the youth here, the notion of free choice is intertwined with a kind of singularity and individuality that is specific to western identity.

Compromise (some of which is gendered and age-contingent) is not imposed by an external patriarchy but rather negotiated in a range of ways within their own families and communities, and the repercussions are not always negative. Indeed, as they point out, choice is and has always been difficult to articulate and analyse, because "one's own preferences and decisions can never be disentangled from the social context within which they are arrived at" (Harris and Dobson 2015, 148), visibly true within this youth sub-community. Some scholars (including Ringrose 2012; Baker 2010) do highlight the need for nuance with such static constructions of free choice as a measure of agency, problematising this notion for young women from "markedly different backgrounds" (Harris and Dobson 2015 149), some of whom story themselves as "'hyper-responsibilised' subjects" (149) in contrast to neoliberal constructs of young women as victims from deficit-framed girlhoods. Yet western notions of agentic and positive girlhoods remain in stark contrast it seems to the kinds of self-constructions these Samoan and South Sudanese youth offer, and while Appadurai and Ahmed have addressed the notion of the melancholy migrant or the 'pastness' framing of traditional cultural identities and practices, the layer of youthness as a kind of western or global futurity requires further examination in intercultural contexts such as these youth groups.

On Technoscapes and Samoan Girlhood

In their introduction to *Youthscapes: The Popular, The National, The Global*, Sunaina Maira and Elisabeth Soep (2005) identify a need for more (and more nuanced) research on the "intersections between popular culture practices, national ideologies, and global markets" (xv), recognising the inextricability of these spheres, the under-theorised literature in this area, and identifying its importance for "developing a new model for youth culture studies" (xv). Their use of the term '(youth)scape' suggests, as does Appadurai's, sites of encounter that are both local and global, and "not just geographic or temporal, but social and political as well" (xv).

The 'fluid and irregular' nature of Appadurai's global cultural flows present in their work are indeed indicative of the increasingly unfixed nature of the lives of young people like Vineta, and the creative and other practices in which they engage. I return to Appadurai in my own work because he speaks lucidly about the ways in which the multi-directional flows of contemporary life are both accelerating and dissolving. While a decade ago we may have imagined that this new century would bring untold mobilities (and it has), we now know that both economically and materially, the digital embodiments that enable new kinds of knowledge and creative exchange do more to reproduce social hierarchies and siloes than they do to flatten them.

For Samoan and South Sudanese (and indeed many other minoritarian) youth, the promise of digital culture has not delivered the kinds of new frontiers and social and cultural mobilities that they promised. Especially for migrant communities and young people growing up in a range of diasporas, the localised forms of sociality that seemed so recently to bound encounters and civic participation seemed set to fall away, but instead the utopian dream of egalitarian digital global mobilities is what has so quickly proven obsolete.

Recent research with Australian migrant young people (Vietnamese, South Sudanese, and Samoan) aged 18–30 from communities in Melbourne's west found they had an ongoing relationship with digital technology that was characterised by a sense of choice that was interactive, accessible, and affordable; had appropriate content that was sensitive to gender; drew on oral, text, image, and sound-based forms of communication; and noted the value of both older and newer forms of technology. Regular and interactive use of social media, mobile phones, and other more recent digital technology was considered an important part of daily life and for staying in touch with friends, family, and others here and in the homeland (O'Mara and Harris 2014), and these uses of digital technology were contingent upon economic, geographical, and cultural access factors.

Vineta and the other young people in this book can be understood as intersectional actors as represented through their creative use of technology both for making and for circulating. They are unique in their cultural, religious, and gendered identities, but also as "a shifting group of people that is simultaneously a deeply ideological category" (Maira and Soep 2005, xvi), and while it is difficult to address in research that all these subjectivities are at play simultaneously and messily, it is crucial to building nuanced understandings. Maira and Soep (2005) distinguish their approach to 'scapes' from Appadurai's by claiming it not so much as a "unit of analysis" (xviii) but rather a set of "local and global practices—including apparently trivial micro-interactions as well as heavily regulated institutionalized procedures—that render youth a viable cultural construction" (xix), which Vineta and her peers certainly are. If "youth, then, are at the center of globalization" (xix), technoscapes surely are too.

One result of this "reflexive modernization" that is characterised by the technoscape is "both self-critique and social critique" (McRobbie 2011, 90). This might involve the kind of social critique that moves beyond sectional analysis and into something like reimagining culture along intersectionally fluid and creatively innovative lines:

> If Leadbeater harnesses talent and creativity for the sole purposes of growth and wealth creation, can sociologists not remind the public of the various histories of these categories, which have been central to the discipline, from Bourdieu and the sociology of art to those working in critical pedagogy. It should also be possible to revitalize creativity in education without forgetting that the most influential Marxist thinkers, from Adorno to Jameson, have argued for the redemptionist, utopian and instructive functions of art.
>
> (McRobbie 2011, 90)

In suggesting ways forward in which the flattening effect of freelance creative labour might be (re)combined with individualized subjectivity or 'differentiated subjectivity', McRobbie suggests that "this is in fact an argument about how individualization can give way to 'new productive singularities'. These in turn would challenge neo-liberalism by showing it to be productive only if truncated" (2011, 91). By combining Foucault's concept of biopower and self-monitoring or self-regulation with Deleuze's and Guattari's "desiring machines as flows of power, the working body becomes a point of intersection with other working bodies" (91). McRobbie asks, "Why should desire or energy not be associated with work? Thus, creative work becomes a site for re-socialization, since it is better done with or for others" (91). Vineta and the Samoan youth commentary highlights this re-socialization, but also demonstrates how this might look. In doing so, they offer material possibilities for McRobbie's re-imagined sociality in their creative and cultural practices.

Recent Australian research (O'Mara and Harris 2014) has found that when using digital technology to communicate on health and self-image, there is a need to differentiate engagement with young people based on their settlement and migration experiences, and cultural preferences for communication. For example, using the internet at school/university or other public access points rather than at home and communicating orally and in Dinka was easier and preferred for young South Sudanese Australians. Samoan migrants were likely to use social media more heavily and record events such as dances and performances. Much of Vineta's discussion about her use of social media for creative or faith-based networking and sharing returns to such discussions of health, body images, and wellbeing. As in earlier excerpts, the following dialogue returns to such discussions and the ways in which Vineta's social media engagements reproduce offline engagements and relationships, thus offering an example of how these youth are using digital media to explore McRobbie's notion of re-imagining sociality:

Anne: *You have a YouTube channel is that right?*
Vineta: *Yeah.*
Anne: *And what kind of stuff do you put up there? One thing I love about you guys is that you just put up a lot of really casual clips right?*
Ana: *Yeah.*
Vineta: *We even did Gangnam style. Yeah we did the exact same you know like the environment of the video clip but they did it in Samoan. So bad.*
Ana: *No, that was Harlem Shake that we did. Samoan style.*
Anne: *Do you put them up on YouTube, or just share them through Facebook or other social media?*
Vineta: *Yeah I put up like a video, like a video of us on YouTube.*

108   *Samoan Mediascapes and Faith-as-Performance*

Joy: *Yeah like the dog smash one!*
Vineta: *Yeah we had a lot of views, not like 100,000 but you know like 500 likes is really big.*
Ana: *You got a lot more than that though.*
Vineta: *Yeah for that video. Only for that video. but it's only the Samoan people. Like no one else goes on there [on their YouTube channel]. So because a Samoan page I think saw the video and then they were like let's share it but that page had Samoans from America and Samoa and New Zealand, everywhere. So they were all looking at our videos and they are all Samoans. So yeah, like it started off like that and then once we started getting these kinds of responses we was like, oh, my gosh, we should make some more videos so that we can connect to our Samoans from all around the world. But then on our second video we did a gospel one and not only did we approach our cultural side but everybody who's Christian and who loves R&B because it was an R&B song as well. So we were sort of connecting to everybody. It all depends on like the songs that we're doing and who would actually like those songs.*
Ana: *We're thinking about audience.*
Anne: *And you're thinking about connecting but also maybe like being a performer that has an audience right? So that sounds like two things: Like one is who can we reach with this artistically, and one is how many other Samoans we can reach culturally or something, is that right?*
Ana: *Yeah that's right. In our first video we like we engaged with our audiences as Samoans I think because it was only Samoans who were responding.*
Anne: *Was it in English or was it—*
Vineta: *It was in Samoan. So it was mostly like Samoan people who responded because it was our old-school Samoan song that everybody loved and we sort of changed it around as well. So that's the other thing that people like because of course the new generations, they're really into old school hip hop as well. So I think because you know how in the old school of my parents in Samoa they only like their Samoan songs, but now we like the hip hop side as well, and we're putting it together and the parents are like oh ok.*
Ana: *All the olden days you know how like now we're into hip hop? Back then they were into country. So all their songs sounded [makes tune] like that. Like it was cool.*
Joy: *I think country was the only kind of music they had connection with.*
Anne: *What kind of old-school R&B is your youth group into?*
Ana: *We're really into harmonies, so Boys II Men.*
Vineta: *UB40.*

Semblance and Praisesong 109

Joy: Beyoncé, Destiny's Child.

Vineta: The things that everyone likes. They, like a lot of Samoan artists, they like to mix that because it's all our favourite sort of genres. So when they mix it together it's like—that's the island beat.

Anne: So it's a distinctive beat that comes from a mashup?

Joy: Yeah. It's happening in Samoa, New Zealand, especially New Zealand.

Vineta: [indicating Joy] You know how you see her in the videos? I force her. That's why she's always at the back. I'm like, 'I'm not going to make you pie for tomorrow and she is like okay, okay', [laughing]. That's how you bribe Samoans, you offer food.

Ana: Works every time [laughing]. Yea but we think about the views and about faith, spreading the faith, those are our motivations. I think it depends on how well your first video goes.

Vineta: So you know how when I did my first video and we had like a big response to it and then our cousins were like, oh, my gosh, you should do another one so we can get more likes. But initially that's not what we wanted. Like it's more of sharing and just you know showing our family as well because we have a lot of family everywhere and my nanna she loves to boast about how talented her grandkids are. 'Put it on her Facebook so your aunty can see', she says. You know it's about family more than—

Ana: Yeah so that's the first thing and then we get that response we go, oh, my gosh, we have to make sure Beyoncé sees our next video, you know. It just gets more and more and more and but like nah, but at first it's more modest. And then we get not modest.

Joy: I keep telling her to join the Laughing Samoans [a performing comedy troupe].

Vineta: Because they think I'm funny.

Ana: Something she's good at.

Vineta: No, it's funny how they think I'm funny, but I'm not funny.

Anne: You are funny.

Vineta: I think people just laugh at me because I'm big [laughing]. Anyway I have this plan so I'm going to lose weight and then the first clip I'm going to have you know have you see the Chris Q Beyoncé clip and he's not hard out dancing and it looks so good. I was going to do because you know all the before and after pictures they're like that's cool, it's like just cool and that I'm like wow that's amazing and when the first picture came out. See now that's old news, I'm trying to think of a more creative way to promote losing weight. So I was like okay Beyoncé so instead of thinking of I want to do this to lose weight, it's like I want to do this to be healthy and to be a better me and to like show people that I can actually do things that I want to do but I think I don't know how to do. So everybody loves Beyoncé, I love Beyoncé and I want to

110 *Samoan Mediascapes and Faith-as-Performance*

> *know how to dance like Beyoncé. Obviously I can't, I get that. So I will be like the first 'before' video and I'm like dancing and then it's not really that great and you can see like the room shaking when I'm shaking as well. Just like for fun, because people love— people love funny stuff. So yeah I can share my funny side on the big side and then I finish that and then I lose weight and then show them all the other things that I want to achieve like through other videos. And then I do an 'after' video when I'm all skinny and so hot, but I'm already hot now [laughing]. So then you put the videos together and the before and after doing the Beyoncé thing, do you get it? And everyone is like wow. And then the video will go viral and then people will be hiring me and then I get money and I help my poor family.*

This discussion of their use of video-sharing technology echoes other Samoan youth who are also using online technologies to link their faith experiences, creativity, and cultural identities in subtle or more overt political ways. One such self-made superstar is New Zealander Joshua Iosefo (see his TEDx Talk *Brown Brother* at Iosefo 2012; Lowrie n.d.). In Joshua's work, he stresses the unknown futures we all face as a great opportunity for creative minoritarian youth. McRobbie extends Foucault and Deleuze to suggest that "the critical knowledges and generative energies that are produced by today's creative workers may allow for new forms of socialization to emerge, and may, in keeping with Hardt and Negri's (2000) views, lead to transnational pressure politics" (McRobbie 2011, 12). While remaining strongly UK-focused, McRobbie articulates some tensions of the creative/cultural economy that bear upon the global south, especially in relation to minoritarian ethnic youth like the Samoan and South Sudanese featured in this book, and others like Joshua.

Homogeneity and Creative Futures

McRobbie's use of *The Green Paper* "brings together three elements: the individual, creativity (now extended to mean 'having ideas') and freedom" (2011, 82), three solidly western tropes which nevertheless offer a good place to begin this discussion of the intersection of cultural and individual creativity evidenced by the youth here. *The Green Paper*, like Australian and other nation-based vision statements articulating a 21st century view of creativity and the emerging workforce, "looks forward to a future generation of socially diverse creative workers who are brimming with ideas and whose skills need not only be channelled into the fields of art and culture but will also be good for business" (82). If creativity continues to evolve toward a use-value definition of creative practice, what will become of the kind of 'praisesong' creativity that also enriches the lives of these young people?

Semblance and Praisesong 111

It is certainly not workforce-oriented, explicitly capital-oriented, or even in most ways aspirational. It is simply an externalisation of faith-based values and community-building through creative expression. In this way, the creative practice of these youth bears almost no similarity to the kind of 21st century creativity discussed here by McRobbie. *The Green Paper* (and others like it, including The Melbourne Declaration and the incoming American Common Core skills and capacities framework) may be seeking socially diverse workers, but they still have no interest in culturally, religiously, or ethnically diverse ones.

If we entertain the possibility that individual agency and collectivist cultural work are not contradictory tasks, and that the "seeming inevitability of local to global neo-liberalism" (McRobbie 2011, 83) could be "redirected as a force for revitalizing the democratizing process" (83), rather than an endangered species, what radical role might creativity play? And while the creative industries' move toward consultancy/self-employment may be a thinly veiled neoliberalisation of the workforce, might those like Vineta and other cultural-creatives find themselves in a powerful position to lead this workforce change? There are nefarious implications, to be sure, in this "double act of neoliberalization: first to minimize social welfare support for those unable to earn a living wage . . . and second, to set individuals to their own devices in terms of job creation so that the large corporations are less burdened by the responsibilities of a workforce" (McRobbie 2011, 83). In this scenario, workers/creatives are on their own to seek so-called self employment when and if they can find it.

Apart from the crushing divestment of government in the social fabric of training and workforce development, it may be a misleading 'carrot' for young people—aspirational or not—who are trying to find their way in an increasingly competitive workforce. In it, "creative work is particularly appealing to youth because of the emphasis on uncovering talent" (83), and yet the unlikeliness of real financial or material reward for creative labour remains high. But the so-called creative economy is groaning under its new market demands, just as the slippery ubiquitous creativity discourse is in ideological terms. Yet for those like Samoan youth who are used to missing out on the few work opportunities available to those in their twenties, could this shift toward self-directed labour markets actually benefit them, as "in Zygmont Bauman's phrase, the labour market melts away, it liquidifies" (McRobbie 2011, 84)?

Such conditions make way for new theories of creative production. McRobbie, for example, theorises[2] a distinct social and marketplace difference between what she calls "first-wave producers" [which she sets as roughly 1985–1999] who were trained and work autonomously and "second-wave de-specialized cultural entrepreneurs (or entrepreneurs of the self)" (84), in which these (often young) workers are not 'new independents' but rather "sub-contracted creative workers, wholly dependent on bigger companies for the services that are now outsourced rather than produced in-house" (84).

112 Samoan Mediascapes and Faith-as-Performance

There is now a familiar intermingling of arts and business, where investment companies (real estate, technology) align with schools of art and independent artists in order to benefit from the cache of the 'cutting edge arts' creative economy, which will have direct material appreciation on their investments (e.g., giving cache to new inner-city warehouse developments, etc.), all to benefit the investors and of no lasting benefit to the creatives. These become institutionalised trends through the ways in which "the commercialization of art is reflected in cultural policy" (McRobbie 2011, 85). Hence creative discourses become institutionalised by making visible the trajectory from fringe/independent arts practices, through scholarly and consultative recommendations (in the UK in this instance, via Leadbeater's notion of the 'cultural entrepreneur'), through to policy. For McRobbie, the 'answer' lies in a conscientization of the creative (working) class who, she suggests, "at present do not sufficiently analyze their own working conditions" and for whom she encourages a change that might "form the basis of new and as yet unimaginable forms of group action" (2011, 89).

While the emerging creative class has been well (and repeatedly) defined by Florida and others before her, McRobbie suggests that this highly educated metropolitan elite is distinct from those who have come before, with "sufficient cultural capital to take risks and test the ground of the new cultural economy with enough material and symbolic resources to fall back on if things go wrong" (89). While I might disagree that this is a new creative elite (based on my own experiences of being a working class interloper into the world of 1990s creative class members during my undergraduate and postgraduate study at New York University, where these claims were certainly in evidence), I will leave McRobbie's definition here because however we define the contemporary creative class one thing is clear: the majority of South Sudanese and Samoan young people of this text do not belong to it according to these (albeit varied) originary definitions.

This leads us to consider McRobbie's call to recritique the "self-flagellating model of Bauman ('must try harder and harder')" (2011, 90) with a call to "'reflexivity' as a tool for forward thinking"—indeed, she claims, "those sociologists who have best developed this concept have done so without a full theory of media, art, culture or communication" (2011, 90). While McRobbie makes a strong argument, I would go further in suggesting that sociological developments regarding reflexivity have done so too, without sufficient attention to the widely divergent material conditions of the young people. Critical education scholars such as Apple, Rizvi, Shor, and cultural theorists like Appadurai have better addressed the gap between material and aesthetic considerations and to the power/powerlessness of reflexivity. As I have suggested by combining the faith-based creative labour and the cultural subjectivities of the Samoan and South Sudanese youth in this book, I am more interested in an intersectional approach to understanding the ways in which digital media work for (or against) them in their contemporary navigation to adulthood.

Semblance and Praisesong   113

For them, aspiration has always demanded an alternative vision of the future, not a simple success trajectory in the white western model. And while creativity is always culturally situated and contingent, I am highlighting the value of focusing specifically on how culture promotes creativity in particular forms and domains and in certain segments of the population and remains not only culture-inflected, but possibly culture-driven. For the youth in Section One of this book, "creativity occurs in dance in Samoa" and through dance and music in Samoan-Australian culture, and that same Samoan culture "provides a set of facilitating and inhibiting conditions for creativity that influence the general level of creative activity" (Sternberg 1999, 347). While such claims may sound anachronistic and culturally essentialising, Sternberg's point bears out in the works of these two groups of culturally hybridised youth, as they forge new hybrid online/offline lives.

Creatively, educationally, and economically, it has been made clear to these young people since even before migration or emergence out of the refugee experience (for the South Sudanese) that these countries of resettlement dominated by white privilege and western values were never here to redeem them, but to assimilate them for economic efficiency. So much critical scholarship concerning both populations remains focused on a singular vision of aspiration of 'transformation' as though aspiration is always toward material success and as though transformation can remain in the realm of the cultural, the spiritual, the holistic, without sufficient concern for the economic.

That is why in this text I have chosen to take an intersectional approach that makes fully transparent the ways in which the creative practices of these youth are focused on other gains as well as market success and economic advancement. They conduct their creative practices with full (if not always westernly articulated) understanding of the deficit ways in which they are framed by majoritarian society, and the unlikelihood of this changing in social, cultural, and symbolic capital terms (i.e., they are well aware of the antagonism of existing social and institutional structures not there for their benefit and in most cases completely impermeable by them). Their spiritual orientation in their creative work, then, takes on another dimension and motivation altogether, one that can be understood as creating an alternate space or 'imagined community' that is multitudinal and multidimensional and not necessarily holding majoritarian community values at its centre—indeed in some ways ignoring white western majoritarian (and creative) economies altogether. This may be its most radical individual and collectivist effect.

Hausman offers a useful definition of intelligibility that encompasses such discrepancies and explains why it is "crucial to the open-ended concept of creativity" (1985, 31). That is, "if we take something to be thus intelligible, we should expect that thing to be interpretable; it must suggest the possibility that it can be classified and placed in external relationships with other things" (31). In this alternate social vision of creative citizenship,

114   *Samoan Mediascapes and Faith-as-Performance*

these Samoan youth offer one new iteration of creative futures, in that "if the non-institutions of the new culture are 'almost unrecognisable', then it follows that whatever political sociality appears will take a different shape" (McRobbie 2011, 90), and (following Hardt and Negri) "perhaps we are thinking about *post-individual political formats*" (McRobbie 2011, 90). Such formations can be seen, at least in embryonic form, in what this dynamic Samoan youth group is doing, not only in their creative practices but in the ways they are thinking about culture and society.

Conclusion

When I returned to the next White Sunday service at the Samoan Methodist church the following year, things felt a whole lot more familiar. I knew the pastor, some of the elders, lots of the youth. I felt comfortable despite my not wearing a hat, or a white dress, or knowing any more words in Samoan than I did the previous year. But as usual, this Samoan church community welcomed me and made me feel a part of things. This time I returned with my video collaborator Alta, with whom I have made several videos in research contexts. The youth and I had decided we wanted to film the White Sunday service in a more professional, polished manner, and they of course would be performing and coordinating the younger kids, so Alta and I came to film.

It was a beautiful day like the year before, but in a different church this time, which afforded more room for moving around at the back of the congregation and getting better shots. In contrast with my experiences of White Sunday the first time around, I felt more at ease during the 2015 service, even though I was perhaps more visible with my camera and accompanied by Alta with her camera. I also felt less distanced from the Samoan youth and the rest of the congregation. They were once again friends, fellow Melbournians, and while I didn't return to Vineta's house this time like I had after my first White Sunday for the incredible sushi and Pasifika feast I had enjoyed last time, I felt like I was revisiting her family in a newly familiar way. While food does not mean that I am now part of this family I have known for ten years, the food, art, Christian praise, cultural diversity, music, and dance certainly weave a web of intimacy that, over time, has brought us closer and made conversations about cultural discomfort and dislocation more possible. These conversations have included gender politics in the church, my queerness, higher education, and more. The fact that we have collectively decided that many of these conversations should not be included in this book also speaks to the intercultural exchange and ability to create 'safe space' in collaborative research relationships.

What these Samoan youth are contributing to Australian and wide global culture cannot be measured, and I am not attempting to do so here. But the feelings, activities, and artefacts that appear and occur at the intersection of their religion, faith, creativity, and youth cultures are certainly powerful indicators of a new kind of agentic subjectivity, one that is inflected with virtual perspectives and lifeworlds, and one that points toward a powerful reintegration of selves that is relevant for all. In Section Two, which follows, I will explore some of these themes within a different context: that of some South Sudanese Christian youth, constructing and populating their own social imaginaries in Melbourne, in very different ways.

Notes

1 See Harris (2013), *The Creative Turn* and Harris (2015), *Creativity and Education*, for example.
2 Note that in this publication (2011), the editors also highlight that McRobbie has (since the essay's earlier form of publication in 2004) theorised a " 'third wave of cultural practitioners' [who] can be distinguished from the general characteristics of second-wave creatives . . . [by] de-specialization, self-reliance and freelance culture . . . [where] unpaid work, internships, project-to-project planning and a transformation of the curriculum of big institutions are accompanied by the suspension of critique" (2011, 92, in endnote #18). The editors point readers toward Angela McRobbie, 'The Los Angelisation of London: Three short waves of young people's micro-economies of culture and creativity in the UK', *Transversal, (January 2001)*, available at **http://www.eipcp.net/transversal/0207/mcrobbie/en.**

Section 2

Religion, Art, and a South Sudanese Post-National Imaginary

Section 2 Overview

Figure S2.1 Rap crew, *Culture Shack*. Photo and copyright, Anne Harris.

>*Tell us the good news, Bible, gossip, magazine . . . Facebook,
>   MySpace and MTV yo.
>Have to decide who I want to be.
>Doctor . . . a celebrity.
>We gotta know our own identity.
>Even if we gotta learn our own personality
>We don't know what to believe yo,
>We don't know what's the truth yo
>But what you do know, is that you believe in yourself.*
>   (Afreem, from *Keeping It Real* music video)

120 *Religion, Art, and a South Sudanese Post-National Imaginary*

For South Sudanese youth living in Australia, social media facilitate (or exacerbate, depending on where you stand) the search for identity in an often-hostile cultural climate. The lyrics extracted above, written by Afreem and her peers, who co-created the hip hop music video *Keeping It Real*, articulate the tensions they experience in countries of resettlement against the constancy of family and their Christian faith, but they also celebrate their enthusiasm for what's to come and the support networks that sustain them. The power of creative practices like songwriting and performing hold these tensions together and allow a public airing of these experiences in ways that neither school, nor family, nor sometimes church alone can do.

South Sudanese Diaspora

"There are now estimates that more than 30,000 South Sudanese migrants have settled in Australia" (Robinson 2011), most having arrived via the United Nations High Commissioner for Refugees (UNHCR) refugee resettlement program, of which Australia is a member. Decades of conflict and two civil wars between 1983 and 2005 resulted in the establishment of the new nation of South Sudan in 2011. Since then, separate from the (largely Muslim) northern country of The Republic of Sudan, South Sudan has continued to be plagued by internal unrest.

While numbers of South Sudanese seeking resettlement have tapered off since the establishment of South Sudan, conditions continue to be difficult, and some South Sudanese continue to seek resettlement in other countries. In Australia a recent census showed that "19,049 Australian residents declared they were born in Sudan, with 5,911 in Melbourne alone" (Australian Bureau of Statistics in Harris 2013a, 3), yet this number excludes many culturally Sudanese, who were born in other countries, to parents already in exile. Other countries of resettlement, including Canada and the United States, host substantial communities of South Sudanese who have, since the largest wave of migration in the mid-2000s, made strong gains in establishing themselves in these new cultures. The United Nations has identified "over 5 million internally-displaced persons (IDPs) in Sudan, the largest number of displaced persons in the world, and that women and children comprise 80% of all refugees in the world" (Harris 2013a, 3).

Most South Sudanese Australians emigrated to this country via Egypt or the Kakuma Refugee Camp in Kenya, neither of which were easy journeys. Many of my earlier publications have detailed the resettlement routes and conditions of South Sudanese Australians, particularly girls. And while the political landscape of Sudan and South Sudan have changed considerably over the past five years, the suffering of the South Sudanese continues to be felt both in the diaspora and at home. Kakuma itself remains a moderate-sized 'city' of tents, shacks, and thatched roof huts in the desert of northwest Kenya, inhabited by more than 90,000 refugees[1] (Sudanese, Ethiopian, and Somali, mostly, but also Congolese, Burundian, Rwandan, and Ugandan). Dating to 1991, it is equally a sanctuary and a prison—once admitted, residents cannot leave without permission of the Kenyan government—and inside its fences, children age into adulthood. The United Nations High Commission on Refugees administers the camp, with aid from a patchwork of international relief agencies, or nongovernmental organizations (NGOs).

(Harris 2013a, 2)

Once in countries of resettlement such as Australia, many South Sudanese continue to experience the racism, if not religious bias, that plagued them at home. There remains a "still-pervasive popular media representation of South Sudanese males as 'dangerous' and females as 'tragic' and 'struggling', yearning for a home to which they can never return (Windle 2008). Such stereotyping has a consistently gendered aspect" (Harris, Marlowe and Nyuon 2014, 1227). Elsewhere, I have noted "the ways in which young people from refugee backgrounds arrive in Australia with high aspirations for educational achievement" (Harris, Spark and Ngum Chi Watts 2014, 371), yet especially young women continue to experience complex challenges both within their communities and interculturally with non-Sudanese Australians.

Apparent improvements in material conditions, including educational opportunities for girls, are not always a simple matter. Many South Sudanese Australians have identified acculturation challenges regarding the ways that their "gains in education carry with them interconnected losses which are difficult to capture, let alone to represent in a cultural context in which higher education tends to be unambiguously associated with the opportunity for personal development, career prospects and individual gain" (Harris, Spark and Ngum Chi Watts, 2014, 373).[2] Gender often remains at the forefront of complex intercultural transitions and border-crossings, and recent research has acknowledged the ways in which "21st-century global flows represent challenges and intersectionalities that are not limited to concerns of race, ethnicity and culture alone, but include gender, age, sexuality and class concerns. African diasporic women's social roles are still often discursively framed to be primarily those of procreator and homemaker" (Harris, Spark and Ngum Chi Watts 2014, 371).

Some of these challenges are discursive, others remain associated with the difficulties of coming from "backgrounds characterized by severely interrupted schooling, especially girls" (Harris 2011a, 732), while others are representational. I have written elsewhere about the links between mediatised beauty and the aspirations of South Sudanese young women, embodied in figures like supermodel Tyra Banks as both a "comforting, maternal, Oprah-like figure" and "the bearer of a magic ticket out of poverty" (Harris

122 *Religion, Art, and a South Sudanese Post-National Imaginary*

2012b, 1). These aspirational role models form part of the mediascape, and as such remain situated within the doxic imaginary explored in Section One. For these South Sudanese youth even more than their Samoan peers, these imaginaries are deeply gendered.

In an annual Melbourne South Sudanese beauty pageant, the media and the young women's lives and imaginaries are intertwined:

> A Sudanese beauty pageant in itself quite literally evokes the media: broadcast pageants, modelling shows, lives of seeming glamour, the ways in which the western media directly link sex and power for young women. . . . Yet there were other interwoven threads of this experience that insisted they be heard: Sudanese young women, disengaged from school, who see modelling, acting and sexual desirability as perhaps their only shot at success . . . but the beauty pageant also suggests something deeper that schools might benefit from: parents' and families' passionate engagement.
>
> (Harris 2012b, 82)

Invisibility from the public record and popular imagination has been an issue since the South Sudanese exile to Kakuma refugee camp in Kenya. While the so-called *Lost Boys of Sudan* became a focus of international empathy, the girls remained invisible and silent. While the UNHCR and other aid and development organisations have noted this invisibility (if only cursorily), "Such invisibility presents a pattern that, once begun in countries of origin and transit, seems to be dangerously replicated in countries of resettlement" (Harris 2010, 47). While some Sudanese commentators have noted that gendered cultural practices positioned the boys differently (and more independently) than the girls, the invisibility was also tied to lower rates of English speaking literacy (impacting on international media representation) and gendered roles in the family, but scholars have noted that "these lost girls have been forgotten twice: upon arrival in Kakuma Refugee Camp, and again when the U.S. refugee resettlement program was started" (Edgerton 2002). In addition, researchers in Australia have observed that overall, South Sudanese young women have less schooling than their male counterparts (Cassity and Gow 2006), and "their isolation and disconnectedness appears to be more severe than for their male counterparts" (Harris 2011a, 733). This is not, however, the whole story.

Religion, Art, and Youth Scholarship

It is easier to find scholarly works on culture and creativity than on faith, spirituality, or religion and creativity, but why? Certainly there is a growth in arts-based and arts-informed scholarship that recognises the power of spirituality expressed through creative research (see Conrad and Sinner 2015; Walsh, Bickel, and Leggo 2015) and the value to scholars of arts and spirituality co-creating in the research experience. Transnational and cross-cultural scholars (Battacharya 2013; Lubart 1999; Ginsberg 1985) continue to write about the ability of creativity and creative methods to transcend cultural boundaries, but not necessarily within the context of youth studies. And so this particular branch of scholarship on religion and creativity—or what some of the youth here prefer to call faith rather than religion (which they believe has too many negative connotations)—remains scarce.

To be clear, we are not talking about religious art per se, or art that primarily addresses religious icons or iconography. In pivotal handbooks on creativity (Kaufman and Sternberg 2010, 2006; Sternberg 1999), cross-cultural creativity is highlighted, and these highlights intersect with the kind of faith-based creativity that can be regarded as spirituality-informed creativity. Yet as Lubart stated in 1999, all forms of creativity are widely accepted to be informed by cultural practices and contexts:

> Concerning a work ethic of accomplishment and achievement, we have already seen how the Western definition of creativity focuses on tangible creative products. The value placed on being active and productive should foster creativity as measured by Western standards. It is worth highlighting that Western creativity tests such as those developed by Torrance specifically note fluidity—the number of ideas produced in response to a problem—as one aspect of creativity. With regard to a belief in progress and optimism toward the future, theorists have proposed that cultures with such beliefs empower people to work on improving the world (Arieti 1976). . . . These beliefs imply a cultural acceptance of change, growth, and movement from the status quo. Those cultures that do not maintain faith in progress and have a pessimistic view of the future are believed to stifle creativity in general.
>
> (Lubart 1999, 345)

These young people's expressions of creativity go beyond mere cultural reductionism, and beyond expressions of their faith. As far back as Stein (1953) and more recently in Rudowicz (2003), scholars have argued that the meeting of creativity and culture is a two-way exchange. While Lubart and Sternberg (1998) are among the most prominent creativity scholars to note the confluence of cognitive and environmental factors in creative processes and products, they have also written clearly nearly a generation ago about the culture-based and co-constitutive differences in both definitions of, and ways of doing, creativity. Cross-cultural understanding is core to a nuanced appreciation of creativity and its socio-cultural functions.

More recently however, Xinfa et al (2013), in a cross-cultural study comparing German and Chinese students' creativity, have found that the relationship between culture and creativity does not indicate measurable or reliable differences, even in the presence of consistent definitions of creativity. For South Sudanese Australians and others who are often conflated into hegemonic categories of 'migrant' or 'brown' or 'Africans' after resettlement, intersections of creativity and culture can also be problematic or at least inconclusive (Harris 2015a). For some, despite their cultural and religious differences, they are reduced in resettlement to 'cultural' performances that reinforce stereotypes and sometimes completely ignore creative skills or deficiencies. For example, South Sudanese youth often get asked to perform as drummers or rappers despite some insisting that they do not know how.

The South Sudanese youth who share their views here continue to find creative ways of not only holding on to culture while integrating into western resettlement contexts, but also of merging strong Christian values with more secular western cultural practices and beliefs here in Australia and elsewhere in the west. While South Sudanese and Somali youth have articulated their different experiences here in Australia, they have also identified many parallel experiences (Gifford, Correa-Velez, and Sampson 2009). Overseas, Murray Forman looks at the ways in which Somali refugee-background youth are 'sutured' into American and Canadian school and public life in Maira's and Soep's (2005) book *Youthscapes*:

> Somali youths [like the South Sudanese youth in this book] generally arrive on this continent with limited 'cultural capital' in relation to international cultural repertoires. They consume the images and styles of their teen counterparts in acts of symbolic creativity, inflecting them with their own relevant meanings in a performative mode with the school conforming to Diawara's notion of a performative space. Clearly, there is a process of reinterpretation and reinvention underway.
>
> (Forman 2005, 17)

This process of reinterpretation and reinvention is both creative and spiritual for the youth in this book. As Carl Leggo (2015) articulates so well, voice is at the centre of being present, both in faith-based praise and in creative flow: "The heart's iamb reminds me *I am*, ontologically located in relationship to all creatures and creation" (Leggo 2015, 160), yet he does not claim that we lose or cannot find our voices, but rather (following Carol Gilligan 2002) that "we lose our desire or courage or will or ability to use our voices to tell our stories . . . so we need to recover or uncover or discover our voices. We need to attend to our souls, our psyches, to the breath and life that is in us" (Leggo 2015, 160).

Appadurai's Post-National Imaginary and Diasporic Public Spheres

As Appadurai tells us, "locality is an inherently fragile social achievement" (Appadurai 1996, 209), all the more precarious as this unfolding 21st century goes on. He makes sense of "modernity as embodied sensation . . . and ended face-to-face with modernity-as-theory" by thematising "certain

Section 2 Overview 125

cultural facts and us[ing] them to open up the relationship between modernization as fact and as theory" (1996, 2). Similarly, here I am hoping that my thematisation of certain cultural facts drawn from my relationships with these South Sudanese youth can be used by readers to open up the relationships between contemporary creativity as fact and as theory, co-constituted by both interculture and faith.

Appadurai distinguishes between migrants like myself, who have moved for reasons of "work, wealth, and opportunity" (6) and those like refugees and others, who move amidst circumstances of despair and terror. Importantly (and often overlooked), he links migratory flows to imagination (and yes, to creativity), in that,

> we may speak of diasporas of hope, diasporas of terror, and diasporas of despair. But in every case, these diasporas bring the force of the imagination, as both memory and desire, into the lives of many ordinary people, into mythographies different from the disciplines of myth and ritual of the classic sort . . . these new mythographies are charters for new social projects.
>
> (6)

One thing that unites these Samoan and South Sudanese young migrants and myself is a popular culture in which "those who wish to move, those who have moved, those who wish to return, and those who choose to stay rarely formulate their plans outside the sphere of radio and television, cassettes and videos, newsprint and telephone" (6), and of course today of primary importance is new and digital media. The relationships for these youth between digital media and their creative expressions are central to Appadurai's linking of the imaginary and post-national identifications, his notion of the altered role of the imagination in modern life:

> The image, the imagined, the imaginary—these are all terms that direct us to something critical and new in global cultural processes: *the imagination as a social practice*. No longer mere fantasy (opium for the masses whose real work is elsewhere), no longer simple escape (from a world defined principally by more concrete purposes and structures), no longer elite pastime (thus not relevant to the lives of ordinary people), and no longer mere contemplation (irrelevant for new forms of desire and subjectivity), the imagination has become an organized field of social practices, a form of work (in the sense of both labor and culturally organized practice), and a form of negotiation between sites of agency (individuals) and globally defined fields of possibility. This unleashing of the imagination links the play of pastiche (in some settings) to the terror and coercion of states and their competitors. The imagination is now central to all forms of agency, is itself a social fact, and is the key component of the new global order.
>
> (1996, 31)

126 *Religion, Art, and a South Sudanese Post-National Imaginary*

That Appadurai was arguing this nearly twenty years ago only highlights the ways in which this imaginary is expanded by our increasingly mediated world, especially for localised young people. For migrants like the South Sudanese in these last three chapters, "both the politics of adaptation to new environments and the stimulus to move or return are deeply affected by a mass-mediated imaginary that frequently transcends national space" (Appadurai 1996, 6). The importance of social media in particular is evident in the commentary of all these youth: Vineta and her Samoan peers in Section One, who are deeply connected to other Samoans through social media, not in spite of the digital media that is so often characterised as alienating and virtual, and for the South Sudanese youth in this final section, who not only use social media for the dissemination of their imaginative creations but also actively form new social imaginaries through the networks they are thus able to maintain.

Their creative and communal uses of social and other digital media applications contradicts what Appadurai claims, including that, in contemporary life, "the imagination will be stunted by the forces of commoditization, industrial capitalism, and the generalized regimentation and secularization of the world"[3] (1996, 6), a late capitalist world in which contemporary global culture is a "space of shrinking religiosity (and greater scientism), less play (and increasingly regimented leisure), and inhibited spontaneity at every level" (6). Appadurai asserts instead that digital technology and mass media in particular "often provokes resistance, irony, selectivity, and in general, *agency*" (7), and the narratives of the Samoan and South Sudanese youth here reflect this. His examples of the ways in which the non-western world or non-dominant cultural actors are using the internet and other mass media in creative, imaginative, and unique ways are not so different from the works and strategies of the young people in this book. Indeed, they represent just such a 'politics of hope' (2013) that Appadurai encourages us to nurture, facilitated (not inhibited) by social and digital media—now more evident than when he first articulated these views.

Instead, Appadurai claims a concrete connection between digital imaginaries and material conditions in that "the imagination has a projective sense about it, the sense of being a prelude to some sort of expression, whether aesthetic or otherwise. . . . Imagination, especially when collective, can become the fuel for action" (1996, 7). And these youth do use their imaginations—both individual and collective—as fuel. In the remainder of this book you'll see examples from South Sudanese young people of the ways in which they increasingly expand into creative social imaginaries that are only beginning to be felt in the global south. By drawing voraciously from across the globe on examples of the kinds of material success and creative agency they wish to embody, regardless of national boundaries and identities, these young people are dissolving nation-state borders as a by-product of their living, their imaginings, and their becoming, finding others who share their values and visions.

Appadurai extends Benedict Anderson (1983) in reminding us of the ways in which mass media can create such senses of community, or what he has called "community of sentiment" (Appadurai 1990), "a group that begins to imagine and feel things together" (Appadurai 1996, 8). This is exactly the kind of grouping that these young people establish and then consolidate in their creative commentaries and activities. More perhaps than any generation before them, these migrant youth can articulate the kind of code-switching increasingly required of tomorrow's globally mobile creative citizens. This is not to minimise the racial and xenophobic bias they encounter on a regular basis, yet there is a kind of forward motion in their creativity and the global future they imagine and create through their families, churches, and artworks.

Appadurai says of his theory of the collective imagination, "My approach to the break caused by the joint force of electronic mediation and mass migration is explicitly transnational—even postnational" (9). By transcending nation-based borders that occupied the thinking and doing of subjectivities and collectivities even a generation ago, these young South Sudanese Australians embody what Appadurai envisioned. Today, while nationhood means different things in different places, and the pressure of global economics means that some states remain more nation-identified than others, digital media continue to at least assist in the project of interrupting nation-based borders (while some would argue erecting others in their place).

Globalism Versus Localism

Like Thomas Piketty's (2014) economic analysis, O'Connor and Gibson (2014) link the local/global and urban/rural continua that they claim must inform a re-balanced and sustainable national functionality:

> Though the erosion of national identity in a globalising world is easily overplayed, it is clear that urban identification—though mobile, multiple, temporary—is becoming a crucial part of contemporary social cohesion. From our perspective, this does not just concern symbolic identification—through various multicultural initiatives and projects—but also the ability to participate directly in that cultural economy. In fact the two are linked: unless there is diversity of production, there will not be diversity in provision.
>
> (2014, 62)

The relationship between the local and global cannot be only economic. If creativity has adopted a neoliberal slant, imagination and its role in nation-building is going in the opposite direction. Appadurai's notion of a new imaginary as "a social structure-in-the-making", and the ways in which "his imaginaries and social structures are co-constitutive", (Harris 2014, 4) may help bridge the imagination/creativity divide as well as the local/global one. For the young people here, creativity serves a praise function, not just an

128 *Religion, Art, and a South Sudanese Post-National Imaginary*

aspirational or aesthetic one, as I have explored earlier with the Samoan youth. Yet imagination plays an equally potent role in this praise work: to a very real degree, the audience for their creative endeavours is not only their fellow religious and creative youth, but their conception of a God itself.

In Appaduraian terms, these youth are using their creative capital in conjunction with a kind of social imaginary that helps them to

> constitute the notion of the imaginary as a social field, which is both future-focused and also already existent. Through intersecting scapes, participant-citizens co-create new modes of social organisation and emergence that are based in current capabilities and identities as well as emergent ones; driven by intersubjectivities and also capital flow structures and nation-states. Creativity is one such flashpoint in contemporary global culture.
>
> (Harris 2014, 4–5)

These young people's creative celebrations of their faith cultures are certainly collectively creating a new social field for themselves. In order to do this, they not only use their communities and own bodies as the sites of that creativity, but they effectively use digital and social media to network the local and global spheres and create their new social field(s). Of course, attention to time and temporality matters here, as an imaginary—Appaduraian or otherwise—is by its nature a future-focused activity or spatiality, and temporality remains an important constitutive tension of creativity yet often goes unremarked in creative economies discourse. Perhaps creativity is the always present and future expression of Appadurai's imaginary, or as Erin Manning has put it, creativity (and novelty) "occurs always in the present: novelty emerges through the time-slip between reality and appearance. Because the present takes form on the threshold of appearance and reality, the present must be conceptualized as operating in the midst of the virtual becoming actualized" (2009, 68). It is this interstitial space between the conceptualised and actualized that these young people and their creative work inhabits.

I want to pick up here a point I floated but did not fully explore in my book *The Creative Turn*, the possibility that "the quest for a reproducible creativity today echoes many aspects of Benjamin's argument" (5), and that by problematising a digital productivity continuum from Walter Benjamin through Marshall McLuhan to today's democratisation and commodification of creativity, we might gain greater insight into "creative reproducibility and the modern productivity imperative" (5), the move perhaps from 'mechanical reproduction' to 'digital reproduction'. The ways in which these youth use digital reproduction of their creative works points to the hybrid identities and creative practices that I discussed in Section One. Like mainstream media, their digital works "also tell us something about our increasingly singular world culture, global flows and knowledge economies" (Harris 2014, 10). While these youth are able to create new kinds of faith practices and communities through their use of digital media, they are also sometimes read as nascent creative products, sometimes but not always accompanied by aspirations for 'fame', 'fortune', and 'success'.

As I have noted, this intersection between growing creative economic markets and this kind of culturally rich creative productivity demonstrates in one way how an "insatiable need for creative products is linked to instantaneous dissemination in digital markets" (Harris 2014, 10). In this way, their expressions of faith- and culture-based creativity provide another kind of example of not only self-made communities through social media and the establishment of new social fields, but also the kind of local/global intersections that are increasingly of interest to creative and cultural industries scholars. They are two sides of the same coin, once again returning to O'Connor and Gibson:

> According to Manuel Castells . . . the division between globalism and localism 'is one of the most fundamental contradictions emerging in our globalised, urbanised, networked world'. This presents opportunities for analyses and approaches to social cohesion policy that cut across typical divisions and issues based on 'old' versus 'new' Australians. New approaches could bring to the fore the challenge of integration into the world of 21st century opportunities, not just for socially excluded migrants, but also—and perhaps even more so—for many Australian-born. They need to account for people and urban spaces that derive their meaning and identity from global mobility and connectedness and those that find them in the local place.
>
> (2014, 57)

Indeed, this relationship between the two can be seen through a "Deleuzian lens on the capitalist and cultural implications of creativity . . . in his notion of 'differentiation' which offers a way of understanding the cultural changes affected by creativity" (Hickey Moody 2013, 129). Adorno too addressed "aesthetics and commodification, including a concern with the hegemonising affects of capitalism on the process and cultural role of creativity" (Harris 2014, 113). Indeed, creativity is always culturally situated, but it is discursively situated too.

I offer this review of the imaginary in relation to the creative industries and cultural economy in order to set the majoritarian scene against which these minoritarian young people live, work, and create: against tensions that are pervasive in discussions of creative capital and commodified notions of contemporary creativity. However, I also ask readers to consider what might be possible if, in our consideration of 'creative capital', we abandon or at least more daringly problematise Bourdieu's approach to accrual and instead look to contemporary (post)feminist critical scholars like Jessica Ringrose[4] (2015), thus moving toward considerations of capital that may be read as decidedly un-capitalist. If O'Connor's main concern with creative

130 *Religion, Art, and a South Sudanese Post-National Imaginary*

industries is its narrowness and unsustainability, it is time to look beyond capital as well, particularly human-focused conceptions of it. O'Connor and Gibson (2014) claim that,

> *Creative Nation* was an attempt to articulate a newer version of the relationship between state and market, nation and cultural identity, in the context of a less deferential, more active, more educated, more diverse and more globally connected citizenship. Its multicultural vision . . . has been relatively successful. . . . Its opening up to commercial popular cultures has certainly become more the norm in the way we value culture, but . . . this embrace of non-state subsidised culture has been all too frequently reduced to an 'economic impact' in the form of the creative industries.
>
> (58)

Kate Shaw (2013) has made a similar point in her analysis of the non-creative-industries-identified creative subcultures in and around Melbourne, Australia, where the two youth communities in this book live and work. But whether creativity can (or should) truly be considered a form of capital, and how it impacts on cultural and youth practices and communities, is a central concern of this book. How does culture intersect these notions of capital, and can it be considered to be changing the notion not only of creativity but of cultural capital too?

I have noted that "if McLuhan believed that digital media would facilitate the establishment of a 'global village', 'dissolving borders and replacing individualistic capitalist print culture' (McLuhan 1962, 158), Benjamin was concerned with the auratic or artistic value of mechanical reproduction" (Harris 2014, 146), and these youth have goals for their creative endeavours that include artistic, spiritual, auratic, and economic ones. Both the Samoan and South Sudanese youth are keenly aware of the kinds of exoticisation that proliferate about them outside of their own communities, stereotypes that at times help advance their creative efforts and at times hold them back or pigeon-hole them into cultural creative ghettos. Yet they still seem to find ways of combining these multiple influences to create their own habitus in a way that works for them. As I have argued:

> The 21st-century turn does not mark a decline in aesthetics but rather a shift in aesthetics based on its 'transitoriness'. What Benjamin saw as secular/religious cults defined by aesthetics or ritual values has been replaced by other cultural practices, in ways that parallel organised aesthetics. . . . Unlike religion and its own accelerating turn toward conservatism, both creativity and aesthetics are characterised by speed, reproducibility and sameness, rather than aesthetic or affective impact. . . . Benjamin notes his 'turn' in both content *and* form

Section 2 Overview 131

(like McLuhan) as a difficult one, saying 'cult value does not give way without resistance' (Benjamin 219) . . . and is typified by works and 'work' (labour) which can be characterised as profitable and transferable, exportable,

(Harris 2014, 132)

or what I consider a shift from human capital to creative capital.

On Capital, Human and Otherwise

How might a conceptualisation of creative capital move beyond the limitations of a humanist nature? Certainly marketplace demands are reshaping definitions of creativity and creative work. As Salehi reminds us:

> If we accept that the formation of a paradigm is related to the context in which it emerges, I believe that both modernist and post-modernist discourses of creativity have been responsive to the needs of capitalism as a system of nomadic power and of constant de/reterritorialization. Today, the process of commodification plays a vital role in the construction and experience of contemporary subjectivity as well as the notion of creativity subjecting people to free-floating and nomadic forms of control. . . . The Deleuzian world is a state of flux, a constant differentiation. Creation, in such a world, is driven by differentiation. The only way to affirm these underlying processes of differentiation is in 'creative becoming'.
>
> (Salehi 2008, 283)

Creative becoming might still be considered a form of human capital, but alternatively it might be proposed as an alternate form of capital. By eschewing a strictly Bourdieuian approach to definitions of capital, creativity may offer a new form of capital in fluid contemporary global contexts. In this book I am interested, for example, in the way Benjamin and others foresaw "aspects of the human and creative capital implicated in the development of digital technology" (Harris 2014, 129), in order to prompt a reconsideration of creativity but also potentially of capital. Forms of capital overlap in the creation and in the experience of habitus, but with the mobility of digital and social media, forms of capital become more malleable. Whereas more traditional definitions of human capital may have pivoted on influences like education and health, productivity can now be regarded as nearly independent of human labour at all, with the emergence of robotic workforce capabilities suggesting a reshift in the 'outsourcing' trend of the last thirty years. If human capital remains contingent in large part upon education and health,

> their economic value lies in the effects they have on productivity: both education and health impact individuals' capacities to be 'productive'.

132 *Religion, Art, and a South Sudanese Post-National Imaginary*

Education and health have a considerable impact on individual wellbeing as well. In addition, global ranking of nation-states remains linked to a large extent to the educational attainment and health status of its population. . . . Three key areas contribute to the social capital of higher education and its positive effects on health promotion: self, context and behaviour. For each of these determinants, the creative aspect . . . has the potential to play a significant part.

(Harris 2014, 101)

I consider context as those factors including environment, social interactions, and social capital, and for these Samoan and South Sudanese young people, those factors are of utmost importance. For minoritarian youth, support and social networks that include peers but extend further (such as the religious communities here) are a crucial component of the context in which they construct their identities and identifications. These networks may be formed in any manner and are no longer limited by geo-locations and provide pivotal shaping and influencing of beliefs, values, and norms (Groot and van den Brink 2006). Dewey and Benjamin taken together offer a commentary on spirituality and creativity that still feels prescient today:

Two years before Benjamin published his famous essay, Dewey published *Art as Experience* (1934) in which he explored more deeply than in any of his later works the connection between aesthetics and the mystical. While I won't be so simplistic as to suggest that he was foreshadowing the confusion over definitions of creativity, art and innovation that are the central concern of this book, he did understand that the modern era would be characterised by a separation, alienation or a decoupling of the connection between art and spirituality that had existed for so long before. The popular appeal of Dewey's search for a connection between art, spirituality and education is one primary reason why his work is still read today—by educationalists if not philosophers. Yet the co-existence in time and space of Dewey and Benjamin between the wars may have something to tell us about the shared aspects of their visions.

(Harris 2014, 130)

We too exist in a time of conflict, and these simultaneous conflicts in the Middle East, in South Sudan, in shifting but frequent sites of terrorist, religious, and racially motivated attacks stimulate (not dampen) our search for affective connection with others. We seek collaborative and meaningful encounters, and our need to understand what makes us human grows stronger. Our interest in belonging, religion, faith-based groups, mindfulness practices, and new materialist, non-human, posthuman, and more-than-human considerations are a reflection of our deep concern for what is most central to being human. Our struggle with human-to-human empathy is only made clearer in our efforts (and frequent failures) at ecological and animal empathy and ethical behaviour. Our obsession with defining and measuring creativity is surely a reflection of our nostalgia for its ineffability and an extension of this yearning for deep experiences beyond use-value.

Previously I argued that creative capital might be comparable to Appadurai's tournaments of value, in that:

> In a formulation that echoes an analysis of creative capital today, Appadurai's tournaments are contingent upon 'not just status, rank, fame or reputation of actors, but the disposition of the central tokens of value in the society in question' (Appadurai 1986, 21). . . . While Appadurai drew on the darker view of contemporary culture evident in Anderson's *Imagined Communities* in his consideration of creative flows, culture and the dying nation-state, Anderson also informed Appadurai's articulation of 'post-national' global flows, ones I have suggested include a new formulation of creativity as capital.
>
> (in Harris 2014, 163–164)

The youth in this book are reflecting a creative capital value that is inclusive of cultural capital, but in new formations. They are extending but also challenging, as they do so, a Floridian conceptualisation of a creative class that pivots on the symbolic value of creativity, and on those who are allowed to perform it:

> Building on the 1990s knowledge economy, and Florida's (2007) articulation of the creative class that characterises our post-industrial culture, this new creative economy portends a shift from production to information, and calls for new 'modes of education' (xvii) to accompany new modes of knowledge. Yet this new creative economy—reflected in schools—is never far from considerations of material conditions and capital. The *Creative Capital Report* (2008) (in Peters and Araya 2010) defines 'creativity in relation to artistic, scientific and economic creativity' (xvii); like Robinson (2011) and Joubert (2001), these are conceptualisations of creativity as 'original ideas that have value'.
>
> (Harris 2014, 19)

Yet in this book my collaborators and I are problem-posing about not only who is defining that value, but how and why it is changing. The very suggestion of static forms of capital in today's accelerated consumer culture is reminiscent of outdated conceptions of nationhood, both of which no longer ring true; the borders between forms and exchanges of use-value (and nation-states) continue to dissolve, and in so doing to suggest new social imaginaries.

Post-national Imaginaries

The South Sudanese themselves are keenly aware of the mercurial nature of borders, for the world's newest state has been betrayed not only from the outside but from within, multiple times in its recent modern history alone. In such zones of liminality and precarity, the social imaginary that Appadurai argues for is in some ways far more recognisable than in more stable political contexts. As such, Appadurai articulates a "postnational imaginary" (1996, 177) in which youth like these South Sudanese and Samoan Australians contribute in important ways to emerging "post-national spaces" in which "the incapacity of the nation-state to tolerate diversity (as it seeks the homogeneity of its citizens, the simultaneity of its presence, the consensuality of its narrative, and the stability of its citizens) may, perhaps, be overcome" (1996, 177). These axes, according to Appadurai, exist along ethnic, religious, and other lines.

If Appadurai's prediction is correct that we are nearing the end of the nation-state as we have known it, his suggestion that "the materials for a post-national imaginary must be around us already" (21), based on the "relation between mass mediation and migration, the two facts that underpin my sense of the cultural politics of the global modern" (21), points us back to these diasporic young people who move so seamlessly (if not easily) between scapes and practices. In particular, we must look closely at what he calls 'diasporic public spheres'. Indeed, the South Sudanese youth you will meet in the following pages are taking public space in creative and agentic ways, and creating new versions of diasporic public spheres that Appadurai himself did not anticipate, but toward which he is moving in his more recent work on materiality and an anthropology of the future (2013). Who best to instruct us in its character and habits than these diasporic youth in our midst?

Notes

1 This number is currently estimated at 179,000 residents, and conditions remain challenging. Indeed, the attention of the global community has decreased since the height of the Sudanese crisis in the mid-2000s, making conditions in some respects harder than ever before.
2 For more, see also Nunn (2010) and Gifford et al (2009).
3 I wrote about the effects on creativity of this mass culture commodification in *The Creative Turn* (2014).
4 Ringrose and her collaborators extend Deleuze, Braidotti, and Grosz combining feminist and postfeminist thinking with new materialist and posthuman scholarship. Her 2015 essay has been helpful to my thinking for this book, especially how she discusses Guattari's 'four-field map of figuring out the coordinates of subjectivity'.

4 Imagining New Individualities/ New Collectivities

Ain't gonna stop . . . cuz I love hip hop
til I reach the top.
I go to school, get good education
To go to college, cuz I need that knowledge
People killing, stealing, getting locked up in
The dealin, so why slide with our crime.
Came to speak my mind
Make sure you all understand my rhymes.

(Queen Imogeen, from *Keeping It Real*
music video)

On Imagining and Imaginaries

In *Studying Urban Youth Culture: Primer* (2008), Greg Dimitriadis (with Lois Weis) writes on how researchers might re-conceptualise a more effective 'research imaginary', through the lens of multimodal and multi-faceted globalisation. Dimitriadis sought ways to think about researching youth cultures, including 'denaturalizing' the youth with "new research imaginaries" (2008a, 109). Included in his analysis were the "new forms of identity work in a time of globalization, including the role and importance of youth culture in a 'post-subculture' moment" (110), and the Samoan and South Sudanese young women featured here are in multiple ways representative of such a moment.

Dimitriadis draws on Appadurai's capacity to aspire, which Dimitriadis summarises as "the capacity to imaginatively link one's own personal problems and issues to a broader set of social, political, and economic forces and pressures—and to work to transform them" (2008b, 126). Such a capacity, claims Dimitriadis, is "necessary for a vibrant public sphere" (125). Dimitriadis deftly links Appadurai's notion of the individual within global flows with a critical education that is truly democratic. This is the kind of education that occurs not only within schools and other formal institutional structures, but also in community-based arts programs like *Culture Shack*, and church groups, arts groups, and youth programs.

136 *Religion, Art, and a South Sudanese Post-National Imaginary*

Like Dimitriadis' youth collaborators and research subjects, these youth and their performances of hybrid identities and 'code-switching' have also "opened up a more flexible notion of ideology critique, one that looked at the interpenetrations of 'class' and 'culture', showing how social actors both resisted and reproduced their class positions in practice" (110). For the South Sudanese young women involved in *Culture Shack*, their code-switching is not limited to African/western or Black/white or even home/resettlement. Rather, they continuously switch between maker/consumer, materialist/spiritualist, and collectivist/individualist. Their self-filmed (ethnocinematic) video clips, which document their creative and collectivist process during the period of the *Culture Shack* program, attest to the ways in which they move in and out of these collectivities, or what some scholars refer to as assemblages. In the following snapshot, the young women play off each other in resistant ways, but in the process reinforce a unity in responding to the ethnographic enquiry of their Samoan group member. It isn't until their facilitator Nantali weighs in with some serious and culturally grounded feedback that the conversation begins to deepen.

Melbourne, Australia

On April 18, 2011, on a brightly lit autumn morning in a mini-van winding through the streets of Footscray toward the multimedia studios of Youthworx Media where the South Sudanese (and one Samoan) young women made their hip hop music video, one of the young people filmed a conversation about 'what have you learned doing *Culture Shack*', the year-long engagement in community-based arts practice leading to a Certificate[1] pathway at the local university and technical college. Being early morning, most of the girls were uninterested in being serious or reflecting, asking Eseta, their Samoan peer and the only non-Sudanese member of the hip hop 'stream' of the program, to get the camera out of their faces. When she insistently asked about what they had liked best or learned during the applied two-week portion of the program, some joked that they had learned how to use Facebook, that they had learned nothing, and some named learning the skills to edit on Final Cut Pro and other software. But when Eseta turned the camera on the stream facilitator, Caribbean-Canadian rapper and educator Nantali Indongo, she had this to say:

Nantali: *I learnt about some history of . . . the Sudanese communities here and about the Samoan. I learnt that Samoan men tattoo from their hip to over their knee. And the women also tattoo their thigh, and it's a very significant symbol. I learnt that if in Sudan a lot of women are pregnant it's great because if you're breast-feeding you can leave your child with another woman who's breastfeeding.*

Achai: *No way, is that true? I didn't know that!*

Imagining New Individualities/New Collectivities   137

Nantali: *I learnt that going from Sudan to Egypt like many of the girls here was not always a fun experience, and sometimes in Egypt people weren't very nice to them, kinda racist at times. I learnt that in Footscray there are moments of violence.*

Afreem: *Moments of it every time!*

Nantali: *I learnt that Afreem and Ayet love each other very much. Like without each other it would be very hard.*

Afreem: *Nah!*

Nantali: *I liked that I met new people, most importantly. I liked that I met young women who are positive, are trying to do something with themselves, young women who are creative and didn't shy away from their creativity. I met some cool people in the community who are doing some good work to help those young people be leaders.*

And in her closing interview with one of the Australian program artists, Nantali had this to say:

> *I learnt a lot about their dedication to God. I'm really really amazed by this, cus I don't have a dedication to God like that, and . . . I'm so happy for them and . . . some of them went so far as to rap about God, and I learnt something in that, that whole religious culture for them, and what it means to them. They rapped about God and they rapped in Arabic and Swahili, so we had cultural exchanges from all those different levels.*

Not long after, a continuation of anti-African violence landed another young South Sudanese man in the hospital after being attacked by a group of young non-African men. In the mainstream media, he was roundly blamed for the altercation, a pattern common in the Australian press at that time. In response, our unit put out a media release which read, in part:

> *Local Sudanese young women recently completed a 2-week intensive with international hip hop star Nantali Indongo of multicultural rap group Nomadic Massive, at Footscray Community Arts Centre. The 14 young women who participated in the program learnt a history of hip hop, wrote original raps, recorded them with the artist's assistance at Kindred Studios in Footscray, and finally made them into a hot new music video with the help of social enterprise powerhouse Youthworx Media in Brunswick. All this while working toward a Certificate 3 in Creative Industries through Victoria University's arts education pathway. Culture Shack, a Victoria University School of Education program, offered workshops in playwriting and animation, in addition to the hip hop work with Indongo.*
>
> *The young women and the project team, led by Dr Anne Harris, are distressed by the recent negative media coverage of the Sudanese community, echoing a similar spate of news spots following the 2007*

murder of Liep Gony in Noble Park. "The Sudanese community in Melbourne is achieving great things, collectively and individually", says Dr Harris. "The fact that negative stories get picked up and positive ones like Culture Shack and the Miss South Sudan annual beauty pageant don't is frustrating to many community leaders, community members and their colleagues and friends".

Such friends include Indongo, who "was blown away" by the commitment of the participants. She says, "This is a community working toward something better", in which Sudanese youth like these are—contrary to some reports—eager to contribute and work hard:

> "Their engagement was spot-on, it was great. And I think they got even more excited and passionate about what they were doing—they were helping each other—I learnt about their experience here in Australia, as new immigrants and about their dedication to God . . . (they rapped about God), and they rapped in Arabic and Swahili, so we had cultural exchanges on many different levels".

I begin this chapter by drawing on both young women's experiences and the scholarship of Greg Dimitriadis on urban youth cultures in North America in order to comment not only on their commonalities, but on the need they highlight for work like Dimitriadis' to continue (2012, 2009). Research communities need it, and these young people need it. In these final chapters, I examine some ways in which these South Sudanese youth imagine new ways of being both individually and collectively, and how these constructions of identity are informed by both their cultural and religious backgrounds, contributing to the global flows which surround them, and in which they are immersed.

Figure 4.1 Hip-hopsters Dona and Rania. Photo and copyright, Anne Harris.

Imagining New Individualities/New Collectivities 139

They represent what Dimitriadis and Appadurai have both called an antedote to the "rise of violent fundamentalisms (including Islamic and Christian) around the world", which "is largely a response to the anxieties of our now firmly globalized and interpenetrated world" (Dimitriadis 2008a, ix). In his scholarly conversation here with Appadurai, Dimitriadis highlights the darker side of globalisation, the flip side of Appadurai's hopefulness, concluding in part that Appadurai's "global flows have not been met, on the whole, with cosmopolitan dispositions. Rather, they have been met with vicious fundamentalisms that aim for new and brutal kinds of clarities" (x). Dimitriadis finds reason for hope in the ways that "young people are crafting new identities and social networks using a range of globally generated and proliferating resources . . . moving both literally and figuratively, crossing national borders with their bodies as well as imaginations, constructing new and unexpected kinds of identities" (x). This is why I find the intersection of creativity, religion, and culture in these Samoan and South Sudanese youth so important and noteworthy: these young people are using all three loci as points of strength, imagination, and transcendence rather than separation and alienation.

'I Didn't Know There Were Black Canadians'

The *Culture Shack* project provided an opportunity to explore tensions in Melbourne's western suburbs (along racial, gendered, religious, and socio-economic lines) where these young people mostly live, as well as tensions within their artworks, which seem to exist between (a) impulses to perform and develop cultural identities; and (b) impulses to commodify culture and identity. The data I'm drawing on here (as with the Samoan youth concerning the *Culture Shack* program) were collected by both facilitators/artists/researchers and the youth-artists themselves over the course of approximately fifteen months throughout 2010–2012 using audio, video, and still recording devices (flipcams, video cameras, still cameras, disposable cameras, tape recorders), including the young people's own devices (phones, etc.) where possible. Interviews were transcribed and, along with observation notes, analysed using situational analysis (Clarke 2005) to identify the key themes and influences contributing to the young people's sense of cultural, educational, and creative success.

Alongside Dimitriadis' and Appadurai's cultural anthropological approaches, I apply in part a Bourdieuian logic and return to a consideration of educational aspirations, institutions, and systems of exclusion which these South Sudanese youth have navigated throughout their lives in this urban centre. Both *Culture Shack* and this book project were two collaborations (out of several we have conducted together) which offer an opportunity to revisit these young people's creative work to imagine and build new futures, despite their uneasy relationship with the 'capitals' required for school integration and dominant discourses of educational and workplace success. This chapter problematises a single incident in the

140   *Religion, Art, and a South Sudanese Post-National Imaginary*

Culture Shack program as emblematic of how creativity and creative practices are emerging as an alternative form of capital (as summarised in the Introduction), but—perhaps more importantly—might suggest alternative use-value structures that function differently from capital in other global flows, or—as Appadurai might have us consider it—along new imaginaries altogether.

I have written in previous chapters and elsewhere (Harris and Lemon 2012) about other critical incidents during the *Culture Shack* program, including about how the Samoan young women performed a dance of thanks for their drama workshop leader, and how it was (largely) misinterpreted by the white western scholars in attendance. Here I will turn instead to a moment between the South Sudanese youth and Nantali, their Caribbean-Canadian hip hop artist and workshop leader. I am not concerned with 'interpreting' such a critical incident for salient answers or foreclosed possibilities; rather, I hope to provoke readers' questioning about whether these aspirations are fragile and contingent, representing vulnerable identities, or if they are resilient aspirational ones that signal a build toward nascent identity formation. These young people used the creation of a hip hop song, lyrics, and ultimately co-created music video in order to synthesise their religious, linguistic, and emergent (multi)cultural identities, and in the process entered into new pedagogical considerations and conversations with their 'teachers', mentors, and peers.

Nantali Indongo, the hip hop artist who worked with our youth participants in the *Culture Shack* program, continues her artistic/educational work in Toronto with youth from refugee backgrounds. The project and book *Mapping Memories: Participatory Media, Place-Based Stories and Refugee Youth* is available online (see *Mapping Memories* in bibliography) and is a powerful example of "first-person narratives by youth with refugee experience" using digital stories, films, photovoice, soundscapes, and oral history. In this program, a number of short-term creative projects provided public and arts-based platforms for refugee-background Canadian youth to comment upon their experiences and share them with wider publics. One such sub-project, *Going Places*, joined forces with the Montreal YWCA to create what they have called "memoryscapes, a method of connecting personal stories to public places. In this workshop participants wrote stories and developed them into story soundscapes, which were shared on a city bus tour. As tour guides, the youth connected the past to the present, personal stories to public spaces, and offered insights into refugee youth experiences" (*Mapping Memories*, 'page' 1). Such creative public projects usefully connect both the place and space of the host community with the temporal continuity of migration and refugee experiences—that is, the process of 'leaving' and 'arriving' and 'integrating' in new communities is not a finite one but rather continues throughout the lifespan, impacting both the migrant and the host community (**http://www.mappingmemories.ca/video/hip-hop-no-pop**).

Culture Shack shared many of these dynamics, goals, and characteristics, but this chapter looks at one particular moment—a question—between Nantali, the South Sudanese young women, and a public audience. In this narrative, Nantali attempts to provoke a group discussion of the ways in which this creative work may be seen as culture-contingent—that is, integrating and synthesising divergent identities—or whether it is relentlessly commodified, even by the youth participants. Such market conditions of the commodified forms (including academic/pedagogical ones) are constantly impacting on their identities. Here I seek to avoid foreclosing ontological and conceptual possibilities but rather to stimulate further unravelling of complex cultural creative acts and interrelationships.

In order to do so, Bourdieu offers some foundations for understanding contemporary intersections of culture, capital, and creativity. His articulation of doxic aspirations, which come from populist mediations and normative productivity (doctor, lawyer), tell these young people what they should aspire to, and how. We know that Bourdieu suggests that values and beliefs circulate in complex ways through everyday lives, constituting logics and values that become "unquestionable for many . . . such logics acquire a taken-for-granted status as 'commonsense' or, in Bourdieu's terms, *doxa*" (Zipin et al 2015, 231). These carry a "power of symbolic violence since they codify the norms, and so select for the success, of those in relatively powerful positions, yet hold sway among others—whose lack of success thus appears justified as the result of 'deficits', or 'lacks', of aspiration or aptitude" (231). Zipin's three key strands extending Bourdieu—1) 'doxic aspirations' (what you should aspire to); 2) 'habituated mediations' (inherited through family culture, what is pursuable, so they pursue); and 3) 'subcultural doxic aspirations'—do not offer a structural solution, but do make transparent the meritocratic underpinnings of the capitalist inequities which these youth are up against.

As I discussed in Chapter Two, Appadurai (and Williams) theorise culture as representing a kind of 'pastness', and Appadurai suggests ways in which culture might be reconceptualised as a futurity of sorts. Aspiration here is linked inextricably with futurity, and what Zipin et al (2012) conceptualise as *funds of aspiration*, I have pointed to in my theorisation of *ethnocinema* (Harris 2015a, 2013a, 2013d), a methodology in which aspirational futures (through intercultural video method) are shared, mutually expressed, and collaboratively achieved. Where Zipin et al (2015) ask 'how, methodologically, can this (re)search for emergent aspirations be staged?', I answer with the suggestion that we can do so by conducting scholarly research that is applied, collaborative, and mutual (like ethnocinema and some other arts-based methods). Where the method is collaborative, the emergent aspiration (whether short- or long-term) will be more collaborative as well, and offer some ways of getting beyond the interview and survey approaches that limit traditional methodological approaches. Where Zipin, Appadurai, and others have sought the means for *capacitation*, which is embedded in "the

142   *Religion, Art, and a South Sudanese Post-National Imaginary*

cultural map in which aspirations are located" (Appadurai 2004, 83), I suggest that by working collaboratively using creative or practice-led methods, researchers are better able to understand not only their participants' cultural map and emplacement, but also their own.

Yet I agree with Zipin et al (2015) that we must "aim not only to research but also to *capacitate* aspirations that young people might hope to pursue" and that we "cannot simply prefer emergent over *habituated* aspirations . . . nor can we simply prefer emergent over *doxic* aspirations—the goals of which have long incited successful upward mobility for *some* from low SES communities" (242). But how best to capacitate is not always clear, and not always met with consensus. For those who move between cultures (especially for identity-forming young people), emergent aspirations are not always and only outside of the doxic aspiration zone. These young people are, after all, both diasporic as well as cohered within ethnic and racial communities.

In *Modernity at Large*, Appadurai asks, 'what does it mean to be diasporic?', and Nantali too provokes a consideration of this question. Does all creative endeavour within/by diasporic communities and subjects then require a kind of ethnically bounded self-reflexivity? There is a powerful contradiction in Nantali's provocation, which suggests not only a going-beyond of culture, but also a possibility of getting outside of the notion of commodity capital, or alternatively suggests a different kind of 'capital'—a creative capital—as I revisited in the Introduction of this book. Yet Zipin et al (2015, 2012) suggest that this kind of perspective might offer a way to go beyond capital itself, through a Funds of Knowledge approach.

I combine populist mediations with a consideration of 'habituated mediations' (in the habitus inherited through family cultures) to understand that which is pursuable for these South Sudanese young women, in relation to their engagement with this program. Within the context of habituated mediations, they connect to and pursue notions of 'hip hop star' because they have seen it (and through Appadurai's mediascapes it becomes real), and therefore it is able to be imagined—and imaginary. Despite a constant encounter with obstacles due to globalisation, workforce precarity, neoliberalism, and changing markets, in this space new imaginaries open up, as well as a more nuanced dynamic that Zipin et al (2015) have termed "*subcultural doxic* aspirations . . . a model of actually achieved aspiration from a marginalized locale . . . a fantasy for most in that, while many may feel called, very few are chosen" (235). While Nantali as 'hip hop star' and facilitator of *Culture Shack* might represent one such doxic aspiration-made-good, this chapter suggests that she does not represent a structural solution but rather an exception, a welcome symbol for these young people of absolution from the *doxa*-ruled and often exclusionary if more everyday success imperatives such as 'doctor', 'lawyer', or even 'teacher'.

Many out-of-reach aspirations for those from economically or racially marginalised communities are reinforced by the mass media's portrayal of the 'self-made man' and other white western tropes. In an educational context, this has repercussions of "symbolic violence that induces low SES students to see themselves as in deficit when not succeeding in pursuit of doxic goals is compounded when policy makers make simplistic judgements that these students and their families lack appropriate strategies" (Zipin et al 2015, 233).

The third kind of aspiration draws on Raymond Williams' (1958) 'structures of feeling' as residual and emergent structures of feeling that are an incipient, grounded form of imagination. Here linked to Appadurai's 'capacity to aspire' in these youth participants' cultural lifeworlds, through programs like *Culture Shack*, they have the ability to imagine new possibilities and new means of achieving them. In closing, I highlight a key tension of affirming cultural habitus and consciousness, and meeting the culture of the new place in ways that aren't just in finding synthesis but also at times through assimilating via popular culture. But in so doing, these young people are able to teach us their lived experiences through an emergent creative capital—lived experience that is multiple in consciousness but also in performativity, crossing dimensions of religion, gender, race, and creative orientations.

Figure 4.2 Lyrics review. Photo and copyright, Anne Harris.

A Complex Creative Moment, and a Fraught Question

Our public sharing day was the culmination of a year-long arts education pathway program and a two-week intensive creative holiday program that these twenty-four young people participated in, working with artists in three

144 *Religion, Art, and a South Sudanese Post-National Imaginary*

streams (detailed previously regarding the Samoan participation, in Chapter One). During the public sharing day, in discussion with the youth-artists, artist-mentors, and public audience, hip hop artist-mentor Nantali Indongo asked the South Sudanese youth a question which many of the young people identified as a turning point in the way they thought about the creative work they had done in that program, and a provocation that altered the direction of the public conversation that day.

While the discussion itself was not tape recorded, so there is no verbatim record of her words, I have paraphrased the question this way: "Is the purpose of all this to explore and further cultural identity of which you girls are members, or is it to become a famous artist?". While South Sudanese youth artist Dona responded affirmatively that it was both, the other young people were more reflective about the implications of the question. Indongo pressed further, querying whether *Culture Shack*'s intention was to help make commercially successful artists, or education pathways for all through the accessibility of the arts, or celebrate the cultural riches of these particular young people from migrant and refugee backgrounds. It was—and remains—an important question for all working within community arts and arts education. How, exactly, do we (and the youth we engage with) *capacitate* these multiple aspirations?

Zipin et al (2012) encourage educators and others to demand educational exchanges (both formal and informal) that "involve moving beyond discussions of futures defined in limited terms of the present or in terms of normative discourses about 'the future' such as those that conjure entrepreneurial individuals or groups pursuing social and economic mobility through capital-building efforts" (188), but also to pursue those outcomes which aspire *"towards potentially new communities-to-come*, characterised by more just forms of sociality . . . *in many creatively imaginative moments* [in order] to exceed the gravity of capital and its historic configuring of 'possible futures' " (188).

Drawing on Appadurai's capacity to aspire (2004), they encourage action, not just imagination, in that "capacities to imagine and aspire thus fuel each other, as activities neither of idle wish nor ideological confounding—nor of 'individual' effort—but as co-labours of *socially materialising productivity*", and they also "usher new forms of social life and relation into the world. In working imaginatively upon rapidly circulating (liquid) flows of imagery, they also feed new imaginaries into global circuits: they create *new funds of knowledge*" (Zipin et al 2012, 189).

Such links between creative endeavour and cultural identities were made clear by the relationship between Nantali and the South Sudanese young women. "As one young participant put it, 'Nantali is our culture queen. She talks about how art and culture fit together, so we talk about ours. She basically got us talking about culture' " (Harris 2013c, 127). What are we doing when we ask questions like Nantali's? I see this as a pedagogical question that may have more than one answer. In the *Culture Shack* project, the participants, artists, and researchers all seemed to recognise

Imagining New Individualities/New Collectivities   145

the interconnection of these happenings due to the world we/they live in, and the wider exchange-value framings of what it means to be an artist as against the use-value of what it means to 'have an education' or to 'be somebody'. For these young women, being somebody has more to do with the public pedagogies of popular culture and hip hop (L. Williams 2010) than it does with being South Sudanese, Christian, and music-lovers. By sharing and situating this thick description of intercultural exchange, I am posing a problematic that I believe can only fully be addressed with both theoretical and artistic approaches. The nature of the problematic/critical incident was both, and therefore can only be answered using both.

What does Nantali's question signify? It is a fraught question as much for her own identity as something between a pedagogue and performer, in that she tries to lead them to think about pedagogy and education in cultural terms, in alternative forms, but they really only want—perhaps can only imagine—the pop cultural frame/fame. Nantali poses her question not only for their artistic and educational futures, but for their identities as well. I am suggesting an alternative reading of this world/moment as a tension between the use-value of creative work for identity and for the creation of imaginaries in which young people already have capacities.

As a successful North American (Canadian) musician and teaching artist, Nantali may also be misreading this (new) world that she is working in, a world that is Australian but is also white/Black and western/non-western as inhabited uniquely by these 'students' of hers. She brings her own experiences (similarities and differences) to this work in a new cultural context, but ultimately only partially recognises that these young people are living as diasporic actors in a still-unfamiliar western context in which they wish 'to succeed'.

As Nantali tried to make explicit links with futures that are not popular-culturally mediated, she gained less uptake than when selling rap: "We were talking about 'you can become great rappers' something like that, and I just injected 'or you can become a great teacher and use rap to teach English writing, or whatever'" (Indongo interview transcripts) and no participants responded. Even for Nantali, who came with such capital in their eyes through her impressive online presence, there were limits and misperceptions. For example, the participants were shocked to learn that she was not African American ('she's Black and she raps'), and her cache as a hip hop artist is in tension with their disinterest in her self-perception and vocation as (and financially informed need to be) a teacher. Through this intercultural collaboration, Nantali too was working through her own intersectional complexities, including cultural ones. When asked if she had experienced it as an intercultural learning, she responds:

> Oh yeah. Yes. Absolutely. All those things that you named, even linguistically. . . . They started speaking to me in Arabic, we were laughing and I said 'people always speak to me in Arabic, I gotta learn' and they

146 *Religion, Art, and a South Sudanese Post-National Imaginary*

were like 'yes you do!'. And they rapped in Arabic as well, in Arabic and Swahili, yeah, so we had cultural exchanges from all those different levels . . . for sure.

In these kinds of critical moments, where a provocateur might ask what role the arts can play, Nantali's case suggests that such questions implicate both the asker and the asked, the witnesses and participants. Can community/ education arts programs like *Culture Shack* be only cultural maintenance, or must they always already also be commodified public pedagogies?

Other Approaches to Agency: Funds of Knowledge

The framework of Funds of Knowledge (developed by Moll et al 1992), "offers rich ways to counter the power of 'capitalising' logics that configure and constrain teaching and learning" (Zipin et al 2012, 179), but also the kinds of creative endeavour that occur in church and community locations such as those in this book. In these contexts, the pedagogical, spiritual, and cultural are intertwined: "Within the prevailing 'neoliberal' policy climate, curriculum is hedged in by multiple logics of capital: cultural, human and social" (179). They define cultural capital as that which is "historically materialised, deeply structuring and covertly institutionalised logic" (180) and which

> carries the accumulation logic of economic capital . . . cultural capital . . . includes 'official' curricula of selected knowledge forms and contents that in turn select for those who embody power-elite cultural capital. It also includes 'hidden' curricula by which learners are differentially regarded and treated by teachers and school systems, due to assumptions about their learning capacities based on attributes that signify 'higher' or 'lower' social position.
>
> (Zipin et al 2012, 180)

For those who ask questions like Nantali's social and creative critique about the 'good' of hip hop as a cultural and capitalist pivot, the Funds of Knowledge movement offers some ways of thinking about those multiple needs as interconnected, in that it

> does not disregard the need for learners to gain better opportunities through schooling to improve their life chances in the capitalising world as historically received . . . however, this is not sufficient . . . and joins a pragmatic need to engage learners . . . and to honour their cultural-historical lives . . . by *recognising a diversity* of cultural knowledge embodied by learners.
>
> (Zipin et al 2012, 181)

Imagining New Individualities/New Collectivities 147

Figure 4.3 Samoan and Sudanese collaborators and friends—Vineta, Achai, Rosada. Photo and copyright, Anne Harris.

Nantali's provocation is to challenge these young people about whether their creative endeavours and dreams are solely focused on working with their desires to be pop stars, or rather something bigger—namely, to advance their cultural locations and identities and funds of knowledge through creative expression. Perhaps it is neither, but rather about finding/creating alternative pathways that are not so alienating, so English-language-based. Such alternative 'funds' of knowledge might incorporate cultural knowledges, but there are many other values of using creative arts that go beyond just this.

The following link from 2012 spotlights Nantali's "Hip Hop No Pop" approach to teaching the historicity of hip hop and provides some insight into her project for hip hop as a culturally grounded public pedagogy:

http://nomadicwax.org/hip-hop-no-pop-workshop/

The fact that the South Sudanese young women in Melbourne brought their intensely religious and faith-based inflections to this work added a component that Nantali had not experienced before, and opened up an additional set of questions about identity. To the Melbourne young women, Nantali was a pop star, but she herself highlighted the power of creative expression as something much deeper than that. Nantali's theoretic about hip hop (not just pop) foregrounded the value of this artform as not just some kind of performance to make its practitioners 'famous', but yet she was able to convey that effectively to the Melbourne youth partly *because* of her 'beautiful', 'glamourous', and 'famous' North American identity.

148 *Religion, Art, and a South Sudanese Post-National Imaginary*

Aspirations are a complex weave of the possible and not-yet-possible, as the commentary from these South Sudanese and some of the Samoan young people showed. In follow-up focus groups and dialogues as part of this book project, several remarked on the shift from manual labour jobs (which they had predicted for themselves) to attending university (some are in community college/TAFE programs now, and some on their first-, second-, and third-round tries at university). For some, they noted, these may be small or incidental moves toward the kinds of aspirations they identified four years ago in that original *Culture Shack* program, yet for them and their families it is a pronounced difference. Vineta, for example, is enrolled in an Arts Management course at a major university here, while some of the others are studying Education, options that for them represent a happy midway between the chimera of medicine and law degrees versus careers in the arts, two extremes which both seemed unreachable.

In other contexts, Robert Hewison (2014) has noted the ways that a kind of chimeric 'creative Britain' shifted from the promise of success for the creative few supposedly to the many, a shift which parallels the turn from cultural to creative industries, and how their funding flows were reduced from the many to the few. Similarly, the 2015 Australian budget drastically reduced funding to our Australia Council in favour of a Federal Arts Minister who was given sweeping powers to change funding patterns and structures in our creative and cultural industries, and whose first act was to signal a turn from funding the many to the few. This neoliberal narrowing can be seen in Zipin, Sellar, and Hattman's (2012) 'many are called but few are chosen' analysis in favour of capacitating aspirations that are possible; yet it reminds us that aspirations are aspirations because they represent dreams, not just probabilities or necessities. Finding the middle ground between the possible and the fantastical is no easy task, and whether it is the job of education or not is a matter for another book; this text documents the ways in which creativity, as a lever for culture, faith, and youth, can build new roads to whatever future comes.

In *Culture Shack*, and in other creative and collaborative communities like church communities, these young people experience sites for synthesising their religions, languages, and recollections of places where they are/were the majority rather than a fragmented minority. Synthesising these deeply personal and unique aspects of their lives—aspects that all too often go unrecognised or are denigrated in countries of resettlement—is what Nantali's question suggested about how this work might be strengthened by its culture-contingent nature. This is in opposition to the program's aim, which was primarily focused on compelling the mainstream education system to recognise the 'market value' of these skills and passions (i.e., academic credit). Yet part of this (perhaps false) binary of cultural/capital is also the individual/collective nature of aspiration discourses. Zipin et al (2015) point out the

Imagining New Individualities/New Collectivities 149

nagging contradiction in aiming such *deficit discourse* at the less fortunate. On the one hand, it is applied to broad-based *social groupings* such as 'low SES'. On the other hand, mainstream invocations of aspiration deficit tend to signify a lack of motivation, in an *individualist* psychological register.

(Zipin et al 2015, 229)

Further, they point out the punitive tone of this individualist discursive strategy, a shift from a commitment to social welfare as in previous eras. Blaming the disenfranchised for what are framed as their 'wasted lives' (Bauman 2004) exonerates the ruling classes from any responsibility for the inequity or the suffering of others, and facilitates wealth-accumulation by the few at the cost of the many. Such global capital flows are the broader contextual canvas against which these Samoan and South Sudanese youth are fighting to gain ground for the contributions they can and want to make. If, as Bauman suggests, mobility is the new capital, these youth are indeed finding new ways of circulating themselves and achieving kinds of mobility that are wholly digital and creative (2006), while retaining their own particular brand of cultural and faith-informed world-views.

Creative Culture/s

Raymond Williams stated that "community can be the warmly persuasive word to describe an existing set of relationships, or the warmly persuasive word to describe an alternative set of relationships" (Williams 1983, 76). Not so different from Nantali's observation that *Culture Shack*, like many of these young South Sudanese women in their churches, created "a community working toward something better, and working toward something better in very similar ways . . . but in diverse contexts (Montreal and Melbourne)".

In one sense, a discussion of programs like *Culture Shack* can be understood as a scholarly analytic in which our data and conceptual tools should assist us in reaching coherent conclusions about these subjects; yet the program might more accurately be understood as a web of complexity of the evolving identities of kids from the power marginalised inner city suburbs of Melbourne along racial, ethnic, and economic lines when they wrestle with an arts project that draws that out. A more reliable analysis, however, might wonder what are the dilemmas of such a project, for the young people, the artists, and the researchers.

Still within the Australian context, Jane Wilkinson has looked at the social capital and networks of support that assist in resettlement of refugee-background youth, particularly how religious and church engagement fostered the students' habitus or disposition toward educational achievement, through building their social and cultural capital in diverse faith-based activities, particularly church youth groups, and their 'imaginings'

150 *Religion, Art, and a South Sudanese Post-National Imaginary*

(Appadurai 2004) for their education futures. Wilkinson and Langat (2012) have found that there is little research on religious involvement and educational achievement in students from refugee backgrounds (one exception was Bankston and Zhou 1994). In the UK context, a survey examining social capital and refugee integration with recent arrivals from refugee backgrounds found that regular support from religious groups was a significant factor in building social capital, and furthermore enhanced the chances of accessing employment and education (Cheung and Phillimore 2013). Wilkinson, Forsman, and Langat (2013) identified multiple out-of-school networks and practices (including religious) that positively impacted educational success of the Sudanese young people in their study.

Their research suggests that despite the 'deficit framing' of African youth from refugee backgrounds, there is considerable capital-building occurring *outside* of schools, yet it remains unremarked in the literature. Unlike Wilkinson, in this text I am not looking at how these areas of connection and endeavour build their overall educational capital, but rather at how it contributes to community-making or what Hickey-Moody has called 'little publics' (more on this in Chapters 5 and 6). But Wilkinson's work has made important links between religious commitment and educational achievement, resilience, and attainment (see also Barrett 2009). Barrett's study of African-American students living in inner urban areas claims that religious involvement can go some way toward compensating for low socio-economic challenges, yet African-American students are not migrant or refugee-background youth living a world away in Australia. Yet transcultural comparisons can offer important global contextualisations too, as Nantali notes in her relationship with her South Sudanese students:

> And then I learnt about their experience here in Australia, as new immigrants. And that kind of put me in a different context as well because . . . my parents are immigrants, but here I'm working with young people who are themselves recent immigrants, and some of their identity stuff resembled some of my identity issues, but then also are very different.

Benedict Anderson, and Appadurai, who has drawn on him extensively, encourage us to be skeptical of all truth-claims (Anderson 2006). If Anderson helped Appadurai theorise ethnoscapes made up of geographically reimagined and reconfigured communities, in this chapter I argue that neither Anderson nor Appadurai went far enough in stimulating a consideration of diverse alterities. Gender and race, for example, emerge and re-emerge in new imaginaries, including creative ones. Building on the 'imagined communities' made possible in new ways through creative use of online

Imagining New Individualities/New Collectivities   151

technologies, the South Sudanese young women featured in this section can be understood through Anderson's skepticism of the nation-state to imagine new ways of expressing and nurturing creative identities.

Appadurai's notion of 'scapes' may be seen as falling short in its ability to respond to a current need to create new aesthetic communities that can serve to organise beyond capital/industrial needs—as Moll et al's (1992) Funds of Knowledge point toward an alternative knowledge structure that goes beyond capital structures. Unlike Anderson's claim that this aesthetic imaginary is a conscious one, both the creative cultural work *and* the doxic aspirations of these young South Sudanese women demonstrate how pervasively and unconsciously commodifying thinking can work. That these young women have dreams of music and dance 'fame', as well as a deep need to share their cultural and diasporic experiences, are not contradictory impulses. Indeed their lives and creative activities evidence both aesthetic and intellectual activism, particularly those from subaltern subjectivities like these who are establishing and commodifying their emergent and reconfigured individual and collective identities for a world market.

Creative Intermediaries and the Economic Imaginary

Seen through a lens of creative and cultural industries, O'Connor has articulated what he calls 'cultural intermediaries'.[2] He borrows from Bourdieu's "discussion of the 'new petty-bourgeoisie' . . . [and which] was subsequently conflated with a small fraction of this class . . . ', most of whom are the producers of cultural programmes on TV (television) and radio or the critics of 'quality' newspapers and magazines and all the writer-journalists and journalist-writers" (O'Connor 2013, 3). Any nuanced discussion of the cultural/creative industries tension must include this attention to the actors or intermediaries who perform these socio-cultural functions, both embodying the difference and also the changing role of creativity in these spheres. Continuing to draw on Bourdieu to argue what I am calling a new form of capital—a creative capital—O'Connor says:

> Bourdieu is rather disparaging of the expansion of a 'middle brow' media sphere reporting on artistic and intellectual matters for the layperson browsing the Sunday supplements, just as he dismisses their attempt to subvert or loosen cultural hierarchies through the destabilization of boundaries of legitimate and popular culture . . . these new cultural intermediaries were more than just critics and producers of cultural programmes in a new expanded media; they were a broader group providing an ever-growing range of 'symbolic goods and services' and . . . we were concerned to validate, to 'create an audience . . . for new symbolic goods and experiences, for the intellectual and artistic

152 *Religion, Art, and a South Sudanese Post-National Imaginary*

way of life' (45) or as Bourdieu (1984) wrote: 'make available to almost everyone the distinctive poses, the distinctive games and other signs of inner riches previously reserved for intellectuals'.

(O'Connor 2013, 4)

These cultural intermediaries, and O'Connor's interest in them, however, are primarily instructive for our purposes here in their attention to class mobilities and "social transformations". This

> popularization of the 'artistic lifestyle' was . . . not just a destabilization of cultural hierarchies but also a disembedding of identity from class-based (and even nation-based) 'common cultures'. For Lash and Urry, postmodern society is no longer organised around the fixed space-time coordinates of the modern industrial nation-state. Following Ulrich Beck and Anthony Giddens, they conceive individuals as faced with proliferating choices demanding increased 'reflexivity'. The grounds of judgment are no longer supplied by the immediate social structures to which one 'belongs' but rather by 'distanciated' information or expert systems'.

(O'Connor 2013, 4)However, whereas for Beck and Giddens these 'expert systems' were informational or scientific-rational, for Lash and Urry this disembedded self is increasingly based on 'aesthetic reflexivity' (in O'Connor 2013, 4). New fields of employment and education are opening up as a result of this reframing of elite cultural and aesthetic knowledge or expertise, and I think the Samoan youth certainly can be (are beginning to be) regarded as such for both dance and vocal expertise, as the South Sudanese are for both music and fashion. But they are also framed as having expert cultural knowledge, an increasingly rare set of practices and understandings against a globally mobile landscape in which coherent sets of traditional cultural practices are breaking down so rapidly. Hence, traditional knowledge is certainly also regarded as 'expert knowledge' in a way that has market value, rather than simply the stereotypical, objectifying, and harmful exoticised 'noble savage' Rousseau-construction which reached its Samoan pinnacle with Margaret Mead's anthropological representations and South Sudanese 'Lost Boys' narratives. O'Connor frames it thusly:

> The fourth aspect of new cultural intermediaries concerned their employment within an expanding sphere of culture. Their employment prospects derived from the specific expertise in the kinds of aesthetic knowledge required to navigate these new fields of cultural production and consumption, and as they 'rapidly circulate information between formerly sealed off areas of culture' they benefit from 'the emergence of

Imagining New Individualities/New Collectivities 153

new communication channels under conditions of intensified competition' (Featherstone 1991, 10). As 'conveyers of culture, elaborating and re-elaborating meanings for the public' (Bovone 1990, 81), they found employment through new and fluid kinds of career openings.

(in O'Connor 2013, 4)

Such career openings, it must be said, have always existed, but were not considered part of any 'career' track at all—in the UK and elsewhere. In fact, O'Connor in drawing on Bovone acknowledges that at the time, the cultural intermediaries as a profession became an "innovative outlet for all those who . . . cannot make a living, as an artist or intellectual in the pure sense of the term. . . . The education curriculum of the 'artist' or 'intellectual' in post-industrial society inevitably makes them into employees or, perhaps, free-lance professionals" (Bovone 1990, 81). These new career possibilities opened up in what O'Connor calls "an expanded field of education, commercial media and new metropolitan cultures" (4). Such so-called careers demanded a new kind of artist-entrepreneur, who had to be "able to occupy and negotiate these new spaces of 'freelance professional' culture. This was not a 'commercialization' of culture, as in Bourdieu, for it brought with it many of the 'artistic' or 'bohemian' demands and aspirations associated with [it]" (O'Connor 2013, 5).

Understanding Creative Capital as Culturally Constituted

Giuffre draws on Bourdieu's claim that scarcity gives value to cultural capital, and I use this same definition to problematise the notion of creative capital as having decreasing value due to its shrinking scarcity in new creativity discourses. That is, as more and more products and services are considered 'creative', their capital or market value decreases, while in Bourdieuian terms, increasingly scarce cultural capital continues to rise. I draw at length on my previous framing:

It may be impossible to define creative capital today without defining it in relation to 'creative industries'. . . . Davies and Sigthorssun tell us that 'the creative industries is a metaphor, which implies that creative production has been industrialised, set up in factory-like structures and managed along the same principles as the manufacture of any other mass-market goods' (2013, ix), in other words as human capital-driven. Yet, 'Adorno and Horkheimer's universal conception of the cultural commodity, where 'the mere existence of an industrial form of production lead them to lump together jazz and comic strips, radio and cinema' (Mattelart and Piemme 1982, 53 in Flew 2012, 62) is an earlier example of the way in which mass production has blurred the lines between aesthetics and commodities. The creative and knowledge

154 *Religion, Art, and a South Sudanese Post-National Imaginary*

economies represent a shift away from human capital to other capital—in other words, it is no longer about the work of people but about a new understanding of creative capital in Bourdieuian terms. 'Urbanists have used the term . . . creative capital to refer to the putative economic benefits for arts spending and creative industries for urban economies' (DiMaggio 2005, 169). If cultural capital has, in the past, been concerned primarily with 'aesthetic knowledge or its 'cultural heritage' (169), creative capital represents a new deployment and understanding of creativity in a 21st-century commodity culture. Yet as undiscovered as this sounds, it remains not so terribly far from Marx's own definitions of capital that prioritised over all else a concern with 'human activity and not the distribution of things. Humans are defined by their creative capacities. To be denied of the process creatively to labour, is to be denied our humanity' (Beilharz 2005, 10). Yet is it possible that in this new explosion of a so-called creative economy that 'mass consumption of mass-produced commodities is not a creative process' (Ritzer 2005, 492) yet might *appear* creative in the sense of being generative; that is, perfectly matched to a commodity culture which has an insatiable need for creating and fulfilling new markets, markets flooded with commodities of sameness?

(Harris 2014, 153–154)

Such commodities of sameness surely will or are increasingly turning to cultural difference as one source of creativity as well as capital. If these Samoan and South Sudanese young people do not consider their creative and faith-based creative labours to be a form of capital, they do explicitly recognise the commodity-based nature of the cultures in which they live, and in which they are trying to make a place for themselves. As O'Connor and Gibson have noted, "Australia's cultural diversity needs to be understood in the context of an enormous increase in global mobility over the past thirty years, a development which is having profound effects on societies and economies around the world" (2014, 51). They point out the ways in which Australia promotes itself as a multicultural society and welcomes culturally diverse tourists and migrants, linked directly to "Australia's location . . . culturally and intellectually in the Asia-Pacific region", an orientation if not identity in which the cultural benefits "could be considered as an end in themselves. But they also feed back into economic benefits: those who are attracted to Australia for cultural reasons are likely also to invest in the country, to develop business exchanges" (O'Connor and Gibson 2014, 54), or to consider it a destination for tourism, a good demonstration of the blurring of lines between economic, cultural, and policy considerations.

They do not, however, conflate or confuse the terms, highlighting the ways in which cultural industries go beyond capital concerns and speak to identity and nation-building: "The cultural industries have an important role

Imagining New Individualities/New Collectivities 155

to play in maximising the advantages which Australia might gain through cultural diversity . . . but they are also more than this, participating centrally in the formation of attitudes, values and modes of understanding" (2014, 55). More nuanced conversations at the local and national level are required in order to really engage with the cultural uniqueness and also cultural capital of Australia and its diverse population and geography, but such a more layered conversation has yet to happen in the still-halcyon era of Australian creative industries. Even the leaders of creative industries research and policy discourse here, Hartley et al (2012) from the Centre for Creative Industries, remind us that the "jargon of flexible creativity and innovation must not be allowed to obscure or sidestep difficult questions about creative labour. We need to get beyond this 'pro' versus 'anti' impasse, to rethink the categories of labour and work more fundamentally" (in Harris 2014, 65).

Others, including perhaps most prominently Erica McWilliam and Shane Dawson (2008, 2007) have written extensively on the role of creative industries to expand higher education more generally, and how creative pedagogies might improve toward increased sustainability. O'Connor and Gibson mostly reject the construct of creative industries outright, yet use it comparatively against a clarification of cultural economy, and for O'Connor, usually as a bellwether of the poor state of Australian government policy on the issue. For example,

> There is currently a major policy and agency vacuum within the cultural economy—or 'creative economy' as it is often called in its commercial varient. . . . Australia has a greater deficit in creative goods and a smaller surplus in creative services than comparable countries. . . . It is disinvesting in arts and cultural economy at a time when the market in the region is growing.
>
> (2014, 72)

Mostly though, they prefer the term cultural economy, which offers greater breadth to describe the interconnectedness of culture, creativity, and economic development. Such an approach to governance, they claim, "is not simply about 'the economics of culture' but an attempt to understand how this complex sector holds together, how it creates and circulates value(s), and how it might form an object of governance" (57). Creative industries, they detail, "is an inadequate descriptor, [as] it reduces cultural value to economic value, and indeed defines this economic value rather narrowly around 'innovation effects'. In addition cultural economy has an international currency, providing a strong base for comparison" (2014, 57). This international currency is the focus of many cultural economy scholars and analysts, but for this overview we will keep our focus fixed on the relationship of global and local in creativity discourses, as the meta-discourse framing the work and reception of the two youth groups featured in this text.

Figure 4.4 In the studio—Andria, Abul, Aluel. Photo and copyright, Anne Harris.

How These Youth Are Redefining the Creative Industries

Throughout this book, I am trying to underline some basic distinctions between contemporary creative industries and cultural industries, which are common to the many different paces at which they are unfolding (and in some cases appearing and disappearing) in different nations and regions. I have done so in order to set the scene for the ways in which these Samoan and South Sudanese young people might suggest that non-majoritarian cultural actors and creative makers are embodying and performing new ways of being creative and cultural professionals. While there are overlaps here with the kinds of creative teaching and learning lifespan that informs my other writing on creative industries and economy, my focus here is different: I am exploring how the material which follows is both creative *and* cultural in ways that are both capitalisable, but also importantly retain their religious and cultural character.

These kinds of examples might offer us a hopeful way forward in a field saturated with ubiquitous but vague notions of a creativity that must function socioculturally to save the planet. Extending my critique of this vagueness and ubiquity of creativity in education, I have stated previously that while "some scholars have sought since then to redefine creativity in education as creative pedagogies, creative learning and most recently creative industries . . . others continue to pursue a cognitive or capital measure of the elusive creativity. Well into the second decade of the twenty-first century,

Imagining New Individualities/New Collectivities   157

it seems clear that creativity is becoming a commodity that is increasingly sought but still not well understood" (Harris 2014, 18), and so I offer this book as another provocation to this question (or more accurately to its many over-simplistic responses). Here, these youth speak eloquently and creatively to how we might move forward in more holistic ways, but ways that also have marketplace 'value'.

They have expertise we can't afford to ignore, and they are empowered in ways for which we often still don't give them credit. Youth studies scholars, including Dolby and Rizvi,

> claim that 'youth move not only within the conditions that they encounter but in the ways in which they are agents of change and *produce* the new conditions for their lives' (2008, 8). As exemplars of these agentic young people, the Samoan young women made their own agency known both to themselves, their collaborators and audience. As such, they will no doubt continue to enact change both within their own cultural communities and global communities at large, shattering previous expectations and performances of embodied selves.
>
> (Harris and Lemon 2012, 430)

But Samoan and South Sudanese young people's creativity is "both performative (Butler 1993) and pedagogical (Ewing 2011) and has an important contribution to make to discourses of global pedagogical flows (Rizvi 2006)" (Harris and Lemon 2012, 430). This impasse offers an opportunity to re-examine the intersection of creativity, culture, and pedagogy in a way that might "interrupt the business as usual of social reproduction", visible in "age-old cultural traditions and their hybrid contemporary expressions which are both embodied and digitised in online worlds" (Harris and Lemon 2012, 430). A hybridisation of these worlds suggests new embodiments, and a pedagogical imaginary of the "public body . . . its movement and its voice" (Butler 2011). Such practices can be seen in diverse contexts, including classrooms, songwriting workshops, and other shared spaces in which "we require one another in dependency and desire" (Butler 2011). This section takes this collaborative examination of their embodied performances of self beyond creativity, beyond culture, and certainly beyond capital. The next chapter features the creative work of the South Sudanese youth and our shared commentary about how their creative, cultural, and faith-based selves are interrelated.

Conclusion

In this chapter I have suggested that creative arts—especially situated in the public pedagogies of community arts contexts—can be a capacitating practice for young people who don't often enough experience successes in a social structure that isn't designed for them. I argue that—more than just a

158 *Religion, Art, and a South Sudanese Post-National Imaginary*

tool for creative imaginaries and self-expression or cultural maintenance—such creative programs can build creative capital which has multiple values; they may provide alternative pathways into mainstream academic success, but can also provide tools for these young people to set their own terms of engagement, expanding social, cultural, and creative capital.

The very notion of culture can thus be challenged by those like these South Sudanese youth who are reconceptualising it through their lived and creative experiences. Here culture is "a very elitist notion of culture [that] exists side by side with another notion of culture—that of a 'whole way of life'" (Dimitriadis and Weis 2008, 17), a culturally vibrant way of life that these youth so dynamically share through their music. Synthesising religious, linguistic, ethnic, and gendered experiences, they can want pure self-expression and capitalist success at the same time—and why shouldn't they? The only difference between them and their western-born peers is that capitalism as a new (and in some ways de-contextualised) game incites them "to leap—without knowing how to choreograph these leaps—into *doxic* aspirations (of both mainstream and subcultural varieties)" (Zipin et al 2012, 242).

In this chapter I have intended not to answer the question of mainstream versus subcultural doxic aspirations, but rather to use one critical moment—a question—in order to look more closely at the multi-strands running through a cultural and creative exchange that seems superficially like 'idol worship' or even 'fandom'. I'm suggesting rather that this moment—and the relationship and exchange it represents—offers a much more complex reading of the multi-layered identity work occurring for both the youth and their artist-mentor. As Anita Harris has noted,

> Nowadays, subcultures are not perceived simply as singular, fixed categories that youth are affiliated to in order to work out their class identities or to resist dominant culture. Instead, theorists talk about neotribes, youth lifestyles, scenes, new communities and so on as momentary and changeable expressions of identity.
>
> (2012, 3)

And this chapter suggests that Nantali's question—and the hip hop music video that it focused on—are one such momentary and changeable flash-point of identity and community.

Appadurai's 'capacity to aspire' helps these South Sudanese youth participants to imagine, to discursively frame, to collaborate, and to pro-actively engage in constructing new forms of citizenship through creative methods like hip hop in the *Culture Shack* program. Following Appadurai, a range of capacities are needed now to thrive, including and importantly a capacity to imagine, especially diasporically. For Appadurai (as for Dimitriadis), diasporic imaginaries develop in pockets, and imagination becomes a social material process that offers necessary strategies for survival and success.

These South Sudanese youth show that creative arts—and music videos in particular—provide powerful tools for imagining their way out of and into new spaces. Yet the ways in which they continue to do this are complex and multi-layered, and include the complexities of their interrelationships with pedagogical and artistic others and audiences. The complexity of this multi-layered act of 'imagining' remains its greatest use-value, and in the next chapter I look at the gendered aspects of this new imaginary.

Notes

1 In Australia, community college (TAFE) qualifications run from Certificate 1 to Certificate 4, which can form a stepped programme into university entry or stand as TAFE terminal qualifications on their own.
2 See his article for a fuller explanation of this group and their role in the cultural and creative economies. O'Connor, Justin. 2013. "Intermediaries and Imaginaries in the Cultural and Creative Industries." *Regional Studies.*

5 The Art of Gender in South Sudanese Mediated Diasporas

Time for our laughter, time for our jokes.
Time for our Lord that we can spend on the phone
But what about the time that we lift up God's name?
He's Number One and it isn't a game.
God is the healer, He is the hero.
Helping the nations through all that I know.
Yes He'll never let go, cuz He sacrificed His son
And we knew the job was done.
But we look through foolish eyes and we heard the world cry.
People of this world, keep up with your prayers.
no time for delays
There's no time for joking, the kingdom of heaven is waiting for
  you!
  . . . people he's the God, people he's our Lord, people He's the one
reason why I'm livin' today.

(Sunday Major, from *Keeping It Real* music video)

Bourdieu made clear the complexity of capital and its relationship to power and use-value. Those theorising a range of notions of human capital attempt to frame all social actors as agentic and full of possibilities for capital, an ideology of late capitalism, regardless of considerations of gender and race. The South Sudanese young women who feature in this section are—like most of their peers—attempting to construct viable lives in social spaces not so relentlessly structured by capitals as those they see around them, as young people of colour, but importantly also as young women. Their efforts are partial and progressive, informed by the intersection of their artistic and faith practices, both of which suggest the possibility of something more.

For them, education and employment may not have captured their 'imaginary' of a new kind of life worth fighting for, yet as the data in this chapter shows, even as their expressions of faith are strong, they are equally drawn to capital, not dismissive of it. They don't have the habitus to fit these new countries of resettlement, as they may have had back home in Sudan (or

Figure 5.1 Writing and recording original raps—Winnie and Dona. Photo and copyright, Anne Harris.

even in transit in Kenya and Egypt). For them, arts practices like fashion, modelling, dance, and musical performance provide a way of experimenting with this unknown youth culture-in-the-making, and a rich way of dancing, singing, and slamming themselves into new imaginaries.

Mediated Creativity and Leapfrogging Doxa

Returning to the events that preceded this public showcase of the youth-artists' work, I would like to look more closely at the video that these South Sudanese young women in the hip hop stream created together, with the help of Nantali, at two local music studios. The video really represents two fluid constructions: the young people who made this video, as identities-in-formation, and the video itself, as an artefact of mediated creativity. By reading the video we are able to see the interconnectedness of the identity work connected to this diasporically fractured community, and the creative means by which they respond to those backgrounds.

By creating the music video *Keeping It Real*, these youth celebrate their gendered, cultural, and religious identities, because Nantali and the creation process leave them the artistic freedom to do that. But they also were (at that time) new arrivals in social spaces that they negotiate through both creative and intercultural performances. On the one hand they live corporeal identities-in-formation, creating their structures of feeling through the

162 *Religion, Art, and a South Sudanese Post-National Imaginary*

combination of interpersonal and creative social critique. But they also perform their imaginaries as generated through their current living situations and into the future, forming a kind of capacities to aspire, as seen in these processes and products. The next section will examine the ways in which Nantali and her technical support team were able to *capacitate* these aspirations in both creative (professional) and cultural (capital) ways.

View the music video *Keeping It Real* at the following link:

http://www.creativeresearchhub.com/#!cryc/h95tt

The 'doxa' for most of these youth represents a series of impossible hurdles, promising a hegemonic success story in which they are rarely present or represented. Yet with the process and products of creative capital, sometimes they can leapfrog these hurdles such as more traditional paths to success, and reach alternative kinds of knowledge and agency. And while Nantali's question represents something of a critical self-reflection, she realises the charismatic effect she has on these young women from the first moment, the moment of her introduction, in which she raps that she has come here to Melbourne to speak as a Black woman to her Black sisters. These are not the kinds of public or creative recognition the young women are used to experiencing.

Nantali began the hip hop workshop with a presentation on the history of the form, and she made it clear that her pedagogy was to tell an erased history of hip hop, not just play around in the form as a pasttime or experiment. The South Sudanese Australian youth-artists told her that they had only wanted to dance, not rap, because for them it was a gendered tradition in which boys rap and girls dance. They also explained this is why none of the boys in their groups or families attended the workshop, as they saw a workshop on 'hip hop' to be a dance workshop for girls.

Nantali's first introduction in the theatre where we would go on to spend the following two weeks together was—unlike the other artists'—an improvised performance in her form, straight off the plane. It was impressive, by any standard. In taking the microphone and introducing herself so, Nantali offered an illustration of a certain kind of agency, an aspiration, a signifier, an image—a node for their imaginaries—in which they shift from a certain corporeally located identity to one that could assimilate them as rap-cool, even as girls, especially as Black. It was a kind of creative capital that appeared to allow her (and by extension, them) literal and figurative mobility.

Nantali also represented a kind of aspirational investment in which she has the capital, but the young women have only the aspiration. Using her re-teach of hip hop as cultural truth, she shows excitement about that fusion, which even as it is occurring still leaves important room for valuing their ability to 're-teach' her North Americanness about their lived experiences, all new and important to her. This kind of cultural exchange, especially facilitated by the creative collaborations they were using (including the

The Art of Gender in South Sudanese Mediated Diasporas 163

ethnocinematic cross-videotaping they also employed), was able to honour multiple and complex realities. But Nantali's question on the final and public showcase day also moves this community-based collaborative arts work beyond public pedagogical value and beyond pure entertainment, and into one which asks 'can this kind of mobilization of complex cultural identity work (which is also emotional, aesthetic, imaginary, aspirational) be used pedagogically so that you don't have to be a beautiful girl in order to work this into some kind of meaningful place in your life?'

In her questioning, Nantali was critically interrogating herself as equally as she was provoking the youth or the audience. In her performance of 'entertainer' but also 'teacher', consciousness is complex, and multiple dialogues are occurring at once.

The aspirations she articulates are not separate from or innocent of the mediascape of daily life, and Nantali as a projection of a subcultural doxic identity (Zipin et al 2012) offers multiple challenges to the youth at once: if she 'misreads' the capital of the hip hop (i.e., challenges its probability as a means out of limited capitalist success futures), she also represents 'Nantali the internet hip hop star' and Nantali as a kind of (falsely imagined) 'American' proselytiser of 'Black power' through the artform of rap and hip hop. I suggest that the pivot point of her public questioning is what she expressed more private questions about: for South Sudanese youth in recent resettlement contexts, whether hip hop stardom is a sufficient way of understanding and perhaps pursuing power within capitalist structures, is an alternative response and strategy, or whether it is a kind of doxic aspiration that is, as Lauren Berlant (2011) would say, a kind of 'cruel optimism', doomed to failure.

It may, however, represent a kind of subdoxic imaginary or series of them that offers an alternative story. In a first possible subdoxic imaginary, Nantali's comment about the pop culture attraction of it is a lever for engaging the young women. Nantali used her 'sexiness' to get them to do something more complex, coax them into some kind of new imaginary, a coalition of hers and theirs, in which she sees the arts, and in some cases the church and other communities like this one, offering 'an important refuge out of the fighting on the streets' (Indongo transcript). However, Nantali's question and commentary both indicated another way in which she takes their lived experiences and creativity seriously: it is a recognition of what she embodies and represents, but also what work she sees as important to do in an ongoing or long-term project, so that these kinds of programs don't continue to be short-term ephemeral experiences.

Dimitriadis celebrated the "growing and important body of ethnographic work on young people and their uses of popular culture" (Dimitriadis 2009, 9), a field that has honoured and included the kinds of "creativity and effort that young people invest in the nonelite arts" (9). The kind of 'convergence culture' (Jenkins 2006) that typifies these South Sudanese young women, who move fluidly between digital devices and platforms like phones, computers, and films, has also been noted by youth scholars like

Figure 5.2 Loosening up and learning how to freestyle from Nantali. Photo and copyright, Anne Harris.

Anita Harris (2013), Dimitriadis (2009, 2008a, 2008b), and Henry Giroux (2005; 1992). However, despite our desire to understand these complex youth terrains, Dimitriadis claims that "the young people in such work remain largely faceless. We have little sense of either particular life courses or valued, local social networks and the institutions young people traverse" (Dimitriadis 2009, 10), and this is a serious charge to those of us claiming to work with 'emerging' identities of youth but not sticking around long enough to see the changes. My work with these groups of (largely female) South Sudanese and Samoan young people has continued for over a decade now, and in that time I have seen changes not only in them but also in the social context around them. These changes have been most marked in creative terms but also in gendered ones. The rest of this chapter then will be devoted first to an analysis of some ways in which the creative context of these young African Australian women is changing, followed by a section on the gendered contexts in which these young creatives live and work.

So Watch Me Rise: Creative Changes

> *How do you like it?*
> *Like it like this, and if you do*
> *grab a copy of Rania's disk*
> *. . . Strange in a way, yeah.*

The Art of Gender in South Sudanese Mediated Diasporas   165

I came to win, to conquer, to thrive,
Came to survive
To prosper, to fly
Don't care about enemies, don't care about friends.
. . . One following the next strength
They start coming, and I start running
Must be surprising cuz I'm just rising,
I fly, survive, I fly so watch me rise.
(Rania, in Arabic, from *Keeping It Real* music video)

"As Deleuze points out, no philosophy of creativity can be considered ahistorically" (Harris 2014, 2). I have been considering and writing about the question of creativity and its present commodification for many years now, and of course this consideration of commodification cannot be separated from a person's class, gender, or values (including use-value, or capital). "After all, the global commodity culture in which we find ourselves – amongst its other undeniable benefits such as social networking and global mobilities - demands data to be mined by corporations, governments and digital innovators, and extends even to ourselves." Nowhere are these questions and concerns—both creative and capitalist—more urgent than for South Sudanese young people. And despite what the great majority of youth-oriented literature (both scholarly and popular) would have us believe, this intersection (or contamination) might be as evident in the lives of the globally stationary as those who are globally (corporeally) mobile.

Indeed, the scholarship concerning creativity, education, and youth abounds with references to global flows, global creatives, educational networks, international data, and mobility, but it always refers to particular kinds of mobilities (in addition to Appadurai, see Rizvi and Lingard 2010; Kenway and Fahey 2009; Rizvi 2006). You could almost be forgiven for forgetting that almost everyone is now mobile (at least virtually), regardless of access to capital. The idea that online lifeworlds are determining more than informing offline communities is itself constrained by the very real material conditions of those who are networking—a point I have made in greater detail in my first book *Ethnocinema: Intercultural Arts Education* (2012), and which I further developed in my book *The Creative Turn: Toward a New Aesthetic Imaginary* (2014), which dealt explicitly with the notion of this new creativity as a form of capital. The young South Sudanese women in this book show with their creative works and their global networks that mobility now has many forms.

Yet many dyed-in-the-wool Bourdieuians bristle at the use of 'capital' when discussing the decidedly commodified turn creativity's cultural function has taken on in the past ten or fifteen years. It is not, they argue, truly comprised of habitus or fields, and therefore cannot be considered a new form of Bourdieuian capital in the manner he defined it. Yet Bourdieu himself was criticised for his schema, which some believe is itself too

166   *Religion, Art, and a South Sudanese Post-National Imaginary*

conceptually vague. Nonetheless, I tried in *The Creative Turn* to make my case for an expansion of his capitals in the 21st century to include creativity, and why I thought so. But increasingly discussions of creative capital, creative industries, and cultural economy are to be considered together but in tension with one another, and this book looks at the ways in which these two groups of young people performing creative labour, through culturally grounded expressions of their religious and faith practices, can be understood as representative of these tensions.

Part of the overarching conversation which contextualises their creative practices is our global south perspectives, which often get subsumed by discussions of hegemonic global flows that seem always to head into or out of the global north. For these South Sudanese and Samoan young people, the non-majoritarian perspectives are integral to the work they are making and the ways in which their mobilities manage to remain both local and global. O'Connor and Gibson tell us that cultural policy has changed dramatically over the past few decades, driven by "the rise of cultural consumption. . . . And though technologies of production, reproduction, distribution and social exchanges around these have been crucial, it is the aspirations toward enhanced and extended cultural participation that are most significant" (2014, 57).

Here I approach the problem from another angle, but remain unwilling to abandon the concept itself. I ask myself what might be possible if I problematise the very notion of 'creative capital' by abandoning Bourdieu's approach to 'accrual' and instead look to contemporary feminist scholars such as Jessica Ringrose, who draw on a different set of tools. Ringrose, for example, has caught my creative imagination by extending Deleuze and Guattari, Braidotti, Grosz, and others on the notion of 'schizofeminism' and Guattari's 'four-field map of figuring out the coordinates of subjectivity' (2015, 399). Considering creative capital as Ringrose does, by translating it into a schema of 'developing research methods', can be useful for thinking about what creativity is doing, both in the academy and in the marketplace.

My justification for pairing creative capital with post-structuralism is that it seems to give breathing room to the rapid marketplace evolutions, which sometimes seem to be proliferating faster than either our education or scholarly understandings of it, relegating creativity scholarship to a role of commentary rather than resistance. If critical creativity scholarship might play a greater role in education and cultural studies scholarship, it must become more fearless, more immediate, and less risk-averse than we are now.

Intersectionality, Creativity, and South Sudanese Youth Cultures

One irrefutable (if now well-documented) characteristic of creativity is the great proliferation of contradictions in definition and practice when trying to tie it down in any useful way (see Harris 2015a). Youth studies scholars

The Art of Gender in South Sudanese Mediated Diasporas   167

have articulated a similar mercurial aspect to the concept and discourses of youth that make it equally hard to apprehend in any systematic manner. Thus creativity and youth studies can be seen as likely bedfellows, and share some common characteristics, like novelty and chaos:

> the combination of chance and directed interest does suggest two general characteristics that, to us, seem evident in creative processes: novelty or the unprecedented, and order, or control and design. A control or design present in the activity and an unexpected or unprecedented appearance of a phenomenon or an entity are two of the marks of creativity.
>
> (Rothenberg and Hausman 1976, xi)

Creativity, like youth, is 'a contested term' (Yip and Page 2013), in which "the experiences and meanings associated with it are socially constituted, varying both cross-culturally and historically . . . underscored by, and interlinked with, other powerful factors, such as gender, class, ethnicity and sexuality" (9). By acknowledging the intersectionality of the lived experiences of contemporary youth (especially those like the migrant youth featured here), Yip and Page bring theory to bear upon everyday practices and communities. Intersectionality, they show, "as a theory and a methodology attempts to map the ways in which one's different identities interact to produce certain outcomes . . . often underpinned by power relations that interact to produce outcomes of privilege and disadvantage" (10), which certainly is true for these youth. Whether it is racist oppression and exclusion they feel in the Australian urban contexts in which they live, or the church-based acceptance and agency they experience through their faith communities, an intersectional approach is integral to their perspectives and identifications; in other words, "it is also about the 'intimate interconnections, mutual constitutions and messiness of everyday identifications and lived experiences . . . a nexus of social location, linked to structural phenomena'" (Yip and Page 2013, 11).

These South Sudanese youth are experts at creative and cultural code-switching and juggling multiple identifications (rather than identities). They do not see the world in fixed ways, nor their own place in it as fixed. Their voices and creative works in this book highlight how scholarship too often inadvertently falsely fixes our collaborators and co-participants rather than allows the strength and complexity of their multiplicities to inform our scholarly work rather than frustrate it. Here we together have sought to remain transparent in order to assist readers to better understand the ways in which these young people have communicated and in some cases performed their multiple identifications and roles. Creativity helps them remain elastic in these movements, and for this reason creativity is at the heart of the other analyses here.

Like Erin Manning, Yip and Page (2013) also make the point that "space comes to take centre stage in understanding young adults' everyday experiences", and these young people are no exception. The lived religion of both the Samoan and South Sudanese young people here demonstrates a wide range of ways in which their faith practices are both individualistic and collectivist, co-constituted and intersubjective, while not necessarily being dogmatic. And as I've argued in Section One, these young people perform their identity-formation in multiple sites, just as they perform their faith-formation and subjectivities. This book has been concerned in part with the ways in which they use hybrid online/offline worlds for performing, extending, and making sense of who they are. While space does not permit me to make extensive use of the growing corpus of scholarship regarding the relationship between online/offline worlds and gendered digital performativity (see Boler et al 2014, for example), my extension of Appadurai's social imaginary highlights some of these effects in both online and offline contexts.

As the creative practices of these South Sudanese young people attest, they gather in and for creative ways, whether that be home, work, school, the shopping centre, or at church—both back in South Sudan as well as in Australia and elsewhere in the 'western' world. They exemplify the ways in which youth not only inhabit spaces (publics), but the ways that spaces are created intersubjectively, and actively, through doing, making, and—in their case—through praising God. The South Sudanese youth in this book not only demonstrate through their creative practices, but also narrate through their reflexive commentaries, this space-making (both social and material), online and offline, sometimes simultaneously. Especially "for religious young adults, space is important, and for them, space is often demarcated between religious and secular spaces. One may be in a 'religious' space at one moment . . . [then] also occupy more explicitly 'secular' spaces, such as school, the workplace, university" (Yip and Page 2013, 11). For these young people, creativity is the bridge between these secular and religious spaces, in often life-saving ways. That creativity might offer a bridge is the focus of this in-depth examination of creativity here, and the ways in which it offers some alternative approaches to not only capital but to faith as well.

Gendered Lives in the Mediascape

Appadurai's notion of the mediascape is one conceptual framing of a 'space' where both religion and creativity can meet. Anna Hickey-Moody, also writing about South Sudanese young women in Australia, offers an account of Appadurai's mediascapes (2013), noting that for her, "Mediascapes thus constitute, and are partly constituted by, dominant discourses about the social groups they come to represent and articulate" (71). While Appadurai does define ideoscapes as including religious beliefs (1996, 35–38), in this chapter I am not as interested in ideoscapes because I'm not looking specifically at the ways in which these enactments may be contributing to citizenship (global or local) per se, or to broader political landscapes, but rather the ways in which these young people are using the intersectionality of their creative, religious, and youth enactments to create alternative (mediated)

The Art of Gender in South Sudanese Mediated Diasporas 169

communities. However, Appadurai stresses the interconnectedness of all five scapes, especially ethnoscapes, ideoscapes, and mediascapes, in that:

> Lived cultures of ethnoscapes are reconfigured in global ideoscapes (moving political ideas) and mediascapes (moving electronic images). These 'scapes' come together to form imagined worlds. Such worlds are 'multiple [and] . . . constituted by the historically situated imaginations of persons and groups spread around the globe'.
>
> (Appadurai 1996, 2)

The five scapes are dimensions of global cultural flows, and in many ways interconnected with O'Connor and Gibson's framing of cultural capital. While all scapes are interconnected in Appadurai's theoretic, mediascapes dominate throughout this book due to the ways in which these young women circulate their mediated artworks and create community in so doing. Hickey-Moody focuses strongly on ideoscapes because for her these are public pedagogies leading to these 'marginalised' youth writing themselves 'into' dominant cultural formations. She argues they "can change communities through facilitating new forms of belonging and they provide frameworks for imagining and performing alternative modes of citizenship" (2013, 72), yet I am not convinced this kind of liberatory discourse is not mere idealism or theoretical hopefulness. This kind of 'transformation' rhetoric about youth arts or arts education risks refocusing away from the continuing unequal material conditions of these minoritarian youth. While it is important to advocate resistance to deficit framing of these young artists, the analysis must remain tied to capital and material conditions. And whether they create "alternative modes of citizenship" and "become known within communities and through which communities come to know themselves" (72), I must still assert the material and racial marginalisation of these youth. For is it, in the end, these 'little publics' that constitute their changed self-knowledge and social positioning, or education and other tools and networks of capital that really make 'transformative' differences in how they are seen by themselves and others?

However, as in Hickey-Moody, the two youth groups in this book were also "characterized through themes of intergenerational pedagogies of tradition, corporeal practices of innovation and cultural fusions that resulted in writing figures of young femininity into the ideoscapes of the local [South] Sudanese refugee [and Samoan] community" (2013, 73). The South Sudanese rappers, for example, wrote rhymes that were simultaneously gendered, racialised, and religious, like this excerpt from Jaklin:

> *Jesus is the one, is standing here with me*
> *Through the tough times and the E-Z*
> *Oh I know you're the one, cuz wherever I go,*
> *However I flow, I feel protected*
> *That's how I know.*
> *Without You my world will be going down.*

170   *Religion, Art, and a South Sudanese Post-National Imaginary*

> *That's why You're here to twist me around*
> *Every time I look at You I feel the spirit rushin down . . .*
> *I just wanna be with You and want You to be with me too*
> *And though I may be lacking in expertise*
> *With You by my side, I know I've found peace.*
> *Yes he's my lord, but only one . . .*
> *I believe in you. And I'm happy cuz I'm Christian.*
> *I believe in you. And I'm happy cuz I'm Christian.*
> *I believe in you. And I'm happy cuz I'm Christian.*
> *I believe in you. And I'm happy cuz I'm Christian.*
> (Jaklin, from *Keeping It Real* music video)

Her language conflates a Jesus figure with a kind of nebulous ghost lover and protector, calling out to God in a way that perhaps she is not able to do directly to a fantasy lover. By declaring "I just wanna be with You and want You to be with me too", the singer can express feelings of loneliness, fear, or confusion in ways that may be more culturally acceptable in her own family or church group. For example, for another young South Sudanese woman, Ashai, creative and arts work should be in service to God:

> *My faith in Christ Jesus as my lord and saviour shapes the way I view everything in the world. For example, people: the Bible says that God created all men in his image and that if we say we love God and hate a brother or a sister we would be lying given that we hate his creation, someone that we can see, and hate Him whom we have not seen yet. . . . Because of my faith in Christ I belong to a family of God in [this] community church where we all encourage each other in every Godly way and basically worship the Lord together as we strive to know Him more and more. This community is the best I have ever been a part of, simply because of the unconditional love that we all have for each other, although we are 'strangers from different nationalities'. My faith lifted my self esteem in the sense that I know I am loved dearly, no matter what I am lacking, so I am now more confident and don't feel the need to become something else to be accepted by the majority. All the young people in my church are encouraged to seek a deeper relationship with God through reading the Bible, attending church and youth group, and having personal devotion time as well as forming godly friendships and not following the popular patterns of the world when it comes to self-expression. Creativity in art forms, music, or dancing are all welcome only as long as they glorify God.*

Amy Dobson and Anita Harris have commented on the commodified nature of girls' roles in mediated culture, where

> The expectations and possibilities for girls and young women today are complicated by the technological and socio-cultural developments around social media, through which girls and young women have become

The Art of Gender in South Sudanese Mediated Diasporas 171

significant producers rather than just consumers of popular mediated femininities. Social media platforms engage diverse groups of young women, positioned within global youth markets and cultures that increasingly promise consumer lifestyles to girls world-wide. . . . In this era, media aesthetics and representations of young femininity rapidly shift and change through commodification processes.

(Dobson and Harris 2015, 143)

Unlike even a decade ago, social media and its global flows are available to almost everyone in the developed world and are increasingly a site of emergent adulthood and the co-construction of global selves. This level of pervasiveness and visibility was beyond Appadurai's imaginary of a mediascape, and yet it has its limitations. Especially for minoritarian youth like the South Sudanese, "the kind of femininities on offer in both social and commercial mediascapes" can reproduce exclusionary and oppressive practices, especially in the "ways in which media address to girls intersect with neoliberal demands on young women to be self-actualizing" (Dobson and Harris 2015, 143), and presume that all young women have equal access to those commodifying and aesthetic constructions. This message alone returns us to the "No Pop" anti-consumerist message of Nantali's hip hop history workshop for these young women: that is, while material conditions and commodified success imperatives are relevant, linked appropriately to some forms of aspiration, and must be honoured, they are not the end of the story. The 'transformation' narrative then is not about anti-capitalism itself, but about alternative forms of capital, or making transparent the limitations of such a singular aspirational approach. But if creativity can provide one alternative form of capital, religion might provide another.

Figure 5.3 Afreem and Andria watching their hip hop video clips. Photo and copyright, Anne Harris.

Can Religion and Creativity be Capital?

In my book *The Creative Turn*, I linked education and health in their impact on productivity, where "Education and health are two central determinants of human capital. Their economic value lies in the effects they have on productivity: both education and health impact individuals' capacities to be 'productive' . . . [and] global ranking of nation-states remains linked to a large extent to the educational attainment and health status of its population" (Harris 2014, 101). Part of the effectiveness of the contemporary creativity discourse is its ability to conflate similarly global concepts like creativity and innovation, creative and cultural industries, creative labour and marketplace use-value. These neoliberal overlays of capitalist and standardized measures of value (including those like Ken Robinson, who still define creativity in terms of its 'use'), are part of what has compelled me to keep arguing for a capitalisation of creativity, or a commodification turn.

In that book and elsewhere, I have noted similarities with how Walter Benjamin saw his own 'mechanical' creative turn, nearly a century earlier, articulated by him as a shift in both content *and* form. He and Marshall McLuhan after him note such passages as culturally complex, saying "cult value does not give way without resistance" (Harris 2014, 219), and today we see the same resistance as notions of creativity give way to a largely digital creative industries. Beyond the overwhelmingly digital nature of contemporary 'creatives', creative labour, and creative industries, creativity is characterised by processes that are profitable, transferable, scalable, and exportable—or what I define in that book as a shift from human capital to creative capital. Digital media serves the ever-expansive virtual marketplace, so in one sense this turn may also be characterised as a shift from the affective or embodied to the possibility of the disembodied 'inauthentic' simulacra, a kind of creativity that is no longer characterised by its tactile and manual nature. The young people in this book demonstrate yet another extension or adaptation of contemporary creativity in their seamless mobility between online/offline worlds which offer a new window on intercultural code-switching and liminal presence. For them, creative expression is, in important ways, both embodied *and* disembodied at the same time.

The young Samoans and South Sudanese in this book characterise a 21st century reconfiguration of community-building and identification. Whereas previously I have argued that "global economic flows are similarly going through a reorganisation of both systems and ideologies" effecting both procedural and relational changes that render "modern education structures and systems similarly *imagined communities*, organised around manufacturing and a human workforce—or human capital" (Harris 2014, 152), here I will explore the non-institutional ways in which young people are forming pedagogical and ideological publics and navigating new ones through the self-circulation of their creative expression, engendering a new form of

The Art of Gender in South Sudanese Mediated Diasporas   173

capital that is intrinsically linked to creativity—even multiple forms and discourses of creativity. To review,

> From 1972, Bourdieu identified and clarified his notion of social, cultural, economic and symbolic capital, and with it changed the way we think about the function of education and its role in culture. For Bourdieu, capital plus field equals habitus. Capital, in Bourdieuian terms, can be economic, cultural and social, but in this chapter I explore the possibility for an emergent creative capital as well. Certainly I acknowledge tensions between multiple interpretations of capital, signalling two main branches of Bourdieu's influence. I am not attempting in this chapter to fully unpack the significance of creative capital as it will differently impact those two branches, but rather deploying the notion of creative capital as a flashpoint for further exploration.
>
> (Harris 2014, 152)

The turn into the 21st century can be characterised by the emergence of a new kind of creativity: creative capital, evolving in discursive terms "(note the numerous texts on the topic, and the rapid proliferation of definitions of even creative capital itself), but also in systemic terms (as the rapid change in economics and education demonstrates). Here I am arguing that the rush to define, understand, and harness creative capital is in fact a desire to colonise it for the purposes of profit; in other words, to identify the nature and market value of a notion of creative capital in order to commodify it" (Harris 2014, 154).

Creativity as a form of capital with a social function is beginning to work its way into socio-cultural conversations. For example, Ritzer states that, "Cultural economists sometimes employ cultural capital to refer to a society's stock of moral and aesthetic knowledge, or its 'cultural heritage'. Urbanists have used the term (or its cognate, 'creative capital') to refer to the putative economic benefits of arts spending and creative industries for urban economies" (2005, 169). Yet concomitant with this emergent creative capital is the symbolic violence exerted by majoritarian actors who reinforce the subjugation of youth of colour, especially from migrant and refugee backgrounds. In persistently symbolically violent western culture that excludes and stereotypes non-western, non-northern, and non-white identifications, the interplay of capital across increasingly overlapping fields suggests some ways in which cultural trends are not changing as much as we like to talk about. Digital media scholars note (far more often than education scholars) that the expansion of online worlds does not necessarily mean that new social orders or patterns will emerge. If Bourdieu has defined symbolic violence as the unconscious enactments of subjugation, often invisible, that accompany social stratifications and social discipline, then the creative maneouvering of these youth suggests ways in which they can circumvent—if not overturn—such persistent oppressions.

174 *Religion, Art, and a South Sudanese Post-National Imaginary*

Creative industries are, in the pantheon of creativity discourses today, a relatively clear-cut example of—if not what creativity *is*—what creativity's social function may be or may be becoming. Davies and Sigthorssun claim that

> 'the creative industries is a metaphor, which implies that creative production has been industrialised, set up in factory-like structures and managed along the same principles as the manufacture of any other mass-market goods' (2013, ix), in other words as human capital-driven. Yet, 'Adorno and Horkheimer's universal conception of the cultural commodity, where "the mere existence of an industrial form of production lead them to lump together jazz and comic strips, radio and cinema"' (Mattelart and Piemme 1982, 53 in Flew 2012, 62) is an earlier example of the way in which mass production has blurred the lines between aesthetics and commodities. Here I am arguing that the creative and knowledge economies represent a shift away from human capital to other capital—in other words, it is no longer about the work of people but about a new understanding of creative capital in Bourdieuian terms. 'Urbanists have used the term . . . "creative capital" to refer to the putative economic benefits for arts spending and creative industries for urban economies' (DiMaggio 2005, 169). If cultural capital has, in the past, been concerned primarily with 'aesthetic knowledge or its "cultural heritage"' (169), creative capital represents a new deployment and understanding of creativity in a 21st-century commodity culture. Yet as undiscovered as this sounds, it remains not so terribly far from Marx's own definitions of capital that prioritised over all else a concern with 'human activity and not the distribution of things. Humans are defined by their creative capacities. To be denied of the process creatively to labour, is to be denied our humanity' (Beilharz 2005, 10). Yet is it possible that in this new explosion of a so-called creative economy that 'mass consumption of mass-produced commodities is not a creative process' (Ritzer 2005, 492) yet might *appear* creative in the sense of being generative; that is, perfectly matched to a commodity culture which has an insatiable need for creating and fulfilling new markets, markets flooded with commodities of sameness? While non-business arts or creative practitioners may be dismayed to think that creativity is indeed being colonised in a new and suffocating way by neoliberal actors and investors, in this book I am taking it as *a priori* and prefer to focus on an examination of the ways in which this might suggest a new aesthetic imaginary.
>
> (Harris 2014, 154)

Like feminist sociologist Clare Hall (2016), Diane Reay (2004) challenges gendering of Bourdieu and 'emotional capital' as an expansion of Bourdieu's "economy of social action because it is a form of capital whose investment is

The Art of Gender in South Sudanese Mediated Diasporas 175

not for the economic benefit of the self, but purely for the benefit of others" (2016, p 125). Hall argues that this capital be extended into publics, outside of the home. Drawing on Amabile's (1982) consensual approach to creativity assessment, Hall's university students measured their musical abilities as perhaps a different kind of 'creative capital' than what I am suggesting is at play with the migrant and refugee youth here, but it bears discernable similarities. Hall says, in this ongoing process of conversion of capitals (emotional for musical, musical for creative, creative for economic capital in the form of a scholarship), that

> The intersubjective assemblage of mother-artist-researcher-teacher enables these pre-service teachers to construct soundscapes of motherhood that to them symbolise their most fundamental and creative self. . . . Because of this, musical mothering is reconceptualised as a source of a range of affective dispositions that these students convert into creative capital that they recognise has value in their future careers in education.
>
> (Hall 2016, 129)

Hall says further that, "Examining individuals' experiences through the lens of competence and capital, rather than incompetence and deficit, reinforces the need to examine creative music learning as highly differentiated phenomena" (129).

Publications grappling with the (not always Bourdieusian) notion of creative capital over the past fifteen years or so are

> not hard to find . . .yet the clear message. . ." that creative capital (also understood as the value of the creative in the social order of things, or marketplace) is clearly distinct from earlier definitions or alignments with arts, aesthetics and affect, and newly and boldly aligned with venture capital (Ante 2008), critical urban theory (Kratke 2012), the creative class and so-called creative occupations (Florida 2007), creative tourism (Wurzburger et al 2009) and creative industries, economies and policy (Flew 2012; Hartley et al 2012; Potts 2011; Henry 2009; Caves 2000). Creative capital, economists and scholars confidently tell us, has replaced human capital (Florida 2007)
>
> (in Harris 2014, 155).

The number of texts endeavouring to define creative capital almost solely in terms of its economic value has proliferated since 2003. The collective exhalation after the turn of the century, as well as a range of conservative contractions in response to both the terrorist attacks and the global financial crisis after them, have contributed to this moment, and "those seeking to define creativity in terms of marketplace concerns are gaining traction" (Harris 2014,155). In terms of finding ways in which creativity

176 *Religion, Art, and a South Sudanese Post-National Imaginary*

can be understood and indeed valued independently of market concerns is at issue in discussions of creative capital. This is not to suggest that creativity is not occurring and also evolving in non-market ways with differing agendas driving them, but the dominant discourse around creativity in diverse sectors (including increasingly education) is firmly rooted in profitability, marketplace concerns, and ways of turning artmaking into business.

Based on these and other patterns that characterise the 'creative turn', I have argued that

> creativity is going through a shift that increasingly resembles Appadurai's tournaments of value. In a formulation that echoes an analysis of creative capital today, Appadurai's tournaments are contingent upon 'not just status, rank, fame or reputation of actors, but the disposition of the central tokens of value in the society in question' (Appadurai 1986, 21). Certainly Herbert and others' arguments indicate that creativity is going through a similar turn as its dispositional role as a central token is under question if not attack. This current transit is all the harder to address given its ubiquitous but increasingly hollow presence in a range of sectors and discourses. While Appadurai drew on the darker view of contemporary culture evident in Anderson's *Imagined Communities* in his consideration of creative flows, culture and the dying nation-state, Anderson also informed Appadurai's articulation of 'post-national' global flows, ones I have suggested include a new formulation of creativity as capital.
>
> (Harris 2014,164)

Further, I argued that new elites and underclasses based on 'creative capital' will come to represent what Walter Benjamin noted in the last century, and Flew and others have reminded us more recently, that:

> while economic capital is associated with possession of goods and services associated with wealth and status, cultural capital revolves around practices of distinction that may be linked to taste and aesthetics, but which operate in a cultural field whose definitional criteria, institutions, rules and practices are highly fluid and contested. At the same time, its patterns of inclusion and exclusion are no less real, and no less keenly felt, than those arising from inequalities of access to economic resources.
>
> (Harris 2014, 168)

By drawing together some remnants of Bourdieu's theoretic, and an approach to commodification of creative making in a capitalist context that mirrors previous commodification turns, it is possible to consider mediated creativity as partly representative of commodity capitalism's resilience. Rather than a simplistic change from manufacturing to knowledge

The Art of Gender in South Sudanese Mediated Diasporas 177

production or curation, creativity provides a kind of test case of the ways in which a single concept which involves labour can be transformed from a manufacturing role to a conceptual one. Benjamin's Marxist analysis "can illuminate aspects of the human and creative capital implicated in the development of digital technology. As Rancière helps us think about subjects as subversive, subjective and positioned (2009, 1), Benjamin too focuses on the 'in-between' potential of technology" (Harris 2014, 129), and it is in this in-between that creativity does most of its contemporary work.

Other virtual commodities also seem to be proliferating, and in this rhizomatic economic and epistemological landscape, adhering to traditional definitions of creativity or capital is not required and indeed is not in some cases desirable. Keller (2015) identifies a hybrid feminist/postfeminist media presence in the online phenomenon of blogger Tavi Gevinson, whom she says wields considerable "subcultural capital (Thornton 1996) that is hip, urban, and pop culture-savvy" (Keller 275). The young women here might be understood too as representing a kind of subcultural capital that is not "primarily white, middle class, and 'cool'" (Keller 2015, 275) but rather—for the Samoan young women—drawing on both mainstream and subaltern Samoan characteristics of humour, nerdy, and rags-to-riches/poor faithful (i.e., done for the 'glory of God'), whereas the South Sudanese draw on fashion, beauty, and African-American symbolic capital. Keller claims that Gevinson is a complicated self-branded subject because she self-identifies as feminist while adopting postfeminist and capitalist tools and strategies. Similarly, these Samoan and South Sudanese young women offer complicated political and social mediatised subjectivities in that they claim an orientation and performativity that is agentically 'for the glory of God' while at the same time participating in some kinds of sexualised self-representations and aspirational claims to fame and fortune.

Feminist Social Imaginary as Habitus?

Yet too often still feminist and youth studies scholars leave race and class apart from their gender analyses. Keller notes that agentic young online subjects like Tavi Gevinson and her analysts risk excluding or ignoring "girls who do not have the race or class privilege to occupy this idealized position" and the oversight regarding how "Gevinson's race and class privilege allow her to perform identity—including a riot grrrl influenced feminist identity—in ways that other girls cannot do easily" (Keller 2015, 279). Keller argues that "we must be better attuned to how the practice of self-branding may limit *which* girls are able to perform feminist identities within a post-girl power context and *who* is able to identify with such alternative girlhood subjectivities" (Keller 2015, 280). Indeed for these South Sudanese young

178   *Religion, Art, and a South Sudanese Post-National Imaginary*

women, who have material as well as intersubjective aspirations for visibility and success, achievement still looks like what is available on mainstream television and internet spaces, and there is still a significant gap between that vision and their lived experiences. One example is Winy's verse from the *Keeping it Real* video:

> *Things I feel, thought I was living in a dream but hold up:*
> *Seems to me, more like a nightmare*
> *People just don't care.*
> *Everywhere, stop and stare, and you know what?*
> *It just ain't fair!*
> *Violence in the streets of Footscray,*
> *I look this way . . . I look that way:*
> *All that I can see is hatred*
> *Confusion, abusin'*
> *People losin'.*
> *Why can't it be loving? We need total freedom,*
> *Get some leadin' yo, get people achieving!*
>   (Winy Anai Majok, from *Keeping It Real* music video)

As Keller summarises, "Feminism, as we have seen with Gevinson, can increase the value of one's brand if performed in a way that is read as 'hip' and avoids threatening the consumer logic of the capitalist marketplace" (Keller 2015, 283). Yet this consumer logic is exacting the kind of regulatory social forces that form part of a counter-discourse to the idea of a social imaginary, one in which social actors both co-construct but also resist or extend current publics. For example,

> According to the Canadian philosopher, Charles Taylor, the idea of a social imaginary involves a complex, unstructured and contingent mix of the empirical and the affective; not a 'fully articulated understanding of our whole situation within which particular features of our world become evident' (Taylor 2004, 21). In this sense, the idea of the social imaginary is akin to Pierre Bourdieu's notion of 'habitus' (1977). A social imaginary is a way of thinking shared in a society by ordinary people, the common understandings that make everyday practices possible, giving them sense and legitimacy. . . . A social imaginary is thus carried in images, myths, parables, stories, legends and other narratives and most significantly in the contemporary era, the mass media, as well as popular culture. It is through this shared social imaginary that relations and sociability among strangers within and across societies become possible. . . . Taylor maintains, however, that a social imaginary is embedded not only in everyday notions and images, but also in theories and ideologies and, by implication, in policies.
>   (Rizvi and Lingard 2010, 34)

The Art of Gender in South Sudanese Mediated Diasporas 179

What are the common understandings amongst these South Sudanese Australians that carry a feminist social imaginary that includes brown women and Arabic and Dinka-speaking rappers, for example? It is not just the doing of that creative work but its circulation, its visibility and accessibility online that helps make it an imaginary and not just an event. If it is through these common understandings that any social assemblage gains 'sense and legitimacy', it is especially problematic that Sudanese female rappers are in short supply online—especially ones from the global south. Any useful social imaginary as a way of thinking—which I have discussed in Chapter One—offers everyday people a way of transcending both their ordinary conditions but also their ordinary affects. Through social imaginaries, or publics, we can co-construct and circulate transgressive images, resistant stories, and counterpublics that offer alternatives to the business as usual of majoritarian culture. The possibility of creative imaginaries (as I argue in Chapter One) offers everyday people (including those featured in this book) a way of reimagining creativity in a new uncommodified way, but also of imagining themselves in a new way through creativity as they perform it. In this way, these young people's stories and creative makings represent an intersection between creative and cultural industries, if not the abstraction of a 'transformation'.

Fema-Creative 'Conjunctures'

Justin O'Connor has argued against the slippage between cultural and creative industries resulting in 1998 from UK's New Labour government's replacement of 'cultural' for 'creative', and the whole host of discursive, epistemological, and policy-based confusions that have resulted. This shift can be partly read as a "shift within the policy field in which government (frequently characterised as 'neoliberal') attempted to use 'culture' to deliver on a range of economic and social objectives previously seen as secondary to its purpose" (O'Connor 2013, 2).

While he has argued extensively on the ways in which creativity might still offer the promise of something better, O'Connor draws on

> Bob Jessop's notion of 'economic imaginaries' which: 'identify, privilege, and seek to stabilize some economic activities from the totality of economic relations and transform them into objects of observation, calculation and governance' (Jessop 2005, 145). Intermediaries actively work within these 'economic imaginaries' and help circumscribe a set of activities which can then become the objective correlate of policy intervention and measurement.
>
> (O'Connor 2013, 2)

This uptake of the concept of social imaginaries[1] within economics discourses mirrors the ways in which I have tried to link culture and economics (that

180   *Religion, Art, and a South Sudanese Post-National Imaginary*

is, with respect to sociality and materiality) in this text, yet as O'Connor points out, this trope, while useful, also fails to "give full justice to how this particular 'creative economy' imaginary had to be carved out not only from other economic activities, but also from a space of 'culture' that had traditionally been set against or apart from the 'economy'" (O'Connor 2013, 2).

Along the spectrum of modern creativity discourses, Pope offered already ten years ago much-needed "alternatives to both the Romantic stereotype of the creator as individual genius and the tendency of the modern creative industries to treat everything as a commodity" (2005, i), and a decade on this distinction is still needed. Many creativity scholars and educationalists seek to remain on one end of this wide spectrum, and a more nuanced and agentic understanding of modern creativity is more closely reached somewhere in between.

While O'Connor situates his discussion of creative and cultural industries further into an economics discourse, his long-term engagement with the creative side of national economic policy (in both the UK and Australia, and more recently in China) makes his work of ongoing relevance to my thinking. His use of imaginaries in these national and global economic flows offers an integrated way of considering the shifting socio-cultural role of creativity, both the language and the doing of it, considering that "the economic imaginary as political project will have crucial moments or turning points, where one imaginary might replace or marginalize another. One might call these 'conjunctures' (Grossberg 2010)" (in O'Connor 2013, 3). I am positioning the creative and affective labour of the youth in this book as representative of one such conjuncture, through my articulation of a 'creative turn' which can itself be considered as one contemporary meta-conjuncture, both aesthetic and economic (see Harris 2014 for more on this).

Importantly as we consider the interrelatedness of the economic, social, and cultural functions of creativity today, the conjuncture of an economic imaginary and a new cultural imaginary (also in part performing itself in new creative ways) offers one path through these complicated sectors and discourses. O'Connor aims "to give a wider historical dimension to the debate around creative industries which tends to focus on the new and emergent at the expense of continuities and 'long waves' (Hesmondhalgh 2007)" (2013, 3). Why, one might ask, is it necessary to consider the 'continuities and long waves' of a creative turn that some might argue seems a recent and opportunistic phenomenon, when so many like these South Sudanese youth continue to be left out of the 'industry' altogether?

For O'Connor, it is necessary to "provide a corrective to cultural economic geographers such as Allen Scott who have tended to portray local imaginaries and indeed place-based semiosis (though he does not use that term) as inputs into local 'cognitive-cultural economies' (Scott 2007)" (O'Connor 2013, 3). Drawing mainly on the UK context (where the origins of both creative industries and cultural industries can be traced to the shift with New Labour in the 1990s), he recognises a discursive and policy-based wave that is now breaking over

The Art of Gender in South Sudanese Mediated Diasporas   181

regions and governments worldwide. This turn to what he calls "the primacy of the economic in the creative industries imaginary (culture as economic resource) remains provisional and contested" and goes beyond mere pragmatism into a more complex and embedded place of culture in which "there is a set of shared assumptions about the changing relationship between culture and economy, a complicity between the cultural and creative industries" (3). This complicity is also a tension at times, and yet by avoiding a simplistic binarised understanding of their relationship and the ways in which they still do or don't speak and function together, we might better understand not only the reason why creativity is so differently experiencing a period of commodification today, but also the social function of that turn.

In the mediated spaces that increasingly dominate these young women's lives, "We see young women taking on and working through a plethora of cultural practices often associated with men . . . we see young women carving out safe spaces in subtle and unpredictable ways, around issues such as disability, technology, and religion" (Dimitriadis and Weis 2008, 120). For them, creativity and its attendant mediated online sociality can offer a shortcut (or leapfrog as suggested earlier) to these organisational and social structures that remain so exclusionary and at times oppressive (racially, sexually, genderly).

Hip hop artist-mentor Nantali celebrated the gendered courage of the young women, in that "they jumped right in, which I was really happy for them as women, trying to rap and perform, as women, something that is often identified as a guy thing, and they just went all in, even if it wasn't great, they kept working at it, and they were helping each other". It's not easy to break through gendered barriers to experiment in new work, especially not in new artforms, but these young women did. Additionally, they use the rap form as a literal praisesong, calling out and transcending the racism and violence that pervades their daily lives. That they attended the program at all is, in some ways, contrary to evidence about cultural industries participation and new migrants. The evidence supports the claims of O'Connor and Gibson (2014), who note that

> The cultural industries typically present higher barriers to entry by 'outsiders' than other industries. Becoming established often requires lengthy periods in unpaid or poorly paid work—a cost that new entrants can generally not afford. Entry in many areas is governed by network contacts, resulting in a tendency to reproduce established employment profiles. State subsidies in the arts can also institute barriers, leading to the formation of arts and culture lobbies more interested in preserving current arrangements than in promoting change.
>
> (55)

Nantali's observation that "when they started writing their rhymes they were writing grafs like 'I love rapping' all over the place", but that the youth

182   *Religion, Art, and a South Sudanese Post-National Imaginary*

then moved on to deeper issues such as religion, family, and race were, for Nantali, "little positive things that [show] that we've done something good here". I would not disagree. But as O'Connor and Gibson note, this narrowness of arts participation in mainstream culture is not just an Australian issue, but an international one and "is consistent with a tendency for recent migrant groups to favour education in more technical fields such as business, science or engineering over humanities, social sciences or the creative arts" (2014, 56). Programs like *Culture Shack* and long-term creative collaborations cultivate (or capacitate) the imaginaries necessary to push through such structural obstacles.

As Dimitriadis and Weis observed in 2008, by using found technology from their lived environments, "young people are creating their own self-styled cultural texts across multiple platforms . . . proliferating in their own specific communities and speaking back to corporate culture in ways that can have constitutive effects on the material production of culture" (120). This material production of culture in rapidly evolving ways is benefitting these young women like Dona, who recognises that the current pathways to artistic, educational, and general doxic success are insufficient for many South Sudanese. She suggests that in addition to exercising their creative muscles, educators and employers should "encourage them and talk to them . . . and go through the pathways, you know? Cuz I'm pretty sure most Sudanese have no idea what the pathways are" (Harris 2012b). Her part of the hip hop video addresses this desire to build community and unity toward a kind of cultural capital that might finally transcend the patterns holding her community back.

Conclusion for Chapter 5

Hickey-Moody calls us to remember the "elastic histories but often brittle present living conditions of migrant and refugee youth. Community and networks of kinship are transnational as well as local for such young people and the complexities of mediating such 'warps' are evidenced in their arts practices" (2013, 69). Their creative processes, whether dance (as in Hickey-Moody) or singing (here) draw inexorably on popular media "as a way of mediating the local and the global, their motherland and their new home" (68).

Whether contextualised against third-wave feminism, contemporary post-feminism, racialised or westernised majoritarian values, or the reproductive nature of the internet, gendered mediations of South Sudanese young women in online/offline worlds continue to offer opportunities for alternative avenues of agency, but also limit the ways in which they are able to be seen, be heard, and perform their emerging identities.

While the South Sudanese and Samoan young people in this book are not plugged into popular culture through social media in the same ways or with the same motivation described by Hickey-Moody, Dimitriadis, and

The Art of Gender in South Sudanese Mediated Diasporas 183

others, gendered popular media constructs still powerfully influence their creative and identity work. For the two subcultural groups represented in this book, recent articulations of 'girl power' bear discursive similarities to 'God power' in that they are emergent, intersectional, and transcultural. For these South Sudanese young women, the notion of God is a comforting, protective but agentic, and decidedly gendered construction that is a powerful but still fluid figure in their lives, meshing with mediated notions of their 'girl' identities as well as their spiritual ones.

Note

1 Although I mostly draw on Arjun Appadurai in this text and elsewhere, the notion of social imaginaries as intersecting with modernity, materiality, psychoanalysis, and late capitalism has been addressed by many, including Charles Taylor's *Modern Social Imaginaries*, Benedict Anderson's *Imagined Communities*, Michael Warner's *Publics and Counterpublics*, in education by Fazal Rizvi and Bob Lingard in *Globalizing Education Policy*, and of course Appadurai's *Modernity at Large*.

6 Meaning and "Madolescence"

ALPHABET RAP—first rap done by the hip hop youth artists with Nantali
A is for actress, that's what I want to B.
B like a butterfly, butterfly I C.
C to celebrate, celebrate with dinner.
Dinner start with D and delicious to eat.
Eat starts with E and rhymes with feet.
Feet is what I've got and I got em from God.
Girl is what I am, and God made me.
I stands for ice and I used to jerk.
Jerk is the dance, made by kids.
Kids love lollies,
And Love their mothers.
Mothers are nice, Nice all over.
Like Overseas, we use to call police.
So Peace out to the queen.
The Queen who rools,
Rules is what I hate but it represents schools.
Schools is education with teachers to teach.
Teaching ain't my thing but I can teach you.
U to understand each other's values,
Values are important especially for the world.
World with different people like different notes like on a Xylophone.
But if you think about it there is a Y in xylophone,
But a very silent one.
Its silent when you sleep except for your ZZzz's!

Jackie, *Culture Shack* rap group

Manning, Massumi, and 'Madolescence'

The two groups of young people in this book remind us that youth is not only about rebellion, risk, and resentment, but can be a time of productive 'madness'. Both the South Sudanese and the Samoan youth here have found creative ways to address the marginalisation that at times dominates their experiences of mainstream culture. By turning to the tripartite intersection of faith, youth, and arts, they are creating valuable communities and alternate 'scapes' where they can thrive. Thriving however, in a frequently ageist, secular, and racist society can sometimes feel like madness or a kind of 'alternate reality'.

By most accounts, imagination remains within the realm of thinking or thinking-feeling (Massumi 2013), while creativity moves us out into doing. If creativity is predominantly in popular culture terms about products, imagination is still about thinking and becoming. This chapter extends the way Manning and Massumi (2014), Manning (2013, 2009, 2007, 2003), Massumi (2011, 2002), and others are exploring affect and embodiment, suggesting new possibilities at the nexus of creativity, technology, and faithed bodies. Here I draw on Manning's and Massumi's shared project of troubling creative relationality rather than strictly aesthetics or discourses, as a critical lens in helping to understand the power of creative capital in the words and works of the young people in this book. For Massumi, interactive art is intrinsically affective, an exchange that invites the Other in each of us to engage with the centre. By examining the ways in which these young people use social media to disseminate but also to co-construct their emerging identities and ideologies, this chapter argues that their virtual embodiments are themselves a creative act.

Many of the South Sudanese young women who collaborated with me in *Culture Shack* and other ethnocinematic projects[1] express feelings of disorientation between marginalising experiences of racism and yet the pervasive success narratives they are told typify the west. Like many others from economically, racially, and gendered minoritarian communities, these young people struggle to find themselves reflected in popular and online media. In addition to leveraging affect and posthumanist scholarship to consider the labour of these youth, I also deploy a more direct youth studies lens in this chapter in order to explore their creative work as affect and embodiment, or what Manning and Massumi have written about as creative practice as a form of thinking (2014).

This is not to say this chapter represents a youth studies analysis, but it is a necessarily situated youth cultures examination, particularly building upon my previous racialised and gendered examination in the two preceding chapters that populate this section of the book. First, some key Australian migrant youth studies context in order to help place these South Sudanese bodies-in-space as emergent creative thinkers and doers in the global south.

Migrant Youth Cultures and Working the Hyphens

Youth studies expert Anita Harris too has found in her recent studies of Australian minoritarian youth that "given the popular image of youth

186 *Religion, Art, and a South Sudanese Post-National Imaginary*

disengagement, a surprising number were, in fact, involved in their local religious centres or places of worship" (Anita Harris 2013, 111). Countering the 'deficit frame' that so often accompanies migrant and refugee-background youth, Dona and the other South Sudanese youth here "may be using the notion of cultural particularity, as expressed through the arts, to position themselves as capable, talented and worthy of respect" (Anita Harris 2013, 63). Their artworks themselves are suffused with images and the language of ascendency, capability, and success. If they are not always clear about the pathways that will lead them there (and in this they are not alone), they are clearly not turning away from culture and family in order to pursue it.

Appadurai reminds us that "the homeland is partly invented, existing only in the imagination of deterritorialized groups" (1996, 49), and through their rap lyrics that tie both religious and geographical histories with the present, these young women exemplify his claim. Emerging from refugee pasts, which in most cases were typified by extreme material deprivation, the homeland is a complex space which is partly in conversation with the opportunities available (to some) in countries of resettlement. For these young women, materiality matters, as it does for everyone. For Asante, our "battle is intense, the struggle we wage for status power is serious and we cannot communicate as equals when our economic position is that of servants" (2008, 49), as is experienced daily by many South Sudanese Australian young women. Asante argues that utopian discourses of transformation and engagement while ignoring the very real material differences are a violence against minoritarian subjects such as the South Sudanese youth here. Despite a strong Christian faith and a commitment to fashion careers, these young women understand that success in their new country will require something more than a slow steady climb to (a mythical) equality beyond race and gender. This chapter asks, rather, whether religious and faith-based practices and spaces can serve a material function for these Sudanese young women, and what its potential as an activist pedagogical community (Giroux 2005) may be. Can it open up the kind of 'interchange' of which Asante speaks, a meeting place between races, genders, and geo-political regions, rather than the extremist alienation that typifies popular media coverage of religion and youth?

These raps and their commentary on contemporary life show materially influenced performances of gender and race as seen from the young women's perspectives, a world in which fashion matters as much as education, and faith is an additional family and global community. When these Black youth look strongly to the United States for models of powerful and successful Black women, they see creativity, sports, and faith play a large role. Where racial and creative identifications intersect, faith-linked practices and performances offer intergenerational links and new ways of 'doing the west', but also doing success. This is not a kind of 'good-enough' deficit

Meaning and "Madolescence" 187

frame that is so often overlayed on them by education and other institutions. It is an engaged citizenship in which the youth strategically read a global popular culture field of possibility and identify potential pathways to success—pathways that education is clearly not providing. In so doing, says Maira, "These immigrant youth model a version of deep citizenship that is not always available to their parents and have become spokespersons about race, religion, and civil rights" (2005, 77), thus performing not only intercultural labour but intergenerational labour as well.

By considering this labour as a truly globally focused while locally grounded labour, and remembering that 'youth' is a culturally situated category construction not necessarily shared in the same way outside of the west (including South Sudan), this chapter recognises "the category of youth as a social achievement, not so much a given category based on biological age but a social position structured by the simultaneous powers of consumption, creativity, schooling, citizenship, surveillance, and social membership" (Lipsitz 2005, xiv).

The hyphens of adolescence then are so multiple considering cultural and developmental movements, one can be glad for the rhizomatic proliferation of the internet, which in so many ways mirrors the 'madness' of adolescence, or offers what Dimitriadis calls a "nexus between the media and common culture: The omnipresent cultural media of the electronic age provide[s] a wide range of symbolic resources for, and are a powerful stimulant of, the symbolic work and creativity of young people" (2008b, 57). A recognition that digital technology expands the online/offline potential of even (and sometimes especially) minoritarian youth often goes under-remarked in discourses about globally mobile (often linked with creative) elites and their 'poor cousins' who remain localised.

As I examined in Section One concerning the ways in which the Samoan youth mobilize themselves through social media and other online pathways, the South Sudanese young women here also use social media to their advantage (for more on this see O'Mara and Harris 2014; Harris 2013c; Harris 2011b).

This text is not unique in examining the ways in which youth subcultures—particularly minoritised youth—find ways of forming community that occur outside of schools or formal institutions. While Dimitriadis looks at this primarily through an urban intercultural lens, and here I look at it in homogeneous cultural groups (Samoan and South Sudanese), there are parallels to be recognised about how youth cultures construct their alliances and affiliations, both as subcultures within the mainstream but also separately from it. Drawing on Robin Sylvan's *Trance Formation: The Spiritual and Religious Dimensions of Global Rave Culture* (2005), Dimitriadis identifies diverse nodes of

> social and personal transcendence—a site where diverse and heterogeneous young people come together to enact (often) life-changing

rituals. Deeply embedded in music, dance, fashion, and other aesthetic registers, these events can be powerful examples of 'unity in diversity' . . . bringing everyone together in an ecstatic unity that transcended these differences.

(2008b, 98)

While far from the rave culture that Sylvan is observing, these Samoan and South Sudanese youth struggle against the 'othering' aspects of coming of age in various global diasporic cultures where they remain so often the outsider. As Dimitriadis calls out, these spaces where youth co-create themselves in aesthetic and political ways "too are pedagogical spaces, spaces where young people enact social, cultural, and religious formations which exceed those ones narrowly delimited in school settings" (2008b, 99). Thus, these aesthetic, (inter)cultural, and religiously homogenous spaces are vital for positive identity-formation of these young people who do not otherwise enjoy cultural capital in new home countries. For despite the opportunities afforded by the fact that "cities are marked by new immigrant groups creating ethnic, racial, and religious enclaves . . . which often force heretofore unimagined kinds of cultural conflicts, dialogues, and synergies" (Dimitriadis 2008b, 12), these youth often do remain within their enclaves. That Melbourne—like most other cosmopolitan cities—is a melting pot of cultures can be exciting but overwhelming too. As many of these South Sudanese youth have narrated, their backgrounds in Sudan, Egypt, Ethiopia, or Kenya were almost always spent in ethnic or language singularities, and indeed the source of much of their persecution was along intercultural lines—either religious or cultural (as Dinka and Christian).

In seeking to understand the multi-directional and multi-layered work of these youth, Anita Harris puts it best perhaps in linking the emergent nature of youth 'work' with Michelle Fine's notion of the hyphen:

because of the expectation of youth as a phase of 'becoming', young people 'work the hyphens' (Fine 1994) of their own identities and ideologies as members of overlapping and clashing networks organised strategically and loosely around culture, gender, age, religion, colour, geography, language proficiency, sexuality, taste and ability. What has been less frequently considered is how, in doing so, they also work the boundaries of community and of the national bond, bringing into question what it means to belong in and make productive a society of considerable cultural diversity. The intersectionality of young people's identities in concert with their non-compliance with tidy ethnic categories necessitate new ways of understanding how they live multiculturalism beyond the politics of both minority recognition and social cohesion.

(Anita Harris 2013, 4)

Here, nation-building and citizenship become work that can be done—that *is* done—by minoritarian youth in diasporic sites, including virtual ones. The move these South Sudanese youth represent from extreme 'localised' community life into multiply 'globalised' ones (and which remain both simultaneously) is deeply characteristic of 21st-century global citizen work for us all, and provides a kind of leadership or innovation in this area, if unacknowledged by the mainstream.

These youth are perfectly placed to lead that work, a kind of curation of self, curation of space as we all juggle the dual concerns of online/offline existence and relationality. The need for such "safe spaces—a term coined by Michelle Fine and Lois Weis for imaginative and literal spaces young people turn to, to 'carve out' space for themselves in often oppressive circumstances" (Dimitriadis 2008b, 107) is only growing. As we know, "these spaces can be in school or out of school, formal or informal . . . they are spaces of healing and nurturance where 'counterpublics' can be formed—often (ironically) in response to the very exclusionary practices of the public sphere today" (Dimitriadis 2008b, 107), and for this reason we look to the glorious creativity, emotion, and momentum of an emergent South Sudanese Australian 'madolescence' for some guidance.

Posthuman Madolescence in Times of Praise

Rosi Braidotti (2013) argues that "posthuman subjectivity reshapes the identity of humanistic practices, by stressing heteronomy and multi-faceted relationality, instead of autonomy and self-referential disciplinary purity" (145). Recognising the presence of this relationship between singularity and relationality in the posthuman subject and intersubjectivity in the creative work of these South Sudanese youth urges readers to consider the ways in which a yearning for faith (as 'something more') and praise (as ecstasy) in western cultures may be answered by these newest members. What the effects of this 'performance of praise' may ultimately have on global culture more broadly is equally of interest in this chapter, as it moves across considerations of time, place, age, and race for a deepening century.

What might the notion of a 'more than human' offer an understanding of the creative and identity work of these youth? The young women often discuss the cultural dissonance of their Sudanese-ness as a collectivist culture, versus their Australian-ness as an individualist one, especially during the adolescent period. For posthumanists, "affect never locates itself once and for all on an individual body" (Manning 2013, 28), and this intersubjectivity is at the heart of how I receive those observations of the South Sudanese youth. Both their collectivity and individuality are interrelationally constructed (as has been well theorised and documented before), but they are also interrelationally experienced, which is perhaps too often overlooked.

190 *Religion, Art, and a South Sudanese Post-National Imaginary*

In Manning's orientation toward process philosophy (rather than phenomenology) to explore questions of the more than human, she contrasts the more than human with the need to deficit frame others (another way of understanding the outsider-making of youth of color like those in this book): "Anything that does not immediately conform to the superficial content of what has been defined as the norm now falls into the more unstable field of the pathological (the sick, the other, the less-than-human), which in effect creates not only a paradoxical pathologization of the individual as such (who never really existed in any stable and reiterable way in the first place) but the more widespread pathologization of experience itself" (2013, 188). As such, the danger, risk, and madness-inflected youth discourses catch (particularly minoritarian) young people in the untenable position of failing as individuals, as collectivities, and even as sets of experiences. According to Manning:

> The pathologization of experience then works to subtract from experience the ineffable more-than, for there is no place for the more-than in an ideology of rationalization or progress or survival or cure (whatever the leading by-line of the time). This not only disqualifies all that does not resemble it—it wrests experience of its incipiency, violently seeking to undermine the complexity of life-living's processual shaping.
>
> (2013, 188)

Of course this dumbing-down or abjecting of life's processual shaping narrows experience beyond that of minoritarian subjects. For example, where does Manning's philosophy of the more than human, and its corollary of the deficit framed, fit with the ubiquity of contemporary creative industries? In "Everyone is Creative: Artists as Pioneers of the New Economy" (2011), Angela McRobbie has argued that the withdrawal of governmental social programs and cultural development support has led, in the creative industries discourse, to an individuation of creative labour, and of artists or 'creatives' as self-responsible and indeed as business people. The social and cultural capital required to build and perform economic self-reliance (as 21st-century creatives or anything else) is unequally available to youth of colour, including particularly migrant and refugee-background youth. In addition to the established exclusionary levers documented so well by these South Sudanese youth in their rap lyrics, these new terms of creative capital engagement add an additional hurdle to their pathways forward.

Manning's process philosophy is one response to these constraints and contradictions. It offers a means of rejecting such limits,

> for the simple reason that the betweenness of human being as it conceives it is not itself human. It is more than human: human plus

Meaning and *"Madolescence"* 191

many-one singular-generic spacetimes of experience; human plus the eventful improvisation of new and emergent vitality affects; human plus contingencies belonging to any number of categories; human plus more than currently human potential, collectively individuation.

(Massumi 2013, xx)

In this framing, the South Sudanese youth are part of a collectivity, but one that is typified by both human and more than human potential, not just pipe-dream aspirations, or those which depend on others to 'capacitate' them.

For Dona and the other youth here, the key to unlocking their potentialities through creative process is interconnectedness with both human and more than human resources around them. Dona's rap lyric excerpt shows her ability to be both fierce and playful in this creative imagining, or what Manning (after Whitehead) calls "self-enjoyment", the creative advance typified by its "coming to subjective form" (Manning 2013, 215).

> . . . *the stars are falling down, it's judgment day.*
> *Bad days, bad times, lookin like the end.*
> *Life is too short to make a better one*
> *Hey you better pray, better do good things,*
> *Pain everywhere, people havin bad times*
> *Bad vibes,*
> *Cuz some are not even baptised*
> *The vision ends with the apple in your eye*
> *The vision ends with the apple in your eye*
> *I've never been a hater, that's the way I go*
> *The way I roll, the way I flow,*
> *I never go low.*
> *And if you need to know—it's time for unity, community*
> *Celebrate, yo!*
> (Dona, in Arabic and English, from *Keeping It Real*
> music video)

Dona's lyrics also demonstrate a productive 'madness' in their ability to transmogrify despair about 'pain everywhere' and too-short lives into a manifesto for unity through community and creative flow. This is not just wishful thinking or creatively conjured social imaginaries; it is what Massumi describes as "philosophy practiced as a concept-creative endeavor that performs in writing the larger process it concerns. It gives the gift of a movement of thought, again as Deleuze and Guattari would say, to a 'people to come'" (Massumi 2013, xiv). Indeed, such creative 'thought in the act' (Manning and Massumi 2014) is a doing not a describing, is a creative conjuring both conceptually and interrelationally, not just imaginatively. And that creative conjuring is imbued with new lifeworld-forming affect.

Figure 6.1 Joyceline and Andria finish recording. Photo and copyright, Anne Harris.

Mama Think I'm Cursed: Affect and Madolescence

> . . . *can't lash out, when I'm hurt and confused*
> *it's just so hard with the years of abuse*
> *think I'll ever be the top? I just can't lose,*
> *I just can't stand being second best,*
> *I'm obsessed, possessed with this lyrical test y'all.*
> *I'm the worst, mama think I'm cursed*
> *I'm the worst, mama think I'm cursed*
> (Achai, in Dinka and English, from
Keeping It Real music video)

The literal and figurative intergenerational conflict found in Achai's rap lyrics are representative of the affective intensities for which hip hop as artform is a vehicle. These young women moved very quickly from believing that rapping was a 'male' creative activity through experimenting with the form in the ABC rap, to contacting these kinds of affective flashpoints in their own individual and collective experiences. Affect offers a site for "the force of becoming that incessantly creates collectivities in the making, collectivities tuning toward an outside where the mutations of difference are most forcefully creative" (Manning 2013, 30). For the creative potential of adolescence and rage, "affect is never exhausted" (Manning 2013, 30). Yet how might incorporating an awareness of the posthuman extend this

Meaning and "Madolescence" 193

'madolescent creativity' beyond rage, or beyond narrowly religious hope? The relationship between Massumi's version of affect and the posthuman offers us one way of bringing together the creative and religious work these young people are doing, but understanding them as in part creative intensities and flashpoints indicative of larger developmental and culturally evolving labour. To do so, however, requires a lateral maneuvering away from Massumi's approach, and for this I turn to Wetherell.

While others including Judith Butler have been critical of Massumi's 'disembodied' approach to affect, Margaret Wetherell (2012) does a great job of poking holes in "what goes awry when bodily responses and discourse melded together in practice are pulled apart in theory" (53). She highlights how Massumi has and hasn't been taken up by other scholars, particularly feminists and cultural geographers. She points out that his 'autonomy of affect' leaves out some crucial foundational elements of affect theory, which, she says "understands affect as a lively virtual force and endorses the most general, 'post-human' definitions of affect" (54), a version of affect theory that has been "decisively formed in contestation with post-structuralist discourse theory" (54). She offers an in-depth examination of this version of affect theory's break with post-structuralism, an examination that offers important pathways for minoritarian youth and their creative futures.

Wetherell deftly critiques Massumi's distinction between

> the 'quality' of an experience and its 'intensity'. Two tracks, he suggests, are set going when the world impinges on the embodied human— the quality track leads to naming and conscious awareness, while the intensity track has very different properties and is better described in terms of its strength and duration. These modes of experience, body and mind, follow very different logics and need to be described in very different ways.
>
> (2012, 57)

For our purposes in this book, I am looking at Massumi's articulation of 'intensity' rather than 'quality', which he typifies as emotions (an "older and more domestic connotation of affects" [Wetherell 2012, 57]). Wetherell's impatience with Massumi's distinction is that it "sharply bifurcate[s] discourse and the body", in which "affect, he argues, is entirely autonomous. Bodies do their own thing" (Wetherell 2012, 58).

Like proponents of non-representational theory (NRT), Massumi's version "may occur beyond consciousness but this does not mean that it is asocial" (Wetherell 2012, 58), and this is why I draw on Massumi's version to look at the creative labour of the South Sudanese youth in this text.

Here Wetherell understands Massumi's version of affect (as Patricia Clough's), to encompass "all of social and material life" (2012, 59), including how a body can be "a rock, a capitalist exchange relation, a cat, a philosophy, a psychotherapy group, a social movement—any whole . . . composed

194   *Religion, Art, and a South Sudanese Post-National Imaginary*

of parts . . . related together in ways that can be characterised in terms of their motion, speed and rest" (59). Considering the hip hop performances and words of the South Sudanese youth here, affect is indeed embodied by them as "a post-personal force exceeding the human" (Wetherell 2012, 59) in a way that is truly "virtual because it sets up and holds as possibility multiple connects and ways of being" (Wetherell 2012, 59). For the faithful and the outraged, these diasporic youth know the collective and processual power of the digital realm and the different affects expressed (and allowed) there.

Wetherell critiques the way that Massumi's association of affect with "potential, becoming and incipience" (2012, 59) is " 'virtual', untamed and inassimilable, always in the process of becoming, and the leading edge of the wave of any engagement with the world before human minds get to it" (Wetherell 2012, 59). This Deleuzian adherence to becoming suggests the kind of never-quite-thereness that often characterises studies of youth. They are always already on their way to something else, carrying with them the hope of something better, the fear of something worse or lost or missed. Studies of youth in scholarship and aesthetics both are characterised by possibility.

Of course, possibilities are always emerging and also always foreclosing, and this foreclosure is at the heart of Wetherell's critique of Massumi's notion of affect, that "these possibilities collapse, however, when discourse, culture, cognition and consciousness come on the scene and develop a story line" (2012, 59). So when Dona and her peers turn rapped imaginaries into narratives about life in the western suburbs of Melbourne, "even if affective possibilities trigger multiple story lines, affect understood as potential has faded and disappeared. The moment selection occurs, potential and the indeterminate turn into the actual and the determinate" (Wetherell 2012, 59).

This, in the South Sudanese hip hop video, is both true and not true, false and more-than-false. Where they articulate intensities (both virtual and embodied) of their seemingly inassimilable lives, they are at the same time embodying assimilation into an emergent 'Australia', an unfixed and imaginary new nation and (through their virtual online video artefact) a beyond-nation existence too. It is absolutely the kind of incipience which Massumi identifies with affect, but avoiding a binarised 'embodiment' or virtuality. Rather, these South Sudanese young women and their performances of self are both incipient and fixed. Through an unfolding series of fixities, affect can remain emergent and untamed.

Both the Samoan youth and their South Sudanese peers demonstrate this points-in-space incipience, a kind of *madolescence* in a field of further-unfolded emergence. There is no demarcation point between the untamed adolescence of these youth and a fully arrived and 'assimilated' adult actualisation. It is a myth, and one which youth studies discourses sometimes uphold. Massumi's approach to affect is one way in which I can consider these young people's *doings* and *becomings* as something more than examples or fixed data or performances or even of some notion of fixed 'selves'. If Wetherell is bothered by some kind of generalising or over-generalising of 'bodies' here by Massumi, I suggest that the generalisation of bodies of minoritarian young people—especially girls and young women—is typical of their experience, and of adult interventions and interpretations of and about them. Yet Wetherell makes the point that "affect . . . over-universalises and risks ignoring the particularity of scenes and relations that have been so central to feminist analyses of the movements of power" (2012, 60).

This is at the heart of Butler's critique too, that "affect seems to be appealing because it appears so 'masculine', contrasted with feminised investigations of domesticated emotion. . . . The turn to affect regularly claims to have moved beyond feminist post-structuralist thinking without engaging with the particulars of that research in even the most perfunctory way (see Tolia-Kelly 2006, and Castree and Macmillan 2004, for other critiques)" (2011, 61). Certainly many feminist and postfeminist scholars (including Braidotti 2013; Ringrose 2012, 2008; Berlant 2011, 2008; Ahmed 2010; Clough 2010; Gill 2007) have been addressing the way that affect expands and potentially explodes feminist theory, including and particularly those who identify as new materialist feminists and posthumanist feminists, or who explore the terrain Donna Haraway has called 'naturecultures' (2008). Braidotti, in particular, identifies a feminist materialism that demands a radical rethinking of fixed sexual differentiation (which she sees at the heart of power inequities), corporeal nomadism, and human-centric subjectivities more generally. So how might Massumi's—or Wetherell's—version of affect theory be deployed usefully to help think about the corporeal, material, and power relations of what these young people are not only doing, but feeling, experiencing, and foreshadowing? Following Warner (2003), what I call *creative counterpublics* may be one way of entering this expanding field of practice.

Faith, Culture, and Creative Counterpublics

My discussion of affect in relation to these young women points to changing notions of place, space, and embodiment, of the new assemblages and intensities that flows across and through these spaces engender. I also point to changing notions of the ways in which these South Sudanese young people not only remain involved with their diverse communities, but "take into account this diversification of identities and the everyday negotiations, within which they become visible, [and] that produce community and nation" (Anita Harris 2013, 4). These young people embody this diversification in ways that produce what Manning has called "the lure for feeling, the lure for the creativity generated at the heart of difference" (2013, 24); creativity as a kind of place-making that is not tied to geographical sites or even static bodies.

Creativity on the Move

Swirski (2013) argues that "creativity is propelling forward amidst the diversification of technological affordances, as well as the complex intertwining of the local and global" (146), and seeks to "anchor creativity in the actions of human beings in their natural and social environment" (132). Such situational understandings of creativity are reminiscent of Anna Craft's 'mini-c creativity' (2011), which describes "the novel and personally meaningful interpretation of experiences, actions and events" (Swirski 2013, 146). But how might the kinds of 'little publics' (Hickey-Moody 2013) or counterpublics (Berlant 1997) of minoritarian groups and communities like these South Sudanese young women understand themselves in relationship with what Manning calls 'the nation-state grouping' (2003), and how might scholarly work poke holes in the membrane between them?

Warner (2003) proposed the notion of counterpublics as a way of responding to a middle class public sphere, which instead might recognise contemporary publics as proliferating, multiple, and overlapping. I extend Warner in combination with current creativity theory that suggests a proliferation of definitions, outputs, and processes (Harris 2014) to consider a new notion of *creative counterpublics*, of which these South Sudanese young women are representative.

Extending Dewey (1927), Hickey-Moody's publics become more generative and are grouped around "religion, race, hobbies (arts and sport), labor, interest" (2013, 19), becoming what she calls 'little publics'. Following Dewey(1934/2005), and then Berlant (1997), Hickey-Moody shows how "citizenship is a creative process that requires subcultures" (Hickey-Moody 2013, 26); yet this logic depends upon an ideology of inclusion of minoritarian actors like the South Sudanese, containing within it a presumption of majoritarian centrism. I suggest that these Samoan and South Sudanese youth ask us to reconsider whether it is still helpful to consider such rhizomatic creativity (that goes beyond gender, race, ethnicity) today as serving or subverting nationhood, or is it forging other kinds of relationships that leave nationhood behind? I am suggesting instead that in creating these socially mediated communities or little publics that these young people are in fact making themselves global citizens and circumventing exclusionary policies, institutional and legislative practices and histories, and an ongoing (maybe increasing) lack of opportunities for traditional forms of capital accumulation in accelerating global flows. They are using their 'little publics' to create their own kinds of global flows and creative classes.

Further, Hickey-Moody develops her notion as an extension of counterpublics (Berlant 1997) to help think about "the ways cultural processes of learning are a part of youth arts practices and are also affected by youth arts performances" (2013, 19). Hickey-Moody suggests a need to 'take more seriously' the creative work of young people, especially minoritarian young people, in that work's ability to influence majoritarian culture; in other words, "that the materiality of their arts practices constitutes a form of citizenship. What begins as affect, style, art practice, effects modes of community attachment that can influence community sentiment and can provide frameworks for policy and legislation" (Hickey-Moody 2013, 19). I have also made a compelling case here, I hope, that the creative works of these young people are of importance to the mainstream as well as the subaltern, in part because it is more in touch with the rapidly proliferating and still-inchoate future of both individualism and collectivity, nationhood and post-nationhood. So I disagree in nuance with Hickey-Moody that they and their work should 'be taken seriously' by some other more powerful actor in this performance of future-making, because it seems to me that our current era is characterised by an inability to know who will ascend and who will decline, in both the near and distant futures. As the last section explored, creativity and its attendant affective landscape no longer must remain location-based, nor body-limited, and for this reason I disagree in logic but not in principle with Hickey-Moody's approach.

In Berlant's discussion of the activist group Queer Nation, she looks at the ways in which its coherence and incoherence as a group can still advance its agenda, indeed how Queer Nation's ability to "exploit internal difference" (1997, 151) has been, she seems to argue, one of its strengths. "All politics in the Queer Nation are imagined on the *street*" and, importantly, "it always refuses closeting strategies of assimilation" (151). While certainly these South Sudanese young women (and their Samoan peers) do not see themselves as a coherent (or incoherent) activist movement, they too refuse the mainstreaming constraints of assimilation, as their creative works show. Berlant maneuvers publics for such minoritarian groups to function in a different way—that publics are not inherently hegemonising, nor do they function the same across online and offline worlds. Indeed, Berlant argues there has been a change in how nationhood and "national publics are characterized and made in an age of mass mediation" (194).

Little Publics, Counterpublics, and Intimate Publics

In a critique of Habermas' construction of publics, Nancy Fraser (1990) claims that "members of subordinated groups . . . have repeatedly found it advantageous to constitute alternative publics" or what she calls "subaltern counterpublics" (11).

But the subaltern counterpublics that school-based (and some community-based) arts activities often self-generate can be used to police and to 'deficit frame' some young people (unevenly applied), particularly youth of colour and migrant youth. Many youth scholars, including Anita Harris (2013, 2008) and Angela McRobbie (2009, 2004), have advanced a gendered analysis of the public versus private spaces that are available to girls versus boys due to parental and institutional control, but note that "young women's activism around consumer citizenship is therefore not limited to culture jamming

198 *Religion, Art, and a South Sudanese Post-National Imaginary*

or the attempted creation of new public spheres through alternative media and the internet" (Harris 2004, 171).

The foregrounding of faith-based and religious subjectivities in the work of the youth here further break down gendered and 'spacetime' binaries that are already entrenched in some online practices. In so doing, their digitally circulated creative work (like girlpower websites, etc.) "may also undo some oppositions that Foucault considered inviolable, such as the division between public and private spaces" (Reid-Walsh and Mitchell 2004, 180).

To consider these public/private online spaces and the creative-cultural work they do, I find Hickey-Moody's articulation of 'little publics' useful in thinking about the ways in which these two youth groups create a kind of private-public space for themselves and audiences. For me, the most compelling aspects of this labour are not necessarily in relation to pedagogy (either public or traditional, as it is for Hickey-Moody), or even citizenship (either global or local). Rather, following Manning, I am collaborating with these young people in order to explore the way they create and experience what Manning calls 'spacetime', or 'a fold of relation', an affective experiential that privileges the ways in which we "sense on top of senses, one sense-experience always embedded in another: cross-modal repetition with a difference" (53).

This is a different kind of encountering and enacting counterpublics, through creativity, in which the very specificity of their digital global/local interaction with their audience-peers seems to me both intentionally intimate, self-consciously public, and a deliberate act of resistance to neoliberal imperatives (as Berlant's Queer Nation similarly understood itself to be doing). Berlant contrasts this idea of an 'intimate public' against Habermas' 'intimate sphere of modernity', as being one in which "domestic and public spheres become merged" (Berlant 1997, 240), and in which it becomes possible for the "hegemonic consuming public to feel that it has already achieved intimacy and equality with the marginal mass population" (104).

Like me, Hickey-Moody sees the "little publics created through youth arts performance . . . [as] local, but they also connect to and articulate through global scapes of 'youth art/s'" (2013, 30), yet she argues this is still a regulatory system of the state, using youth arts to create 'good citizens' who will contribute and produce more effectively than drain the system. I reject this *a priori* positioning or co-option of youth arts in such a discourse; rather it is one way in which neoliberal discourses and institutional agendas assimilate the labour of youth arts, but it is by no means comprehensive or constitutive. For example, Hickey-Moody's tethering of in- and out-of-school youth arts together is what suggests this discourse as ubiquitous, and this is informed by an arts curriculum and education system that is constantly and historically antagonistic to arts education. Her out-of-school framing of youth arts is distinctly more aligned with an analysis of deficit-framing of youth through 'at-risk' narratives about redemption and transformation. Yet again it is important to note that even this second co-option of youth arts is characterised by adult- and institution-driven arts practices. The Samoan and South Sudanese youth groups with whom I collaborate and critically co-reflect here do not share these us/them intergenerational dynamics, and I think it is one reason why their arts practices escape these deficit frames.

Hickey-Moody argues that an "'at risk' youth discourse needs to be understood as a governmental strategy that reproduces selected young people as deviant and thus in need of control. Here, art is a means of governance . . . [and arts are] largely ways that adults control young people" (2013, 21). These South Sudanese and Samoan youths' participation in church activities and creative labour offer a counter-narrative to her argument, which highlights the differences between (in this case) school and community religious sites of youth participation. While she does acknowledge that "there are major distinctions between the natures of the publics formed and/or addressed through various in and out of school youth arts projects" (23), I am suggesting that *all* performances within schools are policed as sites of control of youth, not specific to the arts, as schools are inherently sites of governmentality and discipline. For education scholars like Hickey-Moody, adult intervention and control remain central to the construction and performance of youth and creativity, yet neither this adult-centric view nor approach to youth creativity is always so prevalent. Online publics offer important exceptions to the claim that youth voices are to some degree mediated by adult facilitation/intervention in most publics, but schools remain perhaps the most extreme sites of control of youth bodies and practices, and point to some additional reasons why the *creative counterpublics* of online worlds offer new and expansive potentialities.

Creative Counterpublics

In this last section I suggest the notion of counterpublics might be usefully extended to think about creative labour and also more broadly about "national publics and . . . the corporeal conditions of citizenship" (Berlant 1997, 239). If, as I have traced through Hickey-Moody's analysis, the socio-cultural role of youth arts is changing as this creative labour becomes more multi-sited, more youth-driven, and creativity itself takes on new commodified and collectivist forms, digital media can suggest new frontiers of creative counterpublics as both sites and ways of doing.

In one of her earlier works, Erin Manning explores the private-public relationship through a notion of intimate homes as a counterpoint to the nation-state grouping (2003). Homes become not only spacial but also emotional sites and moments of accommodation of the self, in which experiencing the world and being in the world are not separate activities. Yet in consideration of what I previously termed *madolescence*, or the untamed possibilities of youth creativity, home as Manning articulates it might also be a bridge between the publics of nationhood and the intimacies of selfhood.

200 *Religion, Art, and a South Sudanese Post-National Imaginary*

The counterpublics that offer a set of practices and spaces for belonging (in opposition to the nation or otherwise) might also function as a kind of creative home-making.

If Habermas' public sphere seeks an understanding of the common good, a *creative counterpublic* demands that there is no common good that does not dominate and exclude. "Common sense is too often the dream of consensus that propels the imaginary of the nation and its adjacent narratives of identity and territory" (Manning 2007, 62). These minoritarian youth of colour know intimately the ways in which "this unification of forces for the 'common good' condones domination in the name of a re-balancing of social relations . . . [and in which] intelligibility as a commonality is the primary political articulation within the language of the nation-state" (62). Creativity, for them, can offer bodily and aesthetic "disarticulated remains" (62) that cannot be captured or controlled by the state, by the apparatus of nationhood, whether online or offline traces. So when Rania sings the line

> *Must be surprising cuz I'm just rising,*
> *I fly, survive, I fly so watch me rise,*

it is both a celebration and a challenge to the publics that would exclude her and keep her down, but also to herself as she constructs a living, breathing, new social imaginary. There is tension here. It's clear that this creative conversation must happen intersubjectively, but it also occurs for Raina and her peers as a series of events that become part of their evolving individual-collective selves, about which they set the terms of engagement. According to Manning:

> What is often left unwritten in renditions of the body (-politic) is the notion of antagonism on which the body rests. This antagonism is a mechanism of the reproduction and transformation of subjectivity that produces both effect and affect, troubling the political rationalities sustained within the imaginary of the nation-state.
>
> (2007, 65)

Through both creative and spiritual narratives and enactments, these South Sudanese young women are performing expansive interrelations that—if not yet sustained within the meta-imaginary of the nation-state—represent moves toward new as-yet-unnamed horizons. They exuberantly live out the rich tapestry of themes that Yip and Page (2013) have explored in depth in the British context, including the relationship between faith and young adulthood, and the shifting power relations between religious young adults and religious authority structures. For there is a real difference as articulated by these young people between faith and religion (faith remains largely individual and more an internal, virtual relationship between self and God; religion is a collective external interrelationship with other humans), but also between the adult-controlled spaces of school and church in their lives. Both school and religion (and their separate worlds) have a role, but they serve importantly different functions, and form the basis of different kinds of relationships and practices. It is in these corridors of individual beliefs, values, and expressions of faith and religion that the South Sudanese young women here are making their own self-defined (and fluid) *creative counterpublics*.

Figure 6.2 Long days at the studio. Photo and copyright, Anne Harris.

Conclusion

I opened this chapter with the provocation of *madolescence* as a site of productive and untamed youth counter-narrative to a kind of nationhood that presumes commonality, and a kind of youth that presumes adult and institutional control. Extending Hickey-Moody, I argued beyond a notion of youth arts as public and counterpublic, toward a theorisation of creative counterpublics as a minoritarian strategy that does not depend on relationality with a nation-based or other mainstream, nor exists necessarily in power relationship to it. In order to expand the notion of *creative counterpublics*, I have suggested (following Manning) that it demands a reconsideration of home, of public/intimate spheres, and of affect and the body itself as a primary site of emergence.

Across Section Two of this book, these South Sudanese young women are performing multiple labour with their culture- and faith-infused creative work, going beyond limiting discourses of deficit or liberation. Across these three chapters I have argued that the *creative counterpublics* imagined and populated by these youth and their work offers something more than individualist self-expression, cultural exoticism, or at-risk youth success

202 *Religion, Art, and a South Sudanese Post-National Imaginary*

narratives. The ways in which Hickey-Moody analyses the "pleasure-based citizenship" (2013, 35) of Rock Eisteddfod and other school-linked youth arts is also significantly different from the two youth groups featured in this text. Where Hickey-Moody notes that "there is often great satisfaction in being disciplined enough to rehearse and perform, or make and show, a work" (2013, 35), the South Sudanese and Samoan youth here are driven by very different impulses, partly culture-based (wanting to make their families, parents, elders proud) and also religion-based (for the glory of God). But their work—as their subjectivities—cannot be reduced to a laundry list of impulses and motivations. They are much more and also much less than such representative categories, or as Manning (from Spinoza) frames it, they are bodies "composed of an infinity of particles that express themselves through modulations of rest and movement" (2007, 143), and these rests and movements continue to be both collective and singular, virtual and corporeal.

I close by returning in part to the humanist approach of Dimitriadis, who urges that "even as we look toward and validate the creative practices of youths, we need to understand more specifically how they are negotiating their way—or not—in these new economic times" (Dimitriadis 2008b, 114). But these new times are characterised by more than changed economics. We must now collectively (and collaboratively) attend to the inter/cultural, trans/local, and multi-perspectival agency of these young people as future-makers, rather than remain in "the cultural dimensions of young people's lives, how they explore and elaborate upon their creative impulses in often oppressive sets of circumstances" (Dimitriadis 2008b, 110). Today's accelerations require more, and our need for affective connection demands more too.

But I suggest that a deep understanding of the labour being performed by these youth also requires a more-than-human approach which recognises their relationship to a virtual God-audience and to digital others, all of which transcend national imaginaries and borders. Any such understanding must attend to both the affective and processual domains of that work, and the ways in which not only the youth but also their creativity are both emergent and already-arrived. These Samoan and South Sudanese youth point some ways forward in how youth might "distribute selforganizing creative energies while operatively interconnecting them at a distance. How to connect not simply at the level of content but also at the level of process" (Manning 2013, 36). Their work and creative visions return us over and again to the productive intersection not of nation-states, or cultural, geographical, or gendered alienations, but rather of the creative mashup of youth, faith, art, and a new social imaginary that not only includes but helps co-construct post-national subjects.

Note

1 See *Sailing into Uni!* and others on the website Creativeresearchhub.com.

Conclusion

New Creativity, New Youth Cultures

As Maira and Soep (2005) remind us, "Youth, it seems, are everywhere and nowhere" (xv). This conclusion returns us full circle to a consideration of the ways in which youth experiences of faith, culture, and creativity converge and overlap for these young people in Samoan and South Sudanese Australian worlds. The ability to see the ways in which a rise in faith-based cultures contradicts discourses of religious essentialism can be useful in considering the contemporary obsession with both creativity and also religious extremism. This text, however, has mainly focused on the ways in which these youth use a range of strategies (both online and offline) in order to create communities not bounded by nations or geographies.

By extending Anderson's post-nation-state understandings of community formation, I have considered cultural transcendence as a byproduct of creativity and God-connection. Can the arts practices that these young people from Samoan and South Sudanese backgrounds engage in provide viable channels of transcendence from gendered, aged, and raced marginalities, and do they wish them to? Combining multimodal empirical data and multidisciplinary theoretical frameworks, I have sought to reframe these young people from deficit-framing into a construct of productive madness through my notion of *madolescence*. Building upon Appadurai's understanding of the social imaginary and aspiration, I have suggested that creativity might provide an alternative 'fund of knowledge' or form of capital that is not based in use-value in order to decentre institutional and economic marginalisations of youth of colour, and rather to offer something like *creative counterpublics* in hybrid spaces. These emerging ways of interacting in evolving 'spacetimes' (Manning) offers new possibilities for agency and selfhood that are not as reifying as traditional discourses of arts-based 'transformation' for minoritarian youth.

Anita Harris notes consistently the particularity of these youth from our global south. Australia's unique position in the Pacific Rim, combined with

204 *Religion, Art, and a South Sudanese Post-National Imaginary*

its westward-looking culture, situates migrants differently than those from the same country who might have gone to the United States, the UK, or Canada:

> Owing to particular migration patterns unique to Australia, many terms that describe cultural origin or identity have a contextual meaning that differs from its meaning elsewhere. . . . 'Islander' is a common umbrella designation for people with origins in a range of Pacific Islands (typically Polynesia; for example Samoa, Tonga, the Cook Islands, Niue). Even if they were born or grew up in New Zealand, as many have, they are still commonly identified as 'Islander' or 'PI'. . . . Another umbrella term is 'African', as the more recent arrivals from Sudan, Somalia, Ethiopia, Rwanda and so on are infrequently differentiated by either country or ethnicity.
>
> (Anita Harris 2013, 17)

But these youth are putting their cultural inheritances to work. As I have argued here, Samoan and South Sudanese youth exercise agency through their faith-based creativity, a kind of social capital which can be read as (an emerging) creative capital. Collins (2010) and Runco (2010) have commented extensively on the ways in which this kind of faith-embedded and faith-informed (think a contemporary rhythm and blues, or the more recent Christian rock and country music industry) is coming to be a new kind of capital, especially for minoritarian youth and artists. These versions of capital are increasingly widely theorised in the creative industries literature, as I myself have done (Harris 2014; McRobbie 2011; Pimpa and Rojana-panich 2011; Wilson 2010). Yet in this book I suggest that, as seen in the lives of these youth, creativity offers something more than just a new lever for capital accrual.

If Mitias (1985) lamented that "we still view creativity as a rare commodity characteristic of artists or great scientists! Why?" (1), he might be pleased that global culture is still grappling with both ends of the creativity spectrum—a need for enculturated creativity, as well as a commodified approach. As I have suggested elsewhere (Harris 2015a), creativity has always been linked both affectively and performatively with not only an anthropocentric way of understanding or finding meaning in our lives, but a posthuman and materialist way of enriching and sustaining life too. We still ask, as surely we will continue to do, that if we "suppose that we understand or achieve a measure of agreement on what 'creativity' is, what is the use, in the end, of this understanding?" (Mitias 1985, 1–2). His interrogation of creativity, aesthetics, and affect was prescient, particularly in asking:

> three basic questions: (1) what do we mean by 'creativity', or, what constitutes a creative act or process? (2) Is creativity possible? How can we argue that it is an essential feature of human and natural life? What is

the role of creativity in art, religion, and culture? And more concretely, how can we analyze "some basic types" of human experience—e.g., ecology, love—as creative activities?

(1–2)

The posthuman work of Manning and Massumi (2014) and other new materialist scholars asks similar questions today, and the ecology of creativity is unfolding in exciting new ways. These Samoan and South Sudanese youth demonstrate some ways forward that incorporate and celebrate rich multi-perspectives and multi-layers of such more-than-human creative practices.

Cultural Transcendence, Sexuality, and the God Aesthetic

While this book has not dealt explicitly with sexuality, sexuality is never far from considerations of youth and religion. As Yip says, "Sex saturates society . . . [and] youth are implicated in this discourse and its development" (Yip and Page 2013, 1). I have commented briefly in Section One on my own discomfort with the "twin discourses of increased fetishisation of youth and their association with risk", including the ways in which "the experiences of young people are structured by factors such as class, ethnicity, gender and sexuality" (Yip and Page 2013, 1). White and Wyn (2013) have ensured a global south perspective is part of this international dialogue, yet as Yip and Page point out, "until recent years, religion as a social factor has not generated much attention in the research literature on youth" (4). This book has focused on the gap in literature on the intersection of religion and youth perspectives regarding creativity, and in so doing diverges from so much other scholarship on sexuality—even sexuality and secularity, faith, and religion. For these youth, their primary artistic processes lead them first to questions of fitting in as gendered, racialised, and Christian subjects. They are of course tuned into who does that creative work in 'sexy' ways and who does not, but they are also engaged in other ways with the world and their need for creative expression.

Like them, I rejected the choice of starting from "wellworn assumptions about religion" and sexuality, and instead "decided to start from the lived experiences and understandings of religious young adults themselves, to illuminate the ways in which they navigate" (Yip & Page 2013, 2) these bumpy and intersecting paths.

Battacharya and other Anzalduan scholars who are concerned with spirituality and culture live out intersectional identities that are frequently misunderstood by white western scholars and audience members like me. Yet I too live out my own intersectional identity as a migrant to Australia, as a genderqueer person, as an adoptee who cannot return home (Harris 2014), and indeed I recognise that my attraction to other Others is linked to my own sense of diasporic alienation and longing. As Ray and Anderson assert,

206   *Religion, Art, and a South Sudanese Post-National Imaginary*

"when we travel to a new country, we feel an almost irresistible impulse to smooth over the strangeness, the distinct particularity of the people we meet" (2001, 41), and certainly I have found this particularly true not only as a lifelong tourist, but in a more pronounced way since my migration to Australia nearly eighteen years ago.

For many of us on explicitly diasporic journeys, home can be found in God and God-practices and the communities those practices engender, as in this excerpt from Battacharya's beautiful and evocative poem about migration to the United States, and memory of home:

> Sometimes I don't like masked
> Indian-ness with clothes, jewelry, cuisine,
> All-you-can-get buffet, for everything Indian.
> Main course culture: side orders of religion
> And socialization, generous helpings
> Of comparisons, gossips, and envy—
> All in one weekend.
> I'd rather pray like Papa, in Mumbai.
> How do you find God
> In a high school auditorium? . . .
> In processions, like *Ganpati Visarjans*,
> Decorated brown bodies
> In *sarees, kurtas, salwars*
> In *Tikas, tilaks, and bindis*
> In *Henna, alta, and mehndis*.
> Slums and high rises, side by sides,
> Hearts dancing on the streets.
> I miss how I used to be one of them
> At the crowded Churchgate station.
> Daily passengers, languages blended yet distinct
> Punjabi, Gujarati, Bengali, Hindi, Marathi.
> Their colors, alta red, turmeric yellow, peacock blue
> Chiming like the silver bells
> On an *adivasi* woman's anklet. . . .
> (Battacharya 2013, 617)

Republished with permission of Taylor & Francis, from Battacharya, Kakali 2013. "Voices, Silences, and Telling Secrets: The role of qualitative methods in arts-based research." *International Review of Qualitative Research* 6(4): 604–627.; permission conveyed through Copyright Clearance Center, Inc.

Samoan New Zealander Joshua Iosefo, in his spoken word performance *Brown Brother*, describes the power of invisible borders in keeping us all in positions of less than what we know we can be:

> Now these invisible borders are not geographical borders, they're borders that are both external and internal, they are borders where the people see that they're contained and then where people think and further

believe that they are contained. You see, invisible borders are not just borders that separate South Auckland from the rest of Auckland . . . but they separate your homes from your driveway outside, separates your high school from university, it separates your Facebook from reality, it separates your career from your calling, it separates where you are now to where you're meant to be. It separates your potential from your purpose.

(Iosefo 2012)

Following Yip and Page (2013), I hope this book has advanced scholarly attention on some ways in which migrant and refugee-background youth from the global south are participating in dynamic global networks regarding their faith and creative practices and futures. For them, questions of where they can be themselves, which include but transcend sexuality, are foremost. Like Joshua above, Vineta and her Samoan peers, and Dona and her South Sudanese peers, are keenly aware of the here and now, with eyes firmly fixed on the 'over there'. They see perhaps better than any generation before them the links between themselves as both individuals and members of collectivities, yet they are indeed aiming for something in a different 'spacetime' than the ones they inhabit now. Their ability to have a presence in global online participatory culture is a powerful channel for transcending their local limitations, while taking their local capital with them. As Iosefo says, "Where you really want to be is out there, because out there is where your purpose lies" (2012), but for these young people 'out there' is no good without their 'in here' of family, church, and the arts.

Creative and Cultural Futures

One question this book asks is whether and to what extent those like the Samoan or South Sudanese young people in these communities (not only in Australia but elsewhere around the globe) are actually interested in or able to navigate themselves as freelance professionals, whether they possess the aesthetic or cultural expertise to 'market' these knowledges to their material advantage. If Australia is now approaching the same creative/cultural industries crisis the United Kingdom navigated pre-1990s (O'Connor and Gibson 2014), we might learn from some of the unfulfilled promise of the creative industries turn that ultimately painted itself into a very uncreative corner:

the potential was clearly there for . . . a democratization of culture through both an opening up of the rigid hierarchies of culture to embrace the different codes and possibilities of popular culture, and the expansion of access to cultural production and consumption . . . but also a 'culturalized economy' in which, perhaps, a new 'form-of-life' (Foucault 2005), derived from the 'artistic critique of capitalism', might be developed. This was a powerful emancipatory promise, especially when coupled with a new vision for the post-industrial city.

(O'Connor 2013, 4)

So what is the most important distinction between these agents of cultural versus creative industries, and why must we attend to them in this discussion of intercultural youth, faith/religious practices, and creativity? In Bourdieuian terms, cultural capital morphed into creative capital in perhaps unforeseen ways. Certainly its narrowing from the promise of cultural industries during the heyday of UK's Creative Partnerships program was not wholly anticipated, and the current movement back out toward a broader but perhaps still more commodified cultural economy is evidence of this. As O'Connor reflects, "In a new regime of 'reflexive accumulation' cultural capital became economic capital in a much more literal sense than thought by Bourdieu: it formed a direct input into a new kind of post-Fordist production" (2013, 5). This focus on 'creatifying' production and productivity accelerated into a kind of Frankenstein creative economy discourse that risks destroying everything in its path, resulting in "not just an 'aestheticisation of everyday life' but a 'socialization of culture' " (5) that had some positive but far too many negative repercussions to stem the tide of marketplace pressures.

The dream had been for something much bigger, bolder, and more sustainable. O'Connor waxes lyrical in recalling how "the cultural industries were part of a new economic imaginary, but one in which this economy has been 'culturalized' " (2013, 7). Indeed, "Support for a dynamic local cultural industries sector [in the 1980s in the UK] was not just about economic growth but also about a more democratic, participatory, diverse cultural policy, and both were wrapped up in a new vision for the post-industrial city" (6). What then went so wrong, and how did cultural industries as the context-specific and vibrant cultural base underpinning nation-based development become the emaciated creative industries?

The figure of the 'creative and cultural professional' that O'Connor describes was at that time a "pivotal agent in this project of local transformation, able to work within the new 'freelance professional' cultural industries" (2013, 6), a figure who could not be further from today's creative industrial truth. But where do Samoan, South Sudanese, and other youth cultural intermediaries fit into this picture? What role might they have in contemporary creative industries?

These young people bring a new kind of hybrid 'trans-languaging' approach to their citizenship, religious, and creative practices. Having begun life as solidly transcultural, they now seamlessly incorporate these perspectives into their approaches to making music (mash-ups that creatively combine traditional songs, hip hop, rhythm and blues, and Australian beats are common), and to their approach to practicing their faith (prayers are bi- or multi-lingual, and prayerbooks often are too). Amidst the riches of these cultural and creative practices, what is missing until now, perhaps, is the business side of things, and the kind of financial payoff that the cultural industries promised is nowhere in evidence in the creative industries conception of how a 21st-century professional creative might thrive. These two groups of young people, however, show how in their *thinking* they clearly see a transcreativity that holds their unique cultures at the heart of thriving creative and faith-inflected careers.

O'Connor claims that "the creative industries agenda became differentiated as it was perceived to foreground 'business development'", a move that remains of great concern to governments like Australia's, who wish to be (or be seen to be) competitive internationally. But his argument falsely binarises business development against aesthetics or artistic work, for surely global economies require differentiation along cultural lines as well as profit margins. For example, Korea has been able to successfully brand itself and in so doing differentiate itself culturally and creatively from its Asian neighbours, which has proven both creatively and economically valuable. Yet this "increasing emphasis on economic deliverables at the expense of some of its earlier claims to cultural and social inclusion has been well documented . . . the 'economic imaginary' of the creative industries was contested by those who asserted its wider cultural and social agenda" (O'Connor 2013, 8). Perhaps before looking more closely at the ways in which these Samoan and South Sudanese young people might help expand a creative industries discourse, it is necessary to review my conceptualisation of creative capital as it relates to an economic imaginary.

Creative Capital

In *The Creative Turn* I tried to "problematise the creative explosion we are now seeing as the new organising principle of not only economies but of new kind of creative capital" by articulating "an emergent creative capital" (2014, 152–153). It is a contentious idea, but nevertheless gaining traction in multiple contexts in which

> I acknowledge tensions between multiple interpretations of capital, signalling two main branches of Bourdieu's influence. I am not attempting . . . to fully unpack the significance of creative capital as it will differently impact those two branches, but rather deploying the notion of creative capital as a flashpoint for further exploration. The last ten years can be characterised by the emergence of an age of creative capital, both in ideological terms (note the numerous texts on the topic, and the rapid proliferation of definitions of even creative capital itself), but also in systemic terms (as the rapid change in economics and education demonstrates). The rush to define, understand and harness creative capital is in fact a desire to colonise it for the purposes of profit; in other

210 Religion, Art, and a South Sudanese Post-National Imaginary

words, to identify the nature and market value of a notion of creative capital in order to commodify it.

(Harris 2014, 153)

By linking society, culture, and creativity, the interrelationship between capital and emerging expressions of creativity are easier to see through the ways in which "economic possibilities are informed by the complexion of a society—its cohesion, levels of trust, cultural diversity, capacity for creativity, urban life and distinctive patterns of settlement" (O'Connor and Gibson 2014, 5–6). Readers can see through the creative labour and subjectivities of these Samoan and South Sudanese youth the ways in which "cultural policy has never just been about 'the arts' but about creating citizens", and what role government policy and the commercial sector should play given "the sheer proliferation of cultural consumption and participation in contemporary society and economies [that] has provoked a crisis as to what kind of culture should states support and . . . how they should do this" (O'Connor and Gibson 2014, 6).

In summary, I want to pick up a point I floated but did not have space to fully explore in *The Creative Turn*, the possibility that "the quest for a reproducible creativity today echoes many aspects of Benjamin's argument" (Harris 2014, 5), and that by problematising a digital productivity continuum from Walter Benjamin through/past Marshall McLuhan to today's creative industries discourse, we might gain greater insight into "creative reproducibility and the modern productivity imperative" (5), the move perhaps from 'mechanical reproduction' to 'digital reproduction'.

Extending O'Connor's definition of cultural industries, I'm arguing that more than the instrumental value of understanding and problematising the current creative/cultural industries divide, there is broader cultural value to a closer reexamination of these notions (and industries). In other words, the ways in which "our media also tell us something about our increasingly singular world culture, global flows and knowledge economies; their insatiable need for creative products is linked to instantaneous dissemination in digital markets" (10). Indeed, it is increasingly clear that marketplace-driven redefinitions of creativity *and* culture are changing the way we think about and perform these social functions, not just talk about them. As Salehi reminds us:

If we accept that the formation of a paradigm is related to the context in which it emerges, I believe that both modernist and post-modernist discourses of creativity have been responsive to the needs of capitalism as a system of nomadic power and of constant de/reterritorialization. Today, the process of commodification plays a vital role in the construction and experience of contemporary subjectivity as well as the notion of creativity subjecting people to free-floating and nomadic forms of control. . . . The Deleuzian world is a state of flux, a constant differentiation. Creation, in such a world, is driven by differentiation.

The only way to affirm these underlying processes of differentiation is in 'creative becoming'.

(Salehi 2008, 283)

The cultural/creative industries crisis is not only a marketplace issue, it is a socio-cultural one in which a scholarly tethering of "commodification, imagination and creativity leads us back to epistemologies of globalisation. For Appadurai, 'globalisation is not simply the name for a new epoch in the history of capital or in the biography of the nation-state . . . it is marked by a new role for imagination in social life'" (Harris 2014, 12). Going further, Appadurai pushes us to see how modern consumption culture "seeks to replace the aesthetics of duration with the aesthetics of ephemerality" (Appadurai 1996, 84), a conceptual differentiation that avoids binarising aesthetics and capital but rather problematises the folding in of the two, creating a temporal shift rather than an aesthetic one in the ontology of contemporary creativity.

Elsewhere in seeking to consider aesthetics and commodification together, I have drawn on Massumi's attention to "creative relationship rather than aesthetics or outcomes, as a critical lens in helping to understand the power of creative capital in the words and works of the young people" (Harris 2014, 14) featured in this book and in previous collaborations I have conducted with them. But keeping aesthetics in the foreground or not, cultural economy returns us to a consideration of the particularities of the makers of the work: that is, cultural economies rely on local and cultural specificities, whereas creative economies seem to be a hegemonising move toward no-culture, or a marketplace culture which shares only profit as its singular defining feature. For O'Connor and Gibson,

> Cultural economy is a demonstrable area of economic activity, one which is not inconsiderable and where Australia has shown some international success . . . on the other hand, the cultural economy is also fundamentally cultural: it brings our attention to values that are distinct from the economy and on which the economy relies. There can be no cultural economy without cultural value.
>
> (2014, 6)

I am reminding readers of this more conceptual question about the socio-cultural function of creativity in contemporary times as a necessary context within which we immerse ourselves by entering the denser and more localised worlds of these two groups of extraordinary (and in some very wonderful ways, perfectly ordinary) young people. By framing their creative work and youthful views with considerable contextual unpacking of creativity, cultural industries, and capital, I am highlighting again that this book has set out to look at creativity and religion within these Sudanese and Samoan Australian youth cultures, but that it cannot be done without keeping in

212 *Religion, Art, and a South Sudanese Post-National Imaginary*

mind the meta-narrative of commodified creativity, education, and culture (because these commodifications do co-occur).

Creative Counterpublics

These two youth subcultures (or what Hickey-Moody would call *counterpublics*) offer a view to the ways in which the competing notions of creativity (in all its forms, including creative industries, commodifiable creativity, and the doing of creativity, to name just a few) and cultural economy (culture as a grounding influence, an enfleshing return, a mouth-to-mouth resuscitation of the heart-stopped and dangerously emaciated creative industries/creative economy model) might have something to learn from emergent youth cultures. They both demonstrate in different ways how to be active in creative *and* cultural economies, albeit perhaps not the kind which Richard Florida (2002) and other creativity scholars had envisioned. They perform a kind of hybrid cultural/creative expression of their faith and religious values and communities that have global interest, if not yet the same kind of creative capital generated by majoritarian creative economic outputs.

Nevertheless, the creative practices explored in this book do connect their makers globally, giving them a kind of creative and digital mobility that might still translate into for-profit capital. This kind of market value, it should be noted, is not far from the minds of many of these young people, despite considerable stereotyping about them making music, fashion, and media contributions only for the love of God and for cultural connectivity. It goes far beyond this, as readers will hopefully have seen in their commentary and creative makings.

While the South Sudanese youth certainly approach their creative labour in ways that are importantly different from their Samoan peers, they are still both representative of some ways in which the creative and cultural industries might be re-coupled in Australia and elsewhere. That is, the South Sudanese youth here market themselves (including creativity, culture, and religion) primarily in relation to hip hop and runway model culture out of the United States, whereas the Samoan youth really see themselves as bringing culture and faith into the mainstream of Australian culture, and in so doing allow themselves to stay connected globally to other Samoan diasporic travellers and Christian faithful. In other words (and perhaps it is obvious), these two distinct groups of young people are doing culture, faith practices, and creativity in ways that may look similar but are markedly different. As a cohering (but hopefully not limiting) central question in this book, these two case studies exemplify through distinct lenses how creative youth practices embedded in religion and community are both representative of a contemporary creative industries discourse and yet representative of the ways in which this discourse is insufficient. I have no interest in being prescriptive about what needs to change, or even how, but I hope that readers will find here some examples of the ways in which O'Connor's call to avoid the creative industries trap that has plagued the UK might be reconceptualised elsewhere, including (as here) in Australia.

Changing Creative and Cultural Policy

O'Connor and Gibson make the following explicit recommendation that in any effective national-level policy,

> an ongoing effort should be made to engage regions and populations in Australia beyond those which are predominantly represented in the major cultural industries. While it may be the case that economic output is relatively concentrated in zones of high capital investment near the centre of the major cities, there are also considerable cultural resources in Australia's suburbs and regions and among its indigenous and migrant communities. These resources should be nurtured both for cultural and economic reasons.
>
> (2014, 73)

They also recommend that government should work harder to understand "the cultural economy and the ways it adds value to Australian society" (73), a political investment that can only take place by consulting the "broad range of interests involved in cultural economy—not just the arts and not just the commercial creative sector but including cultural workers, urban policy makers, community sector representatives and academic researchers. A review of the field should involve questions of what is cultural value, how it is produced and what measures are needed to achieve this" (2014, 73). In addition to the need for the kind of high-level consultation described by O'Connor and Gibson, an inclusion of the kinds of innovation being done by these young people and others like them should not be ignored. This is not to suggest that economic or capital value is the primary contribution of these young people's creativity, but it is one aspect that remains underrecognised. But in closing, let me turn to a consideration of how participatory and DIY youth culture, including the digital engagements seen here, might be suggesting new ways forward.

Creative Youth Citizenship

These youth are demonstrating forms of creative citizenship through their layered and diverse creative practices as both a form of citizenship and a kind of post-national transcendence beyond citizenship. While the notion of the 'creative citizen', especially in youth cultures, still has multiple meanings and is variously defined according to region, young people are indeed constructing their own expressions and interpretations of the creative citizen in a range of contexts, including the global south, which is too often still overlooked in mainstream scholarship. This book has tried to critically

214   *Religion, Art, and a South Sudanese Post-National Imaginary*

interrogate whether creative practices do enhance youth voices as a platform for empowerment, or whether they create and populate alternate 'scapes' in which these physically globally local youth are not using their creative digital practices aspirationally but rather resistantly.

Do their digitally mediated communities and voices perform a kind of global citizenship that is informed (or co-constructed) by religious, cultural, and youth-oriented subjectivities? Or do these communities and voices embody a kind of rejection of global mobility/citizenship? The youth themselves throughout this book have described ambivalence on this question. While they are in conversation with popular culture digital representations of 'empowered' creative youth elsewhere around the globe, they primarily seem to use these creative practices and digital tools for reinforcing local, cultural, and religious maintenance rather than seeking 'to become famous', for example.

DIY Culture and '*Va*'

While Anita Harris, Greg Dimitriadis, Anna Hickey-Moody, and Appadurai have written extensively on the topic of intercultural and urban youth, creativity and citizenship, these analyses have still often remained liberatory narratives of 'overcome-ance'. This book has sought to share the work and perspectives of youth from two interconnected culturally minoritarian groups, as representative of other kinds of creative practice that is youth-driven but not in the interest of doxic aspirations of fame, fortune, or social or economic mobility. While the South Sudanese show some ways in which creative practice offers young people a way to work toward improving their present material conditions, it still provides an active point of critique between cultural value and creative citizenship (for more on this see Ratto and Boler 2014). Participatory and do-it-yourself (DIY) maker culture takes on different characteristics through the Samoan youth group's creative music-making and everyday YouTube and social media dissemination (see Burgess and Green 2009 for more in-depth analysis of participatory culture).

Creativity as performed by these youth is both local to their identity-making, family, and church practices and contexts, and at the same time highly networked. What does it mean for them to creatively recreate the notion of citizenship, and how do they understand those practices? My articulation of *creative counterpublics* points to the potential of hybrid online/offline worlds and digital media to network young people who have previously remained both geographically and creatively local. Those like the Samoan youth in this book have adopted that local embeddedness as a strength. The coherence (for some, it must be repeated) of cultural practices, such as dances, songs, food, and religious celebrations, has withstood multiple migrations, fractures, and economic adversity. Yet the economic 'push factors' behind their migration out of Samoa are profoundly different from the civil war that propelled these South Sudanese youth out of their home region. The ways in which they have maintained religious and creative practices are also different, and result in different individual as well as collective subjectivities.

Digital media make these differences visible in ways that they have never been before. The internet offers these young people the opportunity to cultivate local artforms and creative practices while becoming globally networked. Their online creative engagements can run a wide gamut between diasporic family reunions, to Christian proselytising, to for-profit career building in creative industries (Burgess and Green 2009; O'Connor 2013).

One example is autoethnographer Jerodeen Fetaui Iosefo, who, like Joshua, is also from South Auckland in New Zealand. Her innovative and creative masters thesis outlines and draws heavily on "three types of *va* (a Samoan term for 'a space that relates'): The sacred space, the space of relationships, and the respectful space" (J. Iosefo 2014). There are in all thirty-seven types of *va* in Samoan culture, but Iosefo focuses on these three in reminding readers that the work of scholarship is creative, cultural, and faith-filled, expressed in all three types of *va* (spaces). Whether digitally networked, or in offline worlds, attention to *va* has transformative potential for non-Samoans too. Twenty-first century citizenship is still an emergent ideal but one that must be better linked with culturally embedded *va*. Vineta and her peers are clear about the need for strengthening those links, but also about the foundations: "The heartbeat of our group is our family, our culture, and last but not least, our awesome God".

As the book began, I end with an acknowledgement that the threads that bind creativity and spirituality are long and deep, and the things that make creativity both difficult to define and worth pursuing are some of the same (and most elusive) characteristics of faith and spirituality. I don't claim to have written a comprehensive treatment of the spiritual, creative, and cultural lives of these youth, but rather to have offered some provocations to scholarly, non-Samoan and non-Sudanese communities based on the complexity of these creative practices and products. The ways in which these young people find and construct meaning in their lives show the functional value that both creativity and faith practices can serve. What Yip and Page call 'everyday religion' is in abundance within the rich tapestry that scholars might call intersectionality, but which these youth groups acknowledge as a beautiful and valuable inheritance grounded in culture, religion, and creativity, with not a deficit frame in sight. I hope a fraction of that richness is evident in these pages.

References

Abra, Gordon and Abra, Jock. 1999. "Collaboration and competition." In *Encyclopedia of Creativity, Volume One: Online Version*, edited by Mark Runco, and Steven R. Pritzger, 283–294. San Diego: Academic Press.

Ahmed, Sara. 2010. *The Promise of Happiness*. Durham, NC: Duke University Press.

Allen, Kim. 2014. " 'Blair's children': Young women as 'aspirational subjects' in the psychic landscape of class." *The Sociological Review* 62(4): 760–779.

Amabile, Teresa. 1982. "Social psychology of creativity: A consensual assessment technique." *Journal of Personality and Social Psychology* 43: 997–1013.

Ammerman, Nancy T. 2007. "Introduction: Observing modern religious lives." In *Everyday Religion: Observing Modern Religious Lives*, edited by Nancy Ammerman, 3–20. Oxford: Oxford University Press.

Anderson, Benedict. 2006/1983. *Imagined Communities: Reflections on the Origin and Spread of Nationalism*. London: Verso.

Ante, Spencer E. 2008. *Creative Capital: Georges Doriot and the Birth of Venture Capital*. Boston: Harvard Business School Publishing.

Anthias, Floya. 2002. "Where do I belong? Narrating collective identity and translocational positionality." *Ethnicities* 2(4): 491–514.

Appadurai, Arjun. 2013. *The Future as Cultural Fact: Essays on the Global Condition*. London: Verso.

Appadurai, Arjun. 2006. *Fear of Small Numbers: An Essay on the Geography of Anger*. Durham, NC: Duke University Press.

Appadurai, Arjun. 2004. "The capacity to aspire: Culture and the terms of recognition." In *Culture and Public Action*, edited by Vijayendra Rao, and Michael Walton, 59–84. Stanford: Stanford University Press.

Appadurai, Arjun. 1999. "Globalization and the research imagination." *International Social Science Journal* 160: 229–238.

Appadurai, Arjun. 1996. *Modernity at Large: Cultural Dimensions of Globalization*. Minneapolis, MN: University of Minnesota Press.

Appadurai, Arjun. 1990. "Disjuncture and difference in the global cultural economy." *Public Culture* 2(2): 1–24.

Appadurai, Arjun. 1986. *Social Life of Things: Commodities in Cultural Perspective*. Cambridge MA: Cambridge University Press.

Appiah, Kwame Anthony. 2010. *Cosmopolitanism: Ethics in a World of Strangers (issues of our times)*. New York: WW Norton.

218 *References*

Araya, Danial, and Michael A. Peters. 2010. *Education in the Creative Economy: Knowledge and Learning in the Age of Innovation.* New York: Peter Lang.

Arieti, Silvano. 1976. *Creativity: The Magic Synthesis.* New York: Basic Books.

Asante, Molefi Kete. 2008. "Ideological significance of Afrocentricity in intercultural communication." In *The Global Intercultural Communication Reader*, edited by Malafi Kete Asante, Yoshitaka Miike, and Jing Yin, 47–56. New York: Routledge.

Baker, Joanne. 2010. "Claiming volition and evading victimhood: Post-feminist obligations for young women." *Feminism and Psychology* 20(2): 186–204.

Banks, Marcus. 2001/2005. *Visual Methods in Social Research.* London: Sage.

Barad, Karen. 2003. "Posthumanist performativity: Toward an understanding of how matter comes to matter." *Signs: Journal of Women in Culture and Society* 28(3): 801–831.

Barone, Tom, and Elliot W. Eisner. 2011. *Arts Based Research.* Thousand Oaks, CA: Sage.

Barrett, Brian D. 2009. "The 'invisible institution' and a disappearing achievement gap." *Religion and Education* 36(3): 22–38.

Barrett, Margaret. 2011. "Troubling the creative imaginary: Some possibilities of ecological thinking for music and learning." In *Musical Imaginations: Multidisciplinary Perspectives on Creativity, Performance and Perception*, edited by D. Hargreaves, D. Miell, and R. MacDonald, 206–219. Oxford: Oxford University Press.

Battacharya, Kakali. 2013. "Voices, silences, and telling secrets: The role of qualitative methods in arts-based research." *International Review of Qualitative Research* 6(4): 604–627.

Bauman, Zygmont. 2011. *Culture in a Liquid Modern World.* Cambridge: Polity Press.

Bauman, Zygmont. 2006. *Liquid Times.* Cambridge: Polity Press.

Bauman, Zygmont. 2004. *Wasted Lives: Modernity and Its Outcasts.* Cambridge: Polity Press.

Beilharz, Peter. 2005. "Alienation." In *Encyclopedia of Social Theory*, edited by George Ritzer (vol 1), 9–10. Thousand Oaks: Sage.

Benjamin, Walter. 1936/1973. "The work of art in the age of mechanical reproduction." In *Illuminations*, 211–244. London: HarperCollins.

Berlant, Lauren. 2011. *Cruel Optimism.* Durham, NC: Duke University Press.

Berlant, Lauren. 2008. *The Female Complaint.* Durham and London: Duke.

Berlant, Lauren. 1997. *The Queen of America Goes to Washington City: Essays on Sex and Citizenship.* Durham, NC: Duke University Press.

Boler, Megan, A. Macdonald, Christina Nitsou, and Anne Harris. 2014. "Connective labor and social media: Women's roles in the 'leaderless' Occupy movement." *Convergence: The International Journal of Research into New Media Technologies (Special Issue 'New Media, Global Activism and Politics')*, November (20): 438–460.

Bourdieu, Pierre. 2000. *Pascalian Meditations.* Stanford, CA: Stanford University Press.

Bourdieu, Pierre. 1984. *Distinction: A Social Critique of the Judgement of Taste.* Abingdon: Routledge.

Bourdieu, Pierre. 1977/2008. *Outline of a Theory of Practice.* (R. Nice, Trans.). Cambridge, UK: Cambridge University Press.

References 219

Bourdieu, Pierre, and Loic J.D. Wacquant. 1992. *An Invitation to Reflexive Sociology*. Cambridge: Polity Press.

Bovone, Laura. 1990. "Cultural intermediaries: A new role for intellectuals." *Innovations* 1(1): 72–94.

Braidotti, Rosi. 2013. *The Posthuman*. Cambridge: Polity Press.

Bresler, Liora. 2007. "Introduction." In *International Handbook of Research in Arts Education*, edited by Liora Bresler, xvii–xx. The Netherlands: Springer.

Britzman, Deborah. 2003. *Practice Makes Practice: A Critical Study of Learning to Teach* (revised, foreword by Maxine Greene). Albany, NY: SUNY Press.

Burgess, Jean, and Joshua Green. 2009. *YouTube: Online Video and Participatory Culture*. Cambridge: Polity Press.

Burnaford, Gail E., Arnold Aprill, and Cynthia Weiss. 2001. *Renaissance in the Classroom: Arts Integration and Meaningful Learning*. Mahwah: L. Erlbaum Associates.

Butler, Judith. 2011. Judith Butler at Occupy Wall Street [video]. http://www.youtube.com/watch?v=JVpoOdz1AKQ.

Butler, Judith. 1993. *Bodies That Matter: On the Discursive Limits of Sex*. London: Routledge.

Cassity, Elizabeth, and Greg Gow. 2006. "Shifting space and cultural place: The transition experiences of African young people in Western Sydney high schools." In *AARE 2005 International Education Research Conference. Creative Dissent: Constructive Solutions*, edited by PL Jeffrey (vol. 1), 1–15. Melbourne: AARE.

Castree, Noel, and Thomas Macmillan. 2004. "Old News: Representation and academic novelty." *Environment and Planning A* 36: 469–480.

Caves, Richard E. 2000. *Creative Industries: Contracts between Art and Commerce*. Boston: Harvard University Press.

Cheung, Sin Yi, and Jenny Phillimore. 2013. *Social Networks, Social Capital and Refugee Integration*. Research Report for Nuffield Foundation. Accessed September 15, 2015. http://www.birmingham.ac.uk/Documents/college-social-sciences/social-policy/iris/2013/nuffield-refugees-integration-research-report.pdf.

Chi, Sang, and Emily Moberg Robinson. 2012. *Voices of the Asian American and Pacific Islander Experience*. Santa Barbara, CA: Greenwood.

Clarke, Adele. 2005. *Situational Analysis: Grounded Theory after the Postmodern Turn*. Thousand Oaks: Sage.

Clough, Patricia T. 2010. "The affective turn: Political economy, biomedia, and bodies." In *The Affect Theory Reader*, edited by Melissa Gregg, and Greg Seigworth, 206–225. Durham: Duke University Press.

Collins, Hilary. 2010. *Creative Research: The Theory and Practice of Research for the Creative Industries*. Lausanne, Switzerland: AVA Publishing.

Collins, Jock, Greg Noble, Scott Poynting, and Paul Tabar. 2000. "Kids, kebabs, cops and crime." *Pluto Press, Sydney* 10: 251.

Connell, Raewyn. 2007. *Southern Theory: The Global Dynamics of Knowledge in Social Science*. Crows Nest, NSW: Allen & Unwin.

Conrad, Diane, and Anita Sinner (Eds.). 2015. *Creating Together: Participatory, Community-Based, and Collaborative Arts Practices and Scholarship across Canada*. Waterloo: Wilfred Laurier University Press.

Craft, Anna. 2011. *Creativity and Education Futures: Learning in a Digital Age*. London: Trentham.

220 References

Crocombe, Ron. 2001. *The South Pacific*. Suva: Institute of Pacific Studies, University of the South Pacific.

Davies, Rosamund & Sigthorsson, Gauti. (2013). *Introducing the Creative Industries: From Theory to Practice*. Los Angeles, CA: Sage

DeMoss, Karen. 2005. "Washington, DC: Arts education partnership: How arts integration supports student learning: Evidence from students in Chicago's CAPE partnership schools." *Arts and Learning Research Journal* 21: 91–117.

de Plevitz, Loretta R. 2007. "Testing the social justice goals of education: A role for anti-discrimination law." *The Australian Journal of Indigenous Education* 36(Supplement): 98–107.

Dewey, John. 1934/2005. *Art as Experience*. New York: Perigree Books.

Dewey, John. 1927. *The Public and Its Problem*. New York: Henry Holt and Company.

DiMaggio, Paul. 2005. "Cultural capital." In *Encyclopedia of Social Theory*, edited by George Ritzer (vol 1), 167–170. Thousand Oaks: Sage.

Dimitriadis, Greg. 2012. *Critical Dispositions: Evidence and Expertise in Education*. New York: Routledge.

Dimitriadis, Greg. 2009. *Performing Identity/Performing Culture: Hip Hop as Text, Pedagogy and Lived Practice*. New York: Peter Lang.

Dimitriadis, Greg. 2008a. "Series editor introduction." In *Youth Moves: Identities and Education in Global Perspective*, edited by Fazal Rizvi, and Nadine Dolby, ix–x. New York: Routledge.

Dimitriadis, Greg. 2008b. *Studying Urban Youth Culture: Primer*. New York: Peter Lang.

Dimitriadis, Greg, and Lois Weis. 2008. "Rethinking the research imaginary: Globalization and multisited ethnographic approaches." In *Studying Urban Youth Culture*, edited by Greg Dimitriadis, 81–108. New York: Peter Lang.

Dobson, Amy Shields. 2015. *Postfeminist Digital Cultures: Femininity, Social Media, and Self-Representation*. London: Palgrave Macmillan.

Dobson, Amy Shields, and Anita Harris. 2015. "Post-girlpower: Globalized mediated femininities." *Continuum: Journal of Media and Cultural Studies* 29(2): 143–144.

Dolby, Nadine, and Fazal Rizvi. 2008. "Introduction: Youth, mobility and identity." In *Youth Moves: Identities and Education in Global Perspectives*, edited by Fazal Rizvi, and Nadine Dolby, 1–14. New York: Routledge.

Donelan, Kate. 2010. "Drama as intercultural education: An ethnographic study of an intercultural performance project in a secondary school." *Special Issue: Youth Theatre Journal* 24(1): 19–33.

Edgerton, Anne. 2002. "What about the lost girls of Sudan?" *Refugees International, March 11*. Accessed July 17, 2015. http://www.interaction.org/library/detail.php?id=397.

Eisner, Elliot. 2003. "Art and Knowledge." In *Handbook of the Arts in Qualitative Research*, edited by J. Gary Knowles, and Ardra L. Cole, 3–13. Los Angeles, CA: Sage Publications.

Ellsworth, Elizabeth. 1997. *Teaching Positions: Difference, Pedagogy, and the Power of Address*. New York: Teachers College Press, Columbia University.

Ewing, Robyn. 2011. *Australian Education Review: The Arts and Australian Education: Realising Potential*. Camberwell: Australian Council for Educational Research.

References 221

Faleomavaega, Eni F. H. 2012. "Regarding the minimum wage in American Samoa." In *Voices of the Asian American and Pacific Islander Experience*, edited by Sang Chi, and Emily Moberg Robinson, 53–57. Santa Barbara: Greenwood.

Featherstone, Mike. 1991. *Consumer Culture and Postmodernism*. London: Sage.

Fine, Michelle. 1994. 'Dis-stances and Other Stances: Negotiations of power inside feminist research." In A. Gitlin (ed.), *Power and Method: Political Activism and Educational Research*, pp 13–35. London: Routledge.

Fine, Michelle. 2008. "Sexuality, schooling, and adolescent females: The missing discourse of desire." In *Critical Pedagogy Reader*, edited by Antonia Darder, Marta P. Baltodano, and Rodolfo D. Torres, 296–321. New York: Routledge.

Fine, Michelle. 2004. "Foreword." In *All about the Girl: Culture, Power and Identity*, edited by Anita Harris, xi–xvi. New York: Routledge.

Fine, Michelle, Lois Weis, and L. C. Powell. 1997. "Communities of difference: A critical look at desegregated spaces created for and by youth." *Harvard Educational Review* 67(2): 247–285.

Flew, Terry. 2013. *Global Creative Industries*. Cambridge: Polity Press.

Flew, Terry. 2012. *Creative Industries: Culture and Policy*. London and Thousand Oaks: Sage.

Florida, Richard. 2007/2010. *The Flight of the Creative Class: The New Global Competition for Talent*. New York: HarperCollins.

Florida, Richard. 2002. *The Rise of the Creative Class and How It's Transforming Work, Leisure, Community and Everyday Life*. New York: Basic Books.

Foucalt, Michel. 2005. *The Hermeneutics of the Subject: Lectures at the Collège de France 1981–1982*, trans. G. Burchell. Picador: London.

Forman, Murray. 2005. "Straight outta Mogadishu: Prescribed identities and performative practices among Somali youth in North American high schools." In *Youthscapes: The Popular, the National, the global*, edited by Sunaina Maira, and Elisabeth Soep, 3–22. Philadelphia: University of Pennsylvania Press.

Fraser, Nancy. 1990. *Rethinking the Public Sphere: A Contribution to the Critique of Actually Existing Democracy*. Milwaukee: University of Wisconsin-Milwaukee.

Gale, Mary-Anne. 2011. "Rekindling warm embers: Teaching aboriginal languages in the tertiary sector." *Australian Review of Applied Linguistics*, 34(3): 280–296.

Gallagher, Kathleen. 2014. *Why Theatre Matters: Urban Youth, Engagement and a Pedagogy of the Real*. Toronto: University of Toronto Press.

Gallagher, Kathleen. 2000. *Drama Education in the Lives of Girls: Imagining Possibilities*. Toronto: University of Toronto Press.

Georgina, Dianna Mary. 2007. "Performing selves: The semiotics of selfhood in Samoan-Dance." PhD diss., Washington State University. http://www.dissertations.wsu.edu/Dissertations/Spring2007/d_georgina_050307.pdf.

Gifford, Sandy, Ignacio Correa-Velez, and Robyn Sampson. 2009. *Good Starts for Recently Arrived Youth with Refugee Backgrounds: Promoting Wellbeing in the First Three Years of Settlement in Melbourne, Australia*. Melbourne: The La Trobe Refugee Research Centre, La Trobe University and the Victorian Foundation for Survivors of Torture (Foundation House). Accessed March 9, 2015. http://www.myan.org.au/file/file/useful%20resources/report-good-starts.pdf.

Gill, Rosalind. 2007. "Postfeminist media culture: Elements of a sensibility." *European Journal of Cultural Studies* 10(2): 147–166.

Gilligan, Carol. 2002. *The Birth of Pleasure*. New York, NY: Alfred A. Knopf.

222 *References*

Ginsberg, Robert. 1985. "Creativity and culture." In *Creativity in Art, Religion and Culture*, edited by Michael H. Mitias, 98–106. Amsterdam: Elementa/Rodopi Press.

Giri, Ananta Kumar. 2004. *Creative Social Research: Rethinking Theories and Methods.* New York: Lexington (Rowman & Littlefield).

Giroux, Henry. 2005. "Cultural Studies in Dark Times: Public Pedagogy and the Challenge of Neoliberalism." Accessed October 12, 2014. http://www.henryagiroux.com/online_articles/DarkTimes.htm.

Giroux, Henry. 1992. *Border Crossings.* New York: Perigee Books.

Giuffre, Katherine Anne. 2009. *Collective Creativity: Art and Society in the South Pacific.* Farnham UK/Burlington, VT: Ashgate.

Gonick, Marnina, Emma Renold, Jessica Ringrose, and Lisa Weems. 2009. "Rethinking agency and resistance: What comes after girl power?" *Girlhood Studies* 2(2): 1–9. DOI: 10.3167/ghs.2009.020202.

Gray, Jan, and Quentin Beresford. 2008. "A 'formidable challenge': Australia's quest for equity in Indigenous education." *Australian Journal of Education* 52(2): 197–223.

Greene, Maxine. 2000. *Releasing the Imagination: Essays on Education, the Arts, and Social Change.* San Francisco, CA: Jossey Bass.

Groot, Wim, and H. van den Brink. 2006. "What does education do to our health? Measuring the effects of education on health and civic engagement." In *Proceedings of the Copenhagen Symposium.* Accessed March 5, 2015. http://www.oecd.org/education/country-studies/measuringtheeffectsofeducationonhealthandcivicengagement.htm.

Grossberg, Laurence. 2010. *Cultural Studies in the Future Tense.* Durham, NC: Duke University Press.

Grumet, Madeleine R. 1990. "Retrospective: Autobiography and the analysis of educational experience." *Cambridge Journal of Education* 20(3): 277–282.

Hall, Clare. 2016. "Pre-service teachers converting motherhood into creative capital through composing with sound." In *Creative Teaching for Creative Learning in Higher Music Education*, edited by Elizabeth Haddon, and Pamela Burnard, 119–131. Farnham: Ashgate.

Hall, Stuart. 1997. "The spectacle of the 'other'." In *Representation: Cultural Representations and Signifying Practices*, edited by Stuart Hall, 223–289. London: Sage.

Hall, Stuart. 1991. "The local and the global." In *Culture, Globalization and the World System*, edited by A. King, 173–187. London: Macmillan.

Haraway, Donna. J. 2008. *When Species Meet.* Minneapolis: University of Minnesota Press.

Hardt, Michael, and Antonio Negri. 2000. *Empire.* Cambridge: Harvard University Press.

Harris, Anita. 2013. *Young People and Everyday Multiculturalism.* New York: Routledge.

Harris, Anita. (Ed.). 2008. *Next Wave Cultures: Feminism, Subcultures, Activism.* New York: Routledge.

Harris, Anita. (Ed.). 2004. *All about the Girl: Culture, Power and Identity.* New York: Routledge.

Harris, Anne. 2016. *Creativity and Education.* London: Palgrave MacMillan.

References 223

Harris, Anne. 2015a. "Ahmed, affect and the social imaginary in ethnocinema." In *The International Handbook of Intercultural Arts*, edited by Pamela Burnard, and Elizabeth Mackinlay, pp. 81–90. London: Routledge.

Harris, Anne. 2015b. *Video as Method*. London: Oxford University Press.

Harris, Anne. 2014. *The Creative Turn: Toward a New Research Imaginary*. Rotterdam: Sense Publishers.

Harris, Anne. 2013a. *Ethnocinema: Intercultural Arts Education*. The Netherlands: Springer.

Harris, Anne. 2013b. "Peered and tiered learning: Action research as creative cultural pedagogy." *Educational Action Research* 21(3): 412–428.

Harris, Anne. 2013c. "Alphabet rap: Hip hop and the re-coolification of creative pedagogies as research." (article and videos) *New Scholar: An International Journal of the Humanities, Creative Arts and Social Sciences (ejournal)* 2(1): 121–135.

Harris, Anne. 2013d. "Animating failure: Digital collaboration at the intersection of sex, race and culture." *Continuum Journal of Media and Culture* 27(6): 812–824.

Harris, Anne. 2012a. "Blame it on Tyra: Race, refugeity and sexual representation." *Sex Education: Sexuality, Society and Learning* 12(1): 79–94.

Harris, Anne. 2012b. *Sailing into Uni!* (Series of short videos). Accessed June 1, 2015. http://www.creativeresearchhub.com/#!sailing-into-uni-film-clips/ct99.

Harris, Anne. 2011a. "Singing into language: Creating a public pedagogy." *Discourse: Studies in the Cultural Politics of Education* 32(5): 729–743. DOI: 10.1080/01596306.2011.620755.

Harris, Anne. 2011b. *Teaching Diversities: Same Sex Attracted Young People, CALD Communities, and Arts-Based Community Education*. Melbourne: Centre for Multicultural Youth. Accessed February 17, 2015. http://www.glhv.org.au/report/teaching-diversities-same-sex-attracted-young-people-cald-communities-and-arts-based-communit.

Harris, Anne. 2010. "I ain't no girl: Representation and reconstruction of the 'Found Girls' of Sudan." *Race/Ethnicity* 4(1): 41–63. DOI: 10.1353/rac.2010.0030.

Harris, Anita, and Amy Shields Dobson. 2015. "Theorizing agency in post-girlpower times." *Continuum: Journal of Media & Cultural Studies* 29(2): 145–156.

Harris, Anne, and Enza Gandolfo. 2013. "Looked at and looked over or: I wish I was adopted." *Gender, Place & Culture: A Journal of Feminist Geography*. DOI: 10.1080/0966369X.2013.810608.

Harris, Anne, and Andrea Lemon. 2012. "Bodies that shatter: Creativity, culture and the new pedagogical imaginary." *Pedagogy, Culture and Society* 20(3): 413–433. DOI: 10.1080/14681366.2012.712054.

Harris, Anne, Jay Marlowe, and Nyadol Nyuon. 2014. "Rejecting Ahmed's 'melancholy migrant': South Sudanese Australians in higher education." *Studies in Higher Education: 1226–1238*. DOI: 10.1080/03075079.2014.881346.

Harris, Anne, Ceridwen Spark, and Mimi Ngum Chi Watts. 2014. "Gains and losses: African Australian women and higher education." *Journal of Sociology* 51(2): 370–384. DOI: 10.1.177/1440783314536792.

Hartley, John, Jason Potts, Stuart Cunningham, Terry Flew, Michael A. Keane, and John Banks. 2012. *Key Concepts in Creative Industries*. London: Sage.

Hartshorne, Charles. 1985. "Creativity as a Value and Creativity as a Transcendental Category." In *Creativity in Art, Religion and Culture*, edited by Michael H. Mitias, 3–11. Amsterdam: Elementa/Rodopi Press.

224 *References*

Hausman, Charles. 1985. "Originality as a criterion of creativity." In *Creativity in Art, Religion and Culture*, edited by Michael H. Mitias, 26–41. Amsterdam: Elementa/Rodopi Press.

Henry, Colette. 2008. "Women and the creative industries: Exploring the popular appeal." *Creative Industries Journal* 2(2): 143.

Hesmondhalgh, David. 2007. *The Cultural Industries*, 2nd edition. London: Sage.

Hewison, Robert. 2014. *Cultural Capital: The Rise and Fall of Creative Britain*. London/Brooklyn: Verso.

Hickey-Moody, Anna. 2013. *Youth, Arts and Education: Reassembling Subjectivity through Affect*. London: Routledge.

Holman Jones, Stacy, Tony Adams, and Carolyn Ellis. 2014. *Handbook of Autoethnography*. Oxford: Oxford University Press.

Iosefo, Jerudeen O. F. 2014. "Moon walking with the Pasifika girl in the mirror: An autoethnography on the spaces of higher education." PhD diss., University of Auckland, NZ. Accessed September 30, 2015. http://edtalks.org/video/moonwalking-pasifika-girl-mirror.

Iosefo, Joshua. 2012. Brown Brother. *TedxTalk*. Accessed October 3, 2015. https://www.youtube.com/watch?v=S-SKYOwjIGU.

Ito, Mizuko. 2008. 'Mobilizing the imagination in everyday play: The case of Japanese media mixes'. In Kirsten Drotner and Sonia Livingstone (Eds.), *International Handbook of Children, Media and Culture*, pp 401–412. London: Sage.

Jenkins, Henry. 2006. *Convergence Culture: Where Old and New Media Collide*. New York: NYU Press.

Jessop, Bob. 2005. "Cultural political economy, the knowledge-based economy, and the state." In *The Technological Economy*, edited by Andrew Barry, and Don Slater, 142–164. London: Routledge.

Joubert, Mathilda Marie. 2001. "The art of creative teaching: NACCCE and beyond." In *Creativity in Education*, edited by Anna Craft, Bob Jeffrey, and Mike Leibling, 17–34. London: Continuum.

Kaufman, James C., and Robert J. Sternberg. (Eds.). 2010. *The Cambridge Handbook of Creativity*. New York: Cambridge University Press.

Kaufman, James C., and Robert J. Sternberg. (Eds.). 2006. *The International Handbook of Creativity*. New York: Cambridge University Press.

Keller, Jessalynn. 2015. "Girl power's last chance? Tavi Gevinson, feminism, and popular media culture." *Continuum: Journal of Media & Cultural Studies* 29(2): 274–285.

Kennelly, Jacqueline Joan. 2009. "Youth cultures, activism and agency: Revisiting feminist debates." *Gender and Education* 21(3): 259–272.

Kenway, Jane, and Johanna Fahey. (Eds.). 2009. *Globalizing the Research Imagination*. New York: Routledge.

Kincheloe, Joe L. 2005. "The curriculum and the classroom." In *Classroom Teaching: An Introduction*, edited by Joe L. Kincheloe, 85–103. New York: Peter Lang.

Kokkos, Alexis. 2010. "Transformative learning through aesthetic experience: Towards a comprehensive method." *Journal of Transformative Education* 8(3): 155–177.

Korn-Bursztyn, Carol. 2005. "Crossing Institutional Cultures: Brooklyn College and Lincoln Center Institute." In *Community in the Making: Lincoln Center Institute, the Arts, and Teacher Education*, edited by Madeleine Fuchs Holzer, and Scott Noppe-Brandon, 45–57. New York: Teachers College Press, Columbia University.

Kratke, Stefan. 2012. *The Creative Capital of Cities: Interactive Knowledge Creation and the Urbanization Economies of Innovation.* Malden: Wiley Blackwell.

Kumashiro, Kevin K. 2009. *Against Common Sense: Teaching and Learning toward Social Justice.* New York: Routledge.

Lassander, Mika. 2012. "Grappling with liquid modernity: Investigating postsecular religion." In *Postsecular Society*, edited by Peter Nynäs, Mika Lassander, and Terhi Utriainen, 239–267. New Brunswick: Transaction Publishers.

Lather, Patti. 2007. *Getting Lost: Feminist Efforts Toward a Double(d) Science.* Albany: SUNY Press.

Leggo, Carl. 2015. "Loving language: A poet's vocation and vision." In *Arts-Based and Contemplative Practices in Research and Teaching: Honoring Presence*, edited by Susan Walsh, Barbara Bickel, and Carl Leggo, 141–167. New York: Routledge.

Lipsitz, George. 2005. "Foreword: Midnight's children: Youth culture in the age of globalization." In *Youthscapes: The Popular, the National, the Global*, edited by Sunaina Maira, and Elisabeth Soep, vii–xiv. Philadelphia: University of Pennsylvania Press.

Littlewood, Roland. 2004. "Commentary: Globalization, culture, body image, and eating disorders." *Culture, Medicine and Psychiatry* 28: 597–602.

Lowrie, Alex. (n.d.). "Joshua Iosefo." *The Graduate.* Accessed October 4, 2015. http://www.thegraduate.net.nz/our-people/profile/sample-profile.

Lubart, Todd I. 1999. "Creativity across cultures." In *Handbook of Creativity*, edited by Robert J. Sternberg, 339–350. Cambridge: Cambridge University Press.

Lubart, Todd I. 1990. "Creativity and cross-cultural variation." *International Journal of Psychology.* (published online 2007), 25(1): 39–59.

Lubart, Todd I., and Robert J. Sternberg. 1998. "Creativity across time and place: Life span and cross-cultural perspectives." *High Ability Studies* 9(1): 59–74.

Ma Rhea, Zane. 2012. "Partnership for improving outcomes in Indigenous education: Relationship or business?" *Journal of Education Policy* 27(1): 45–66.

MacDonnell, Judith A., and Geraldine Jody Macdonald. 2011. "Arts-based critical inquiry in nursing and interdisciplinary professional education: Guided imagery, images, narratives, and poetry." *Journal of Transformative Education* 9(4): 203–221.

Mageo, Jeannette. 2008. "Zones of ambiguity and identity politics in Samoa." *Journal of the Royal Anthropological Institute* N.S. 14: 61–78.

Maira, Sunaina. 2005. "The intimate and the imperial: South Asian Muslim immigrant youth after 9/11." In *Youthscapes: The Popular, the National, the Global*, edited by Sunaina Maira, and Elisabeth Soep, 64–82. Philadelphia: University of Pennsylvania Press.

Maira, Sunaina, and Elisabeth Soep. 2005. "Introduction." In *Youthscapes: The Popular, the National, the Global*, edited by Sunaina Maira, and Elisabeth Soep, xv–xxxiv. Philadelphia: University of Pennsylvania Press.

Manning, Erin. 2013. *Always More than One: Individuation's Dance.* Durham: Duke University Press.

Manning, Erin. 2009. *Relationscapes: Movement, Art, Philosophy.* Boston: MIT Press.

226 References

Manning, Erin. 2007. *Politics of Touch: Sense, Movement, Sovereignty.* Minneapolis: University of Minnesota Press.

Manning, Erin. 2003. *Ephemeral Territories: Representing Nation, Home and Identity in Canada.* Minneapolis: University of Minnesota Press.

Manning, Erin, and Brian Massumi. 2014. *Thought in the Act: Passages in the Ecology of Experience.* Minneapolis: University of Minnesota Press.

Mapping Memories: Experiences of Refugee Youth (no author). "Chapter 3: Going Places: Connecting personal stories to public places." Accessed August 8, 2015. http://www.mappingmemories.ca/book.

Margolis, Joseph. 1985. "Emergence and creativity." In *Creativity in Art, Religion and Culture*, edited by Michael H. Mitias, 12–25. Amsterdam: Elementa/Rodopi Press.

Mason, Jennifer, and Angela Dale. 2010. *Understanding Social Research: Thinking Creatively about Method.* New York: Sage.

Massumi, Brian. 2013. "Prelude." In *Always More Than One: Individuation's Dance*, edited by Erin Manning. Durham: Duke University Press.

Massumi, Brian. 2011. *Semblance and Event: Activist Philosophy and the Occurrent Arts.* Boston: MIT Press.

Massumi, Brian. 2002. *Parables for the Virtual: Movement, Affect, Sensation.* Durham: Duke University Press.

Mattelart, Armand, and Jean-Marie Piemme. 1982. "Cultural industries: The origin of an idea." *Cultural Industries: A Challenge for the Future of Culture*: 51–61.

Matthews, Judy H. 2008. "Developing creative capital: What can we learn from the workplace?" *Proceedings Creating Value: Between Commerce and Commons.* Brisbane: QUT Digital Repository. Accessed October 12, 2014. http://eprints. qut.edu.au/.

McDowell, Andrew J., and Malcolm J. Bond. 2006. "Body image differences among Malay, Samoan, and Australian women." *Asia Pacific Journal of Clinical Nutrition* 15: 201–207.

McGuire, Meredith B. 2003. "Why bodies matter: A sociological reflection on spirituality and materiality." *Spiritus: A Journal of Christian Spirituality* 3(1): 1–18.

McLuhan, Marshall. 1962. *The Gutenburg Galaxy: The Making of Typographical Man.* Toronto: University of Toronto Press.

McRobbie, Angela. 2011. "'Everyone is Creative': Artists as pioneers of the new economy?" In *Culture and Contestation in the New Century*, edited by Marc James Leger, 41–50. Chicago: University of Chicago Press.

McRobbie, Angela. 2009. *The Aftermath of Feminism: Gender, Culture and Social Change.* Los Angeles: Sage.

McRobbie, Angela. 2004. "Notes on postfeminism and popular culture: Bridget Jones and the new gender regime." In *All about the Girl: Culture, Power and Identity*, edited by Anita Harris, 3–14. New York: Routledge.

McWilliam, Erica, and Shane P. Dawson. 2008. "Teaching for creativity: Towards sustainable and replicable pedagogical practice." *Higher Education* 56: 633–643.

McWilliam, Erica, and Shane P. Dawson. 2007. "Understanding creativity: A survey of 'creative' academic teachers." *A Report for the Carrick Institute for Learning and Teaching in Higher Education.* Canberra: Australia.

Mead, Margaret. 1959. "Creativity in cross-cultural perspective." In *Creativity and Its Cultivation*, edited by Harold H. Anderson, 222–239. New York: Harper.

References 227

Mezirow, Jack. 2003. "Transformative learning as discourse." *Journal of Transformative Education.* 1(1): 58–63.

Mitias, Michael H. (Ed.). 1985. *Creativity in Art, Religion and Culture.* Amsterdam: Elementa/Rodopi Press.

Moll, Luis C., Cathy Amanti, Deborah Neffe, and Norma Gonzalez. 1992. "Funds of knowledge for reaching: Using a qualitative approach to connect homes and classrooms." *Theory into Practice* 32(2): 132–141.

Montuori, Alfonso. 2008. "The joy of inquiry." *Journal of Transformative Education* 6(1): 8–26.

Nash, Daphne. 2009. "Contingent, contested and changing: De-constructing indigenous knowledge in a science curriculum resource from the South Coast of New South Wales." *The Australian Journal of Indigenous Education* 38(supplement): 25–33.

Nayar, Usha S., and Amita Bhide. 2008. "Contextualizing Media competencies among young people in Indian culture: Interface with globalization." In *The International Handbook of Children, Media and Culture*, edited by Kirsten Drotner, and Sonia Livingstone, 328–335. London: Sage.

Netzer, Dorit, and Nancy Mangano Rowe. 2010. "Inquiry into creative and innovative processes: An experiential, whole-person approach to teaching creativity." *Journal of Transformative Education* 8(2): 124–145.

Niu, Weihua, and Robert Sternberg. 2001. "Cultural influences on artistic creativity and its evaluation." *International Journal of Psychology* 36(4): 225–241.

Nunn, Caitlin. 2010. "Spaces to speak: Challenging representations of Sudanese-Australians." *Journal of Intercultural Studies* 31(2): 183–198.

O'Brien, Angela, and Kate Donelan. 2008. "Introduction." In *The Arts and Youth at Risk: Global and Local Challenges*, edited by Angela O'Brien, and Kate Donelan, 1–12. Newcastle upon-Tyne: Cambridge Scholars Press.

O'Connor, Justin. 2013. "Intermediaries and imaginaries in the cultural and creative industries." *Regional Studies.* DOI: 10.1080/00343404.2012.748982.

O'Connor, Justin, and Mark Gibson. 2014. *Culture, Creativity, Cultural Economy: A Review.* Prime Minister's Science, Engineering and Innovation Council (PMSEIC). Accessed January 5, 2015. https://www.academia.edu/8368925/Culture_Creativity_Cultural_Economy_A_Review.

O'Mara, Ben, and Anne Harris. 2014. "Intercultural crossings in a digital age: ICT pathways with migrant and refugee-background youth." *Race, Ethnicity and Education.* http://dx.doi.org/10.1080/13613324.2014.885418.

Ong, Aihwa.1997. "Chinese modernities: Narratives of nation and of capitalism." In *Ungrounded Empires: The Cultural Politics of Modern Chinese Transnationalism*, edited by Aihwa Ong, and Donald Nonini, 171–202. New York: Routledge.

O'Sullivan, Edmund V. 2002. "The project and vision of transformative education." In *Expanding the Boundaries of Transformative Learning*, edited by Edmund V. O'Sullivan, Amish Morrell and Mary Ann O'Connor, 1–12. New York: Palgrave.

Peters, Michael A., and Daniel Araya. 2010. "Introduction: The creative economy: Origins, categories, concepts." In *Education in the Creative Economy: Knowledge and Learning in the Age of Innovation*, edited by Daniel Peters, and Michael A. Araya, 13–30. New York: Peter Lang.

Peters, Michael A., and T. Besley. 2008. *Why Foucault? New Directions in Educational Research.* New York: Peter Lang.

228 References

Piketty, Thomas. 2014. *Capital in the Twenty-First Century*. Cambridge: Harvard University Press.

Pimpa, Nattavud, and Ponsan Rojanapanich. 2011. "Creative education, globalization and social imaginary." *Creative Education/Scientific Research* 2(4): 103–108.

Polamalu, Tafea. 2009. "Diasporic dream: Letter to grandfather." In *The Space between: Negotiating Culture, Place, and Identity in the Pacific*, edited by A. Marata Tamaira, 62–63. Occasional Paper Series 44. Honolulu, Hawai'i: Center for Pacific Islands Studies, School of Pacific and Asian Studies, University of Hawai'i at Mānoa.

Pollock, Mica. 2005. "Race bending: 'Mixed' youth practicing strategic racialization in California." In *Youthscapes: The Popular, the National, the Global*, edited by Susaina Maira, and Elisabeth Soep, 43–63. Philadelphia: University of Pennsylvania Press.

Pope, Rob. 2005. *Creativity: Theory, History and Practice*. New York: Routledge.

Potts, Jason. 2011. *Creative Industries and Economic Evolution*. Cheltenham: Elgar.

Pratt, Mary Louise. 1998. "Arts of the contact zone." In *Negotiating Academic Literacies: Teaching and Learning Across Languages and Cultures*, edited by Vivian Zamel and Ruth Speck, 171–185. Mahwah, NJ: Lawrence Erlbaum.

Pratt, Mary Louise. 1992. *Imperial Eyes: Travel Writing and Transculturation*. London: Routledge.

Raina, M.K. 1999. "Cross-cultural differences." In *Encyclopedia of Creativity, Two-Volume Set: Online Version*, edited by Mark Runco, and Steven R. Pritzger, 453–464. San Diego: Academic Press.

Rancière, Jean. 2009. *The Aesthetic Unconscious*. Cambridge/Malden: Polity Press.

Rao, Vijayendra, and Michael Walton. 2004. "Culture and public action: Relationality, equality of agency, and development." *Culture and Public Action* : 3–36.

Ratto, Matt, and Megan Boler. 2014. *DIY Citizenship: Critical Making and Social Media*. Boston: MIT Press.

Ray, Paul H., and Sherry Ruth Anderson. 2001. *The Cultural Creative: How 50 Million People are Changing the World*. Minneapolis: Three Rivers Press.

Reay, Diane. 2004. "Gendering Bourdieu's concepts of capitals? Emotional capital, women and social class." *The Sociological Review* 52: 57–74.

Reid-Walsh, Jacqueline, and Claudia Mitchell. 2004. "Girls' web sites: A virtual 'room of one's own'?" In *All about the Girl: Culture, Power and Identity*, edited by Anita Harris, 173–184. New York: Routledge.

Reynolds, Richard. 2005. "The education of Australian Aboriginal and Torres Strait Islander students: Repair or radical change." *Childhood Education* Fall 82(1): 31–36.

Riggs, Damien W. 2007. "How do bodies matter: Understanding embodied racialised subjectivities." *Dark Matters 2*. Accessed February 7, 2015. http://www.dark matter101.org/site/2008/02/23/howdo-bodies-matter-understanding-embodied-racialised-subjectivities/.

Ringrose, Jessica. 2015. "Schizo-feminist educational research cartographies." *Deleuze Studies* 9(3): 393–409.

Ringrose, Jessica. 2012. *Postfeminist Education? Girls and the Sexual Politics of Schooling*. New York: Routledge.

Ringrose, Jessica. 2008. " 'Every time she bends over she pulls up her thong': Teen girls negotiating discourses of competitive, heterosexualized aggression." *Girlhood Studies* 1(1): 33–59.

References 229

Ritzer, George. 2005. *Encyclopedia of Social Theory, Vol 2.* New York: Sage.

Rizvi, Fazal. 2014. *Encountering Education in the Global: The Selected Works of Fazal Rizvi.* Abingdon: Routledge.

Rizvi, Fazal. 2006. "Imagination and the globalization of educational policy research." *Globalization, Societies and Education* 4: 193–205.

Rizvi, Fazal, and Bob Lingard. 2010. *Globalizing Education Policy.* Abingdon: Routledge.

Robinson, Julie. 2011. "Sudanese heritage and living in Australia: Implications of demography for individual and community resilience." *Australasian Review of African Studies* 32(2): 25–56.

Rothenberg, Albert, and Carl R. Hausman. (Eds.). 1976. *The Creativity Question.* Durham: Duke University Press.

Rudowicz, Elisabeth. 2003. "Creativity and culture: A two-way interaction." *Scandinavian Journal of Educational Research* 47(3): 273–290.

Runco, Mark A. 2014/2010. *Creativity, Theories and Themes: Research, Development and Practice,* 2nd ed. London: Elsevier.

Runco, Mark A., and Steven R. Pritzger. 1999. *Encyclopedia of Creativity, Two-Volume Set: Online Version.* San Diego: Academic Press.

Salehi, Soodabeh. 2008. "Teaching contingencies: Deleuze, creativity discourses, and art." PhD diss., Queen's University Ontario, Canada. Accessed March 3, 2015. http://qspace.library.queensu.ca/handle/1974/1209.

Savage, Glenn. 2010. "Problematizing 'public pedagogy' in educational research." In *Handbook of Public Pedagogy,* edited by Jenny Sandlin, Brian Schultz, and Jake Burdick, 103–115. New York: Routledge.

Scott, Allan. 2007. "Capitalism and urbanisation in a new key? The cognitive-cultural dimension." *Social Forces* 85(4): 1465–1482.

Shaw, Kate. 2013. "Independent creative subcultures and why they matter." *International Journal of Cultural Policy* 19(3): 333–352.

Simpson, Leanne R. 2004. "Anticolonial strategies for the recovery and maintenance of indigenous knowledge." *American Indian Quarterly* 28(3): 373–384.

Singh, Parlo, and Catherine A. Doherty. 2008. "Mobile students in liquid modernity: Negotiating the politics of transnational identities." In *Youth Moves: Identities and Education in Global Perspectives,* edited by Fazal Rizvi, and Nadine Dolby, 115–130. New York: Routledge.

Smith, Linda Tuhawai. 2006. *Decolonizing Methodologies: Research and Indigenous Peoples,* 9th ed. New York: St Martins Press/Palgrave.

Spencer, Steve. 2011. *Visual Research Methods in the Social Sciences: Awakening Visions.* Abingdon: Routledge.

Spivak, Gayatri. 1990. *The Post-Colonial Critic: Interviews, Strategies, Dialogues.* London: Routledge.

Stein, Morris I. 1953. "Creativity and culture." *Journal of Psychology* 36: 311–322.

Sternberg, Robert J. (Ed.). 1999. *Handbook of Creativity.* Cambridge: Cambridge University Press.

Swirski, Teresa. 2013. "Third-generation creativity: Unfolding a social-ecological imagination." In *The Creative University,* edited by Michael A. Peters, and Tina Besley, 145–160. Rotterdam: Sense.

Sylvan, Robin. 2005. *Trance Formation: The Spiritual and Religious Dimensions of Global Rave Culture.* London: Routledge.

Taylor, Charles. 2007. *A Secular Age.* Cambridge: Harvard University Press.

230 References

Taylor, Charles. 2004. *Modern Social Imaginaries*. Durham and London: Duke University Press.

Taylor, Charles. 1992. *The Ethics of Authenticity*. Boston: Harvard University Press.

Tisdell, Elizabeth J. 2008. "Critical media literacy and transformative learning: Drawing on pop culture and entertainment media in teaching for diversity in adult higher education." *Journal of Transformative Education* 6(1): 48–67.

Tisdell, Elizabeth J., and Derise Tolliver. 2003. "Claiming a sacred face: The role of spirituality and cultural identity in transformative adult higher education." *Journal of Transformative Education* 1(4): 368–392.

Thomson, S. 2009. "Putting a big thing into a little hole: Teenage girls' accounts of sexual initiation." *The Journal of Sex Research*, 27(2): 341–361.

Thornton, Sarah. 1996. *Club Culture: Music, Media and Subcultural Capital*. Middletown: Wesleyan University Press.

Tolia-Kelly, Divya P. 2006. "Affect—An ethnocentric encounter? Exploring the 'Universalist' imperative of emotional/affectual geographies." *Area* 38: 213–217.

Torrance, E. Paul. 1997. *Reflection on Emerging Insights on the Educational Psychology of Creativity*. Unpublished manuscript. Athens: Georgia Studies of Creative Behavior.

Tupuola, Anne-Marie. 2004. "Talking sexuality through an insider's lens: The Samoan experience." In *All about the Girl: Culture, Power and Identity*, edited by Anita Harris, 115–126. New York: Routledge.

Tupuola, Anne-Marie. 2000. "Learning sexuality: Young Samoan women." In *Bitter Sweet: Indigenous Women in the Pacific*, edited by Alison Jones, Phyllis Herda, and Tamasailau M. Sua'ali'I, 61–72. Dunedin: University of Otago Press.

Vacchelli, Elena. 2011. "Geographies of subjectivity: Locating feminist political subjects in Milan." *Gender, Place and Culture: A Journal of Feminist Geography* 18(6): 768–785.

Velde, Beth P., Peggy P. Wittman, and Vivian W. Mott. 2007. "Hands-on learning in Tillery." *Journal of Transformative Education* 5(1): 79–92.

Vertovec, Steven, and Susanne Wessendorf (Eds.). 2010. *The Multiculturalism Backlash: European Discourses, Policies and Practices*. London: Routledge.

Walsh, Susan, Barbara Bickel, and Carl Leggo. 2015. *Arts-Based and Contemplative Practices in Research and Teaching: Honoring Presence*. New York: Routledge.

Warner, Michael. 2003. *Publics and Counterpublics*. Brooklyn: Zone Press.

Weis, Lois, Michelle Fine, and Greg Dimitriadis. 2009. "Towards a critical theory of method in shifting times." In *The Routledge International Handbook of Critical Education*, edited by Michael W. Apple, Wayne Au, and Luis Armando Gandin, 437–448. Hoboken: Routledge.

Wetherell, Margaret. 2012. *Affect and Emotion: A New Social Science Understanding*. London/Thousand Oaks: SAGE.

White, Rob, Santina Perrone, Carmel Guerra, and Rosario Lampugnani. 1999. *Ethnic Youth Gangs in Australia, Do They Exist? Report No. 2, Turkish Young People*. Australian Multicultural Foundation.

White, Rob, and Johanna Wyn. 2013. *Youth and Society, Third Edition*. Melbourne: Oxford University Press.

Wigglesworth, Gillian, Jane Simpson, and Deborah Loakes. 2011. "NAPLAN language assessments for Indigenous children in remote communities: Issues and problems." *Australian Review of Applied Linguistics* 34(3): 320–343.

References 231

Wilkinson, Jane, Liselott Forsman, and Kiprono Langat. 2013. "Multiplicity in the making: Towards a praxis-oriented approach to professional development." *Professional Development in Education* 39(4): 488–512.

Wilkinson, Jane, and Kiprono Langat. 2012. "Exploring educators' practices for African students from refugee backgrounds in an Australian regional high school." *The Australasian Review of African Studies* 33(2): 158–177.

Williams, Lance. 2010. "Hip-hop as a site of public pedagogy." In *Handbook of Public Pedagogy: Education and Learning beyond Schooling*, edited by Jenny Sandlin, Brian D. Schultz, and Jake Burdick, 221–232. New York: Routledge.

Williams, Raymond. 1983. *Keywords: A Vocabulary of Culture and Society*. New York: Oxford University Press.

Williams, Raymond. 1958. "Culture is ordinary." In *Conviction*, edited by N. Mackenzie, 74–92. London: McGibbon and Kee.

Wilson, Nick. "Social creativity: Re-qualifying the creative economy." *International Journal of Cultural Policy* 16(3): 367–381.

Windle, Joel. 2008. "Racialisation of African youth in Australia." *Social Identities* 14(5): 553–566.

Wurzburger, Rebecca, Tom Aageson, Alex Pattakos, and Sabrina Pratt. 2009. *Creative Tourism: A Global Conversation*. Santa Fe: Sunstone Press.

Xinfa Yi, Weiping Hu, Herbert Scheithauer, and Weihua Niu. 2013. "Cultural and Bilingual Influences on Artistic Creativity Performances: Comparison of German and Chinese Students." *Creativity Research Journal* 25(1): 97–108.

Yip, Andrew, and Susan Page. 2013. *Religious and Sexual Identities: A Multi-Faith Exploration of Young Adults*. Farnham: Ashgate.

Youdell, Deborah. 2012. "Fabricating 'Pacific Islander': Pedagogies of expropriation, return and resistance and other lessons from a 'Multicultural Day'." *Race, Ethnicity and Education* 15(2): 141–155.

Zhou, Min, and Carl L. Bankston III. 1994. "Social capital and the adaptation of the second generation: The case of Vietnamese youth in New Orleans." *International Migration Review, Winter Issue*, 20(4): 821–845.

Zipin, Lew, Sam Sellar, Marie Brennan, and Trevor Gale. 2015. "Educating for Futures in Marginalized Regions: A sociological framework for rethinking and researching aspirations." *Educational Philosophy and Theory* 47(3): 227–246.

Zipin, Lew, Sam Sellar, and Robert Hattam. 2012. "Countering and exceeding 'capital': A 'funds of knowledge' approach to re-imagining community." *Discourse: Studies in the Cultural Politics of Education* 33(2): 179–192.

Index

activism 9, 93, 151, 197
aesthetics 53, 129, 130, 132, 153, 171, 174, 175, 176, 185, 194, 204, 209, 211
affect, affective 53, 63, 67, 71 83, 97, 101, 126, 129, 130, 132, 172, 175, 178–180, 185, 189, 191–198, 200–202, 204
African, African American, African Australian 5, 10, 33, 57, 94, 121, 124, 136, 137, 145, 150, 163, 164, 177, 204
Anderson, Benedict 1, 10–12, 127, 133, 150, 151, 176, 183, 203
anthropology 5, 78, 93, 134
Appadurai, Arjun 1, 3, 5, 6, 9, 11, 12, 18, 31, 33, 35, 43, 44, 58, 60, 63, 67–68, 72–75, 77–80, 88–91, 94, 95, 99, 100, 102, 104–106, 112, 113, 124, 125–128, 133–135, 139–144, 150–151, 158–159, 165, 168–169, 171, 176, 183, 186, 203, 211, 214
arts 4, 9–12, 19, 22, 24–28, 36, 43, 45–51, 53, 57–60, 63, 67, 68, 80, 95, 103, 112, 122, 135, 137, 140, 141, 143, 144, 146–149, 154–155, 157, 159, 161, 163, 165, 169, 170, 173–175, 181, 182, 184–186, 194, 196–199, 201–203, 206, 207, 210, 213
arts-based pedagogy 48
arts-based research 206
arts education 25, 46, 48, 50, 137, 143, 144, 165, 169, 198
Asia, Asians, Asia Pacific (also Asia-Pacific) 2, 5, 9, 11, 13, 20, 31, 32, 34, 57, 154, 209

aspiration(s), aspirational xii, xv, 8, 9, 11–13, 44, 46, 49, 57, 59, 63, 67, 72–75, 80, 95
autoethnography 31, 32

Battacharya, Kakali 123, 205, 206
Bauman, Zygmont 111, 112, 149
Benjamin, Walter 12, 91, 128, 130–132, 172, 176–177, 210
Berlant, Lauren 104, 163, 195, 196–199
borders xiii, 66, 126, 127, 130, 133–134, 139, 202, 206, 207
Bourdieu, Pierre 1, 11, 43, 45, 47, 48, 53, 55, 60, 79, 106, 129, 131, 132, 139, 141, 154, 160, 165–66, 173–78, 208, 209
Burgess and Green 214, 215

capacity to aspire 1, 9, 11, 43, 60, 62, 63, 72–75, 77–80, 95, 97, 99, 135, 143, 144, 158
Caucasian 27; see also White
Christian xi, 2, 3, 5, 8, 9, 11, 25, 32, 35, 38, 39, 63, 71, 85, 87, 88, 100, 108, 114, 115, 120, 124, 139, 145, 170, 186, 188, 204, 205, 212
church i, xv, 9, 10–12, 17, 19, 20, 21, 22, 25, 32, 37–44, 50, 52, 53, 59–61, 64, 69, 72, 74–78, 80–86, 88, 89, 92, 95–97, 100–103, 114, 115, 120, 124, 127, 135, 146, 148, 149, 163, 167, 168, 170, 199, 201, 206, 207, 214
cine-ethnography 21
citizenship, creative citizenship 35, 63, 102, 113, 130, 158, 168–169, 187, 189, 196–199, 202, 208, 213–215

234   *Index*

collective/individual xii, 3, 12, 40, 43,
   57, 59, 66, 68, 89, 90, 98, 102, 114,
   126, 127, 128, 138, 148, 151, 175,
   191, 192, 194, 200, 202, 215
collectivities 13, 127, 135, 136, 137,
   190, 192, 207
commodification, commodifying,
   commoditization, commodity xii,
   10, 35, 46, 47, 72, 73, 78–80, 90,
   126, 128, 129, 131, 134, 139, 141,
   142, 146, 151, 153, 154, 157, 165,
   170–174, 176–177, 179–181, 199,
   204, 208, 210–212
community-building xi, 3, 9, 13,
   111, 172
connectivity xi, xii, 10, 212
cosmopolitanism 12, 88
counterpublics xii, 34, 179, 183, 189,
   195–201, 203, 212, 214
creative becoming 3, 29, 131, 211
creative capital xi, 1, 3, 11, 12, 28,
   31, 44–48, 50, 52–53, 59, 60, 63,
   128, 129, 131, 133, 142, 143, 151,
   153–154, 158, 162, 166, 172–177,
   185, 190, 204, 208–209, 211,
   212, 217
creative class 4, 35, 112, 133, 175, 196
creative communities 4, 11, 13, 88
creative counterpublics xii, 34,
   195–196, 199, 201, 203, 212, 214
creative futures 110, 114, 215
creative industries 2, 4, 6, 8, 27, 50,
   53, 72, 88, 89, 90, 111, 129, 130,
   137, 148, 151, 153–156, 159, 166,
   172–175, 179, 180, 181, 190, 204,
   207–213, 215
creativity studies 2, 4, 91
creative imaginary 33, 35
creative partnerships (UK) 59, 208
critical education 2, 112, 135
cultural capital 2, 11, 53, 68, 74, 112,
   124, 130, 132, 133, 146, 148, 149,
   153–155, 169, 173–177, 182, 188,
   190, 208
cultural identity i, 10, 31, 96, 130,
   144, 163
cultural industries xii, 8, 10, 12, 88,
   95, 129, 148, 151, 154, 156, 172,
   179–181, 207–213
cultural intermediaries 151–153, 208
cultural maintenance 3, 11, 19, 100,
   146, 158
Culture Shack xv, 1, 8, 20, 25, 27–28,
   35, 45, 46–60, 70, 82, 103, 119,

   135–144, 146, 148, 149, 158, 182,
   184, 185
ciaspora, diasporic 5, 31, 106, 120,
   125, 160
ciasporic youth xi, xiii, 3, 11, 134,
   194, 207
cigital cultures 2, 9, 207

Dimitriadis, Greg xv, 1, 6, 9, 18, 30,
   135, 136, 138, 139, 158, 163, 164,
   181, 182, 187–189, 202, 207
DIY culture, DIY ethic 4, 10, 213, 214
Dobson, Amy 5, 36, 100–105,
   170–171, 207
doxa 141, 142, 161, 162, 207
doxic aspirations 141, 142, 151,
   158, 214
drama i, 6, 10, 21, 23–25, 27, 47,
   49–52, 55–57, 124, 140

ethnicity 12, 20, 100, 121, 167, 196,
   204, 205
entrepreneur/ialism xii, 111, 112, 144,
   153, 196
essentialising, essentialism 3, 11, 12,
   28, 31, 60, 99, 103, 113, 203
ethnocinema 5, 21, 49, 57, 136, 141,
   162, 165, 185
ethnography 6, 21, 29–32
ethnoscapes 95, 97, 100, 150, 169

faith xi, xii, 2, 3, 7–13, 15, 18, 20–28,
   30, 32, 33, 35, 38, 40, 43, 44, 52,
   59, 63, 66, 76, 78, 86–90, 93,
   95–97, 100–103, 107, 109–112,
   114, 120, 122–125, 128, 129, 145,
   147–149, 154, 157, 160, 166–168,
   170, 177, 185, 186, 189, 194, 195,
   198, 200–205, 207–209, 212, 215
feminism, feminist, postfeminism,
   schizofeminism 18, 20, 29, 31, 66,
   97, 100, 101, 103, 104, 129, 134,
   166, 174, 177–179, 182, 193, 195
feminist social imaginary 177, 179
fundamentalist/isms 7, 139
funds of knowledge 142, 144, 146,
   147, 151

Gallagher, Kathleen xv, 6, 9, 21
gaming i, 10
gay 8, 25, 27, 83, 86, 87
gender 1, 2, 4–12, 20, 25–27, 31, 35,
   37, 54, 55, 58, 68, 100, 101, 103,
   105–106, 114, 121, 122, 139, 143,

150, 158–162, 164, 165, 167–169, 174, 177, 181–183, 185, 186, 188, 195–197, 202, 203, 205
geographies 203, 20, 35
geo-political 4, 10
girlhood 5, 36, 105, 177
global flows (global capital flows, global citizen, global culture/s, global mobilities, global networks) 149, 152, 154, 155, 157, 165, 166, 168, 169, 171, 172, 175, 179, 180, 182, 183, 186–189, 196, 198, 203, 204, 205, 207, 209, 210, 213–215
globalisation 9, 89, 106, 122, 135, 139, 142, 211
global south 2, 3, 6, 7, 20, 28, 35, 110, 126, 166, 179, 185, 203, 205, 207, 213
God, god 23–25, 33, 35, 38–40, 62, 68–69, 75–76, 81, 82, 84–85, 87, 93, 95–98, 101, 103–104, 128, 137–138, 160, 168, 170, 177, 183, 184, 200, 202, 203, 205, 206, 212, 215
gospel music i, 10, 24, 108

habitus 3, 11, 59, 130, 131, 142, 143, 149, 160, 165, 171, 177, 178
Harris, Anita 1, 5, 18, 20, 34, 35, 93, 94, 103, 158, 164, 170, 185, 188, 195, 197, 203, 204, 214
Hickey-Moody, Anna xi, 67, 150, 168, 169, 182, 196–199, 201, 202, 212, 214
hip hop 9, 10, 22, 41, 42, 47, 48, 51, 55, 57, 63, 108, 120, 135–138, 140, 142, 144–147, 158, 161–163, 171, 181–182, 184, 192, 194, 208, 212
hybridisation, hybridity xii, 7, 9, 12, 20, 31, 34, 35, 61, 63, 70, 79, 100, 113, 128, 136, 157, 168, 177, 203, 208, 212, 214

imagined community/ies i, 1, 10, 11, 113, 133, 150, 172, 176, 183
intercultural 4, 24–26, 28, 30, 35, 37, 43–45, 49, 51, 52, 56–60, 65, 68, 77, 80, 83, 85, 93, 94, 104, 105, 114, 121, 136, 141, 145, 161, 165, 172, 187–188, 214
intersectionality 2, 9, 10, 11, 44, 136, 166–168, 188, 215
intimate publics 197

Iosefo, Jerudeen / Joshua 20, 110, 206, 207, 215
Islander / Pacific Islander 10, 28, 42, 57, 58, 94, 204

little publics xii, 150, 169, 196–198
local (local class, localised, localities, glocal) 2, 6, 7, 10, 12, 26, 33, 34, 35, 43, 44, 46, 49, 52, 56, 59, 63, 67, 68, 80, 88 89, 93, 105, 106, 111, 124, 126–129, 136, 137, 142, 155, 161, 164, 166, 168, 169, 180, 182, 186–187, 189, 196, 198, 202, 207, 208, 211, 214, 215

McLuhan, Marshall 128, 130, 131, 172, 210
McRobbie, Angela 36, 72, 80, 103, 106, 107, 110–112, 114, 115, 190, 197, 204
madolescence xii, 184, 187, 189, 192, 194, 199, 201, 203
Maira & Soep 4, 31, 33, 105, 106, 124, 187, 203
maker culture, makers xv, 4, 10, 12, 23, 36, 66, 95, 121, 136, 143, 156, 202, 211–214
Manning, Erin 3, 5, 13, 17, 18, 100, 128, 167, 184, 185, 189, 190–192, 195, 196, 198–203, 205
Massumi, Brian 5, 11, 25, 88, 185, 191, 193–195, 205, 211
materialism, materialist, new materialism 5, 98, 132, 134, 136, 195, 204, 205
materiality 134, 180, 183, 186, 197
mediascapes 3, 11, 15, 18, 20, 63, 80, 88, 89, 100, 142, 168, 169, 171
mediation 33, 43, 51, 127, 134, 141, 142, 182, 197
Methodist xv, 17, 38, 63, 80, 83, 84, 114
migrant 2, 4, 5, 7, 23, 29, 34, 46, 50, 51, 60, 67, 70, 78–80, 95, 101, 105–107, 120, 124–127, 129, 138, 140, 144, 150, 154, 167, 173, 175, 182, 185–189, 197, 204–205, 207
migration 5, 6, 33, 35, 85, 107, 113, 120, 127, 134, 140, 204, 206, 207, 214
minoritarian 31, 34, 60, 71–74, 79, 105, 106, 110, 129, 132, 152, 169, 171, 185–187, 189, 190, 193, 195–197, 200, 201, 203, 204, 214

236 *Index*

Mitias, Michael 9, 98, 204
mobilities, mobility 26, 34, 35, 63,
    73, 89, 105, 129, 131, 142, 144,
    149, 154, 162, 165, 166, 172,
    212, 214
multicultural 1, 10, 22, 26, 29, 34,
    35, 75, 83, 93, 94, 127, 130, 137,
    154, 188
multimodal 11, 30, 135, 203
music 11, 31, 34, 42, 63, 66, 86, 95,
    108, 113, 114, 119, 135–137, 140,
    145, 151, 152, 158, 159, 160–162,
    165, 170, 175, 178, 188, 191, 192,
    204, 208, 212, 214
Muslim / Islam, Islamophobia 8, 39,
    88, 120, 139

networks, networking xi, 7, 26, 47, 88,
    120, 126, 132, 139, 149, 150, 164,
    165, 169, 182, 188, 207
new materialist *see* 'materialism'

O'Connor, Justin 2, 10, 17, 20, 27, 88,
    127, 129, 139, 151–155, 159, 166,
    169, 179–182, 207–213, 215
online / offline 140, 145, 150, 157, 165,
    168, 172, 173, 177, 179, 181, 182,
    185, 187, 189, 194, 197–200, 203,
    207, 214–215

Pacific, pacific rim *see* global south
participatory culture 4, 51, 140, 207,
    208, 213, 214
pedagogy 6, 43, 45, 46, 48, 53, 59, 70,
    106, 145, 147, 157, 162, 198
performance xi, 2, 4–6, 10–12, 15, 17,
    18, 20, 22–28, 30, 32–34, 36, 38,
    40–44, 47, 52, 59, 64, 67, 75, 85,
    86, 89, 90, 95, 96, 100, 101, 103,
    107, 124, 136, 147, 157, 161–163,
    186, 189, 194, 196–199, 206
posthuman, posthumanism 12, 98, 132,
    134, 185, 189, 192, 195, 204, 205
post-nation, post-nationhood, post-
    national, post-nation-state xii, 12,
    100, 117, 124, 125, 133, 134, 176,
    202, 213
post-structuralist 2, 29, 100, 102,
    193, 195
practice-led research 10, 21, 29, 142
praisesong 12, 81, 110, 181
precarious / precarity 6, 124, 134, 142
prosumer cultures 4

publics xii, 34, 36, 67, 68, 73, 88, 140,
    150, 168–169, 172, 175, 178, 179,
    183, 189, 195–201, 203, 212, 214;
    see also counterpublics; little publics

queer, genderqueer, LGBTIQ 8, 86,
    114, 153, 197, 198, 205

R&B 10, 22, 24, 42, 63, 108
race, racism, racist xii, 2, 5, 7, 11, 12,
    18, 20, 28, 29, 33, 34, 57, 66, 94,
    101, 104, 121, 137, 143, 150, 160,
    167, 177, 181, 182, 185–187, 189,
    196, 203
rap, rappers 124, 136–138, 145–146,
    161–163, 169, 179, 181, 184, 186,
    190–192, 194
refugee-background youth 4, 5, 13, 46,
    51, 70, 79, 93, 95, 113, 120–122,
    124, 125, 140, 144, 149, 150, 169,
    173, 175, 182, 186, 190
relationscapes 3
Runco, Mark 17, 27, 204
Ringrose, Jessica 18, 105, 125, 134,
    166, 195
rituals i, 3, 8, 10–12, 125, 130, 188
Rizvi, Fazal 18, 26, 29, 35, 68, 112,
    122, 157, 165, 178, 183

sacred 2, 25, 74, 122, 215
Salehi, Soodabeth 131, 210, 211
Samoan xi, xv, 1, 2, 3, 5–8, 10–11, 13,
    15, 17–19, 21–50, 52–60, 63, 64,
    68–85, 88–96, 98–114,122, 126,
    128,130, 132, 134, 136, 139, 140,
    147, 149, 152, 154, 156, 157, 163,
    164, 166, 168, 169, 172, 177, 182,
    185, 187, 188, 194, 196, 197, 199,
    202–212, 214, 215
secular (post-secularity, secularisation,
    secularity) 2, 4, 7, 8, 9, 63, 103, 124,
    126, 130, 168, 185, 205
semblance 81, 88
sexuality 12, 27, 81, 104, 122, 167,
    188, 205, 207
social 28, 31, 45, 47, 132, 149,
    150, 204
social imaginary 1, 59, 68, 73, 88,
    94, 128, 134, 168, 177–179, 200,
    202–203
social media 10, 11, 17, 18, 21, 26, 36,
    63, 64, 66–67, 70, 88, 89, 102–104,
    106–107, 120, 126, 128–129,

131, 170, 171, 177, 182, 185, 187, 214, 218
southern hemisphere 4, 12, 163; *see also* global south
South Sudanese 93, 95, 99, 104, 105, 106, 107, 110, 112–113, 115, 117, 120–128, 130, 132, 134–142, 144–152, 154, 156–174, 177–180, 182, 183, 185–191, 193–197, 199, 200–205, 207–210, 212, 214
spacetimes 191, 203
spiritual, spiritualist, spirituality 1, 2, 8, 9, 21, 25, 38, 63, 74, 76, 80, 92, 96, 113, 122–124, 130, 132, 136, 146, 183, 187, 200, 205, 215
subaltern xi, 11, 99, 151, 177, 191, 197

Taylor, Charles 9, 74, 178, 183
technoscape 88, 89, 105, 106
Torrance, E. Paul 2, 91, 123
totemic value 12, 91
transcultural xii, 51, 68, 150, 183, 208
trans-languaging 28, 208
trans/local 207 (see also 'local')
transnational xii, 31, 110, 123, 127, 182
Tupuola, AM 20, 37

urban, urbanists, urban theory, urban youth 1, 6, 9, 33, 127, 129, 135, 138, 139, 150, 154, 167, 173, 175, 177, 187, 210, 213, 214

Va 185, 215
video 3, 8, 10, 21, 33, 36–37, 49, 57, 64–65, 68, 87, 92, 93, 102, 107–110, 114, 119, 125, 135–137, 139–141, 158–162, 165, 170–171, 178, 182, 191, 192, 194
virtual, virtuality 66, 68, 77, 88, 115, 126, 128, 165, 172, 177, 185, 189, 193, 194, 200, 202
visibility / invisibility 104, 122, 171, 178–179

White 5, 7, 18, 24, 25, 28, 29, 30, 33, 36, 39, 70, 71, 76, 81, 82, 83, 85, 86, 94, 101, 102, 113, 136, 140, 141, 145, 173, 177, 205; *see also* Caucasian
White Sunday 25, 32, 39, 40, 41, 56, 62, 81–84, 114
Wilkinson, Jane 149, 150
women 8, 20, 21, 23–29, 32, 35–37, 43, 44, 49, 52, 54, 66, 68, 84–86, 93, 96, 100–105, 120–122, 135–138, 140–145, 147, 149, 151, 157, 160–165, 168–171, 177–179, 181–183, 185–187, 189, 192, 194–197, 200–201

Yip, Andrew (Yip and Page) 88, 97, 98, 167, 168, 200, 205, 207
youth of colour 101, 173, 190, 197, 200, 203
youth studies xii, 2, 88, 95, 100, 103, 123, 132, 157, 166, 177, 185, 194